The Loves of Their Lives

The Loves
of Their Lives

Enduring Romantic
Relationships
From Antony and Cleopatra
to Today

Louis Baldwin

A Birch Lane Press Book
PUBLISHED BY CAROL PUBLISHING GROUP

A Birch Lane Press Book
Published by Carol Publishing Group
Birch Lane Press is a registered trademark of Carol
Communications, Inc.
Editorial Offices: 600 Madison Avenue, New York, N.Y. 10022
Sales & Distribution Offices: 120 Enterprise Avenue, Secaucus,
   N.J. 07094
In Canada: Canadian Manda Group, P.O. Box 920, Station U,
   Toronto, Ontario M8Z 5P9
Queries regarding rights and permissions should be addressed to
Carol Publishing Group, 600 Madison Avenue, New York, N.Y. 10022

Carol Publishing Group books are available at special discounts
for bulk purchases, for sales promotions, fund raising, or
educational purposes. Special editions can be created to specifications.
For details, contact: Special Sales Department, Carol Publishing
Group, 120 Enterprise Avenue, Secaucus, N.J. 07094

Manufactured in the United States of America
10 9 8 7 6 5 4 3 2 1

Library of Congress Cataloging-in-Publication Data

Baldwin, Louis.
   Loves of their lives : enduring romantic relationships from Antony
and Cleopatra to today / by Louis Baldwin.
      p.   cm.
   "A Birch Lane Press book."
   ISBN 1-55972-190-1 (cloth)
   1. Love. 2. Sex (Psychology) 3. Intimacy (Psychology)
4. Interpersonal relations. I. Title.
HQ801.B13   1993
306.7—dc20   93-24141
                                                     CIP

To Ginnie, with love

Contents

Foreword

~❧~

The word *love* is used loosely in the following pages because it is used loosely in language—this language and others. Love includes the sentiment we feel for cute little puppies and the motivation of the soldier who falls on a live grenade to save his comrades. It covers a multitude of virtues as well as sins, a myriad of human emotions springing from the infinite variety of human personalities. It is a *many*-splendored thing.

It appears in many guises in these sketches—selfless devotion, deep affection, passionate desire, emotional dependence, obsessive attachment, infatuation, adoration, and occasionally cool calculation, all mixed in various proportions. We see it in the enduring ardor, punctuated by angry hostility, that sparked the thirty-year flirtation between Elizabeth I and Robert Dudley. Throughout those years, it survived his opportunism and her royal caution, their competitive liaisons, their conflicting ambitions, their political maneuvering. They fought and made up only to fight again; they separated only to be re-united; they hated only to return once again to their love. Elizabeth, political animal that she was, dedicated to England as she was, could never share her throne with him. As the queen, she held him at arm's length, even if only figuratively. Yet in the moment of her greatest triumph as queen, his final departure brought tears to her eyes.

For contrast, we can consider the love of Eleanor for Franklin Roosevelt. For Elizabeth, her affair with Dudley was a prolonged, intermittent dalliance, but dalliance, prolonged or otherwise, is not the kind of conduct one can readily associate with the plain and proper lady who resided in the White House during those eleven tumultuous years. For her, making love was a duty, a distasteful aspect of being in love (as she clearly was), even when her partner was a handsome, debonair, devilishly attractive fellow very much in love with her. This gave their relationship a kind of sobriety that doubtless would have driven Elizabeth up the arras. Yet Eleanor could be very affectionate, tenderly considerate, loyal, and self-sacrificing. For Franklin's sake she was solicitous, even obsequious, toward his formidable mother. For his sake she managed the grueling social side of his political career. And for his sake, after his terrible encounter with polio in 1921, she dedicated herself to his recovery, his long-term therapy, his return to politics, his comfort and happiness. She provided the leg power he no longer had. She was his ambassador, his assistant, his indispensable helpmate, even after learning of his affair with Lucy Mercer. From that time on, she protested, she was motivated by her love for the country, not for the man. But lifelong feelings, like old habits, cannot be lightly discarded.

Zelda Sayre's love for F. Scott Fitzgerald was something else again. It burned more intensely than Elizabeth's and more passionately than Eleanor's, and it was much more deeply rooted in emotional dependence. The manic-depressive aspect of their love, laced with alcohol, led to scenes of deeply touching passion alternating with clamorous marital donnybrooks that were the talk of their neighborhoods on both sides of the Atlantic. As her mental health deteriorated and her vivid, fascinating character seemed almost to drain away, she lived, like an image projected on a column of smoke, in her love for Scott. And he reciprocated, in his own fashion. Even when she was institutionalized and he was living with another woman a continent away, he wrote to her faithfully, supported her emotionally and financially as best he could, and proved himself to be the friend that she so desperately needed. Long after the romance was gone, long after the passion had subsided, the love surely was still there.

Winston Churchill's darling Clementine offered him love that gave him hope in his darkest moments, courage in his perilous ones, and warm admiration in his triumphs. Napoleon Bonaparte's *chérie* Josephine did not so much offer love as return it, especially after he forgave her for her extracurricular activity during his absence in Egypt, yet her hold on his affections remained strong even after his second, political marriage and her death. Marion Davies' love for William Randolph Hearst began as the love of a chorine for her sugar daddy, but she was still with him, nursing him, caring for him, more than a quarter century later. Golda Meir's love for Morris Meyerson, like Elizabeth's for Dudley, came second after her love for her country, but, like Elizabeth, she lived to have some doubtful regrets.

Love, John Lyly wrote four centuries ago, knows no laws. The heart is not the seat of wisdom. Unlike the head, it is not bound by logic, consistency, uniformity. It resists stereotyping. As these sketches indicate, it is a very individual, very personal, very mysterious thing.

The Loves of Their Lives

Cleopatra and Marc Antony

Although the most skilled lovemakers in the ancient world were reputedly the women of Egypt, the woman whose reputation in this respect has survived for twenty centuries, inspiring two great plays by Shakespeare and one by Shaw, was a Greek. Cleopatra VII of Egypt was the last of the Greek dynasty established by Alexander the Great in 323 B.C. for the ruling of Egypt under his doughty general Ptolemy and his descendants, and she was a stunner. Her physical beauty may not have been as overwhelming as some legends suggest, but she may well have been one of those women who, because of other attributes, seem more beautiful than they are, at least in the eyes of enraptured beholders. In the movies she has been played most recently by two great beauties, Vivien Leigh and Elizabeth Taylor, although she probably looked more like Barbara Stanwyck or Barbra Streisand. Not that there's anything wrong with *that*.

But even if she had looked like the wicked witch of Oz, her other attributes may have made her quite captivating. She was attractively educated, dexterous in conversation, proficient in languages (she was the only Ptolemaic ruler who could, and did, speak Egyptian), sharply intelligent, perceptive in handling male egos, and well versed in the arts of the bedchamber. Doubtless part of her personal charm was a weakness in her regal character, for she could be as captivated as she was captivating, especially in connection with powerful men. In the first of her two most celebrated love affairs, both of them with the most powerful womanizers in the Western world at the time, she utterly captivated Julius Caesar in Alexandria but later eagerly joined him in Rome, where she was living when he was assassinated. In the second affair, she virtually enslaved Marc Antony yet followed him quite loyally until it was too late to escape their mutual doom.

She had met Antony in Alexandria, the very Grecian capital of Egypt, when he was on Caesar's staff, but she had been too preoccupied with the Roman demigod to pay much notice to a Roman subaltern. When she *really* met him six or seven years later, in 41 B.C., she was twenty-eight, had been queen for ten years, and had learned a great deal about the unscrupulous uses of power, pomp, and circumstance. He was forty-two, a seasoned, colorful, and celebrated battle commander, a rough-hewn Adonis, and ruler of the rich eastern half of the Roman empire. (Octavian, Julius Caesar's young nephew, adopted son, and presumptive heir, held the western half by uneasy agreement.) When he arrived in Tarsus in Asia Minor on an expedition to push the imperial frontiers still farther eastward, he summoned Cleopatra from Egypt for a discussion of her loyalty to Rome's manifest destiny, a loyalty subject to some doubt at the time.

She delayed her response long enough to maintain her regal dignity but not long enough to cause trouble. She arrived in Tarsus gliding up the Cydnus River in the magnificent barge made famous by Shakespeare, all purple and gold and sweet with incense, propelled by silver oars in time with music from flutes and lyres. Amid boys dressed as cupids and girls as nymphs, she herself was costumed, diaphanously we must suppose, as the goddess of love. The word spread among the goggle-eyed people along the river, Plutarch tells us, that Aphrodite had arrived to revel with Dionysus and thus promote the happiness of Asia. Others equated them with Isis and Osiris.

The first issue to be settled between them rings familiar to modern ears: "Your place or mine?" He, as host, invited her to dine with him, but his messenger returned with an invitation to him to dine with her, and he amiably accepted. Of the ostensibly independent kingdoms associated with the young empire, hers was the most important, and he had no wish to offend her. He had reason that evening to be glad that he had not done so, for he was delightedly overwhelmed by the sumptuous, elaborately splendid affair that she arranged for him. Garish and overdone, perhaps, but that was to his taste. This was not an age noted for social restraint among the ruling classes. At his party for her the next evening, he spent much of the time genially apologizing for his relatively shabby performance as host.

Yet her performance as hostess was only an overture to her overtures. For much more personal reasons, he forgot all about his eastern expedition and about his wife, Fulvia, who was in Rome using her unique political talents in his behalf. He and Cleopatra spent the winter of 41–40 B.C. together in Alexandria. She knew about Fulvia, of course, and about his indiscriminate addiction to women in general, and the competition spurred her to make his time with her more attractive than any alternative he could think of. She did, it was, and he thought of none. When he was forced to leave Alexandria late that winter by news of a Parthian invasion of the empire's eastern border, she was pregnant.

He would not return to her until the autumn of 37. On his way to join his troops in the east he learned that Fulvia had fomented an aborted rebellion against Octavian, after which Antony was kept prodigiously busy trying to make up for her indiscretion. After her death in Greece, to which she had fled, he marched to Rome and, after some brief hostilities, concluded the Treaty of Brundisium with Octavian (and the third, smaller wheel of the triumvirate, named Lepidus), essentially continuing the status quo for at least the next three years. To seal this bargain, he married Octavian's recently widowed sister, Octavia, who was a beautiful, accomplished woman younger than Cleopatra. In the palace at Alexandria the air was thick with consternation.

He had plenty to keep him busy in Rome, what with his need to raise money and troops for another eastern adventure, as well as to strengthen his hand in the political competition with Octavian. It was not until mid-37 that he arranged a settlement with this rival once again, this time in the Treaty of Tarentum, under which he turned over one hundred twenty of his ships to Octavian in return for a promise of some twenty thousand troops. When he sailed for Syria that autumn, he took Octavia along but about halfway there sent her back to Rome for reasons of ill health, pregnancy, child-rearing, and moderation of her brother's ambitions. On his arrival in Syria he wasted no time inviting Cleopatra to join him. There they spent the winter, cosily together again.

There, too, they did some bargaining. Octavian's promise of troops was showing no signs of fulfillment (and never would), and Antony needed the support of Cleopatra's rich and powerful kingdom. In exchange for that support, he had some of her internal adversaries eliminated and gave her lands throughout the Near East, which rendered her kingdom almost as extensive and potent as the Greater Egypt of her forebears. He also cooperated in bringing Eastern mysticism to bear on their relationship and status. The two lovers promoted their own divinity and that of their three-year-old twins, Alexander and Cleopatra, allowing her son by Julius Caesar to drop several notches on the official exaltation scale. When he headed east again in May of 36, they were firmly in the divinely regal saddle, he was looking forward to a sweeping conquest, and she was pregnant with their third child.

But he made the mistake of outrunning his supplies, leaving behind too small a force to protect them. When his enemies destroyed his baggage trains and heavy siege equipment, he had to turn tail. After another winter in Syria, he and Cleopatra returned with their three children to Alexandria amid some growing resentment over his failure to attend to business and her too alluring role in that failure. By this time Octavia's conscientious mothering of his children in Rome had earned her a reputation of solid Roman respectability, while Antony's long-term dalliance with his oriental paramour gave him the reputation of an irresponsible satyr. And in contrast with his low fortunes, Octavian was riding high, having brought the western empire well under his control, chiefly through recognizing the extraordinary talent of his new general-admiral, Agrippa.

It was this Agrippa who would carry out Octavian's, and indeed Rome's, revenge upon Antony for his military failures, his gifts of Roman provinces to a foreign queen, his shabby treatment of Octavia, and his un-Roman addiction to Eastern luxury. As for Cleopatra, even though she could not be wedded to Antony under Roman law, her fate was by now wedded to his, inseparably. She was at his side constantly, in military councils as well as in more relaxed circumstances; she had contributed two hundred of his five hundred warships, as well as untold materiel, and she had every right and reason to share in the preparations for Octavian's inevitable attack. In May of 32, the Greek coastline being considered most suitable for a naval engagement, they sailed for Athens. That autumn they moved west and established headquarters at Patriae in the middle of their defensive bases along the western coast, to await the confrontation.

But Agrippa bided his time, allowing them the pleasures, and their soldiers and sailors the discomforts, of another winter together. When he struck, he did so unexpectedly in March, concentrating on a single important base, the one at Methone at the southwest tip of the Peloponnesian peninsula. Having captured that base with professional dispatch, he then used it effectively to harass other naval stations and the supply lines from Egypt. Antony and Cleopatra, in some alarm, moved with their troops out of Patriae to Actium, about fifty miles north, just west of the present town of Vonitsa on the Gulf of Amvrakia. There they found their fleet bottled up by Octavian's troops on the gulf's northern shore and Agrippa's warships at its entrance.

After some sparring revealed that they faced greatly superior forces, both military and naval, they decided to make a run for it. They did, and they escaped (the story that she deserted him during the battle at sea appears to be groundless). But when they arrived back in Alexandria some weeks later, although she orchestrated some spectacular pageantry to make their return seem a triumphal one, they had only sixty ships left out of their original five hundred—and no troops at all, having lost their army mostly through desertions and surrenders. A kind of fatalistic dejection took over at the palace, where the ceaseless partying became an elaborate form of whistling in the dark. Despite all the forced revelry, their last winter together was a miserable one.

Octavian's victories had impoverished him. He needed the wealth of Alexandria. His approach during the spring and summer of 30 was unstoppable, and in August he took the city (commemorating the event in his new title, Augustus Caesar). While his troops were occupying the palace, Antony, separated from Cleopatra and misinformed that she had committed suicide, ran like a true Roman upon his sword. When she heard of this, she had him brought to where she was hiding in her mausoleum, but it was too late to do more than say farewell as he died in her arms. After the soldiers had forced entry into the building and captured her, Octavian allowed her to arrange for her lover's burial.

Octavian did not want to make a martyr out of her by execution, nor a pitiful spectacle of her in his triumphal entry into Rome. He simply wanted to get rid of her. Counting on her dread of being hauled in a cage through Roman streets, and on her oriental familiarity with poisons, he used intermediaries to convince her that there was a mobile cage in her future, and she cooperated. Although she probably did not use an asp, she did poison herself. Octavian had her buried, in a respectful ceremony, beside Antony as she had requested.

But Egypt now became part and parcel of the Roman empire.

Héloïse and Abelard

Rape has been described as not so much an act of lust as an act of violence, asserting physical dominance. Seduction might be described similarly as an assertion of a kind of intellectual dominance, using cunning to overpower the will of a fellow human being. Such, it seems, was the seduction of Héloïse by Peter Abelard in the year 1116.

It was not out of character for him. Not that he was a lecher; on the contrary, outside his family he had never known a woman before, probably in the literal and surely in the biblical sense. Since 1092, when he was only thirteen, he had been absorbed in philosophy, in study and disputation, leading a kind of life in which women of the time almost never participated. Indeed, his brilliance in scholarly debating and contentious logic-chopping had given him not only a formidable reputation among European intellectuals but also a towering opinion of himself. He evidently had a low opinion of whatever women he had encountered, since none were well enough educated to have much, if any, idea of what he was inclined to talk about.

Héloïse, however, evidently rivaled his acumen and even to some extent his erudition, although she was only sixteen and he was thirty-six. Her convent education must have been a good one, her absorption of intellectual input from the stimulating atmosphere of Paris (where she lived with an uncle) must have been prodigious, and her mind must have been astoundingly retentive and agile. Certainly Abelard found it so. Others did, too—she had required a reputation for dazzling intelligence—but none with such delight as Abelard. Here at last, he must have felt, was a woman bright enough to appreciate him. Nor did her loveliness in face and figure put him off at all.

He saw her; he inquired about her; he approached her uncle and offered him a proposition: let me live in your house, since I am teaching at a school nearby, and in return I'll devote my free time to the further education of your remarkable niece. The uncle, a cathedral cleric named Fulbert, being ambitious for Héloïse and hoping some day to reap rich fringe benefits from a splendid marriage, readily agreed. And so Abelard moved in, and soon he and Héloïse were lovers.

It was a sly, beguiling plan for seduction, using Fulbert's greed and Heloise's innocence as principal keys to its success. But Abelard in his way was as naive as Héloïse was in hers (and Fulbert was in his), for he failed to factor in the risk of falling in love. Yet he did fall in love, as did she, and soon the study of philosophy gave way to the study of each other.

Whatever the depth of their intelligence, they were clever enough to indulge themselves in Fulbert's house for several months before being found out. When they were found out, the circumstances were unmistakable, and the enraged Fulbert, his fondest hopes shattered, ordered Abelard to leave at once and never to darken any door of his again. The lovers were reduced to surreptitious letter-writing, and soon in one of her letters Héloïse informed Abelard that she was pregnant. She was rapturous at the thought of bearing his child but also nervous at the thought of Fulbert's reaction to the news. Abelard decided to act before Fulbert could react. At the first opportunity— at night, during Fulbert's absence—he spirited her away to his home province of Brittany, lodging her with his sister until after the doubt-fully blessed event. It was a boy, and they named him Astralabe.

Abelard's conduct in this episode makes it clear that he had not simply been toying with a maiden's affection. He might well have gotten away with leaving her to her own devices, which did not in-clude those of a modern abortion clinic. He was enough of a schemer and a celebrity to evade his responsibility. Instead, he embraced it, without hesitation. And instead of relegating Héloïse to the care of a Paris midwife, he went to considerable trouble to entrust her to a reliable and compassionate relative.

He went further. He asked Fulbert to discuss the situation with him personally. This must have taken some courage and resolve, be-cause Fulbert, ever since his niece's unexpected departure, had been chronically and almost literally foaming with rage. He managed to bring himself sufficiently under control, however, to agree to the meeting at which Abelard told him the whole, painful story and asked his forgiveness. He offered to marry Héloïse, but secretly in order to protect his status and reputation as a cleric and philosopher. (Mar-riage of a minor cleric, though permitted by canon law, was widely considered, in that ostensibly celibate-dominated society, as a rather squalid compromise.)

A public marriage might have satisfied Fulbert, or at least have mollified him. The self-centered Abelard could not see that a secret marriage, from the uncle's viewpoint, was as bad as no marriage at all. Nevertheless Fulbert agreed to the arrangement, perhaps because he expected that Abelard's marital status would be irrelevant to the revenge he may already have had in mind. In addition, Abelard, as his son-in-law, would probably be more reliably accessible for any re-venge, whatever it might be.

The agreement reached, Abelard set off for Brittany to bring Héloïse back for the wedding. As a dedicated male egocentric, he had not consulted her beforehand. He was therefore astonished to hear her decline the nuptial bliss he was offering, and on grounds that he himself might have proposed. The marriage would ruin him profes-sionally, she argued; even if it could be kept secret, the most splendid mind in Europe should not be distracted by the burdens of family life. She marshaled her arguments as he might have, calling on essayists of ancient Rome and on Fathers and Doctors of the Church for support. She even offered, as a final desperate ploy, to live with him as his mistress, so that he would be free to return to a life of restraint at some later time. All to no avail.

She agreed to marry him, Abelard explained in his memoirs, because she could not bring herself to offend him, to seem not to love him, to prevent him from honoring his pledge to her uncle. The wedding, needless to report, was an extremely quiet affair, with very few relatives and friends, and no fanfare. When it was over, the lovers parted, seeing each other thereafter only on those rare occasions when secrecy could be maintained.

The arrangement did not last long. The marriage soon became public, through the studied indiscretion of her side of the family, led by Fulbert. To protect Abelard, Héloïse resorted to a lustrously white lie, denying her marriage to all who asked. When Abelard heard that Fulbert was abusing her for this defiance, he arranged for her to move to the convent where she had stayed as a child. (Their son was with his sister in Brittany.) This so infuriated the Fulbert camp that they immediately activated their plan for revenge. In the dark of the night, some hired thugs crept into Abelard's house, seized him, and castrated him.

Abelard could take the pain but not the humiliation. A man of aggressive ego rising out of insecurity, he feared ridicule above all else. Withdrawing to the famous local abbey of Saint-Denis, he became a Benedictine monk, perpetual vows and all. Héloïse, at his characteristically peremptory bidding, but willingly because she wanted to share in his distress, became a Benedictine nun, perpetual vows and all, at her convent a few miles away. She clearly was stunned, overwhelmed by the realization that they would never really be together again as long as they lived.

Abelard the contentious was not built for the close quarters of monastery life. The undisciplined behavior and corruption among the monks at Saint-Denis offended him, and he naturally had to express his disdain. This created such a persistent ruckus of hostility among the "religious" that he was finally given permission to leave his brothers and settle on a piece of land in the country, where he built a crude hut for solitary contemplation. But the most popular teacher in Europe was not likely to enjoy such solitude for long. Sure enough, his retreat was discovered, and students descended on him from all directions, at first constructing their own simple mud huts but before long graduating to stone. They built him a modest church for community prayer, which he dedicated to the Holy Spirit— thereby drawing the fire of his ever watchful critics, who eagerly accused him of thus questioning the unity of the Holy Trinity. This sort of harassment, some of it much more severe and official— condemnations, book burnings, brotherly attempts at murder by dirk and poisoned cup—was to be his lot throughout his life. His punishment went far beyond fitting the crime.

When Héloïse's convent was closed in 1131 and the nuns were dispersed during a clerical hassle over real estate, Abelard acted promptly to take care of her, obtaining the permission of the local bishop to deed some of his property to her and any nuns who wished to be with her. Thus was founded the convent Le Paraclet (significantly, the Holy Spirit again), of which Héloïse was appointed mother superior, or abbess. It is another of history's many ironies that now, between these two religious houses dedicated to the celibate life, between an abbot and an abbess, there were exchanged some of the world's most celebrated love letters.

She started the correspondence with a report that she had seen a copy of his memoirs—entitled, unsurprisingly, *Historia Calamitatum*, or *An Account of My Misfortunes*—and that he had salted rather than eased her wounds with his almost casual, offhand references to her role in his life and to their love. She reproached him, too, for not writing to her. He still meant everything to her, she wrote; she still ached for him, yearned for him in body and mind. She longed to see him, to talk with him, to know that he was alive, to share some of his life, his experiences, his thoughts and feelings, even if only through letters. Since he was still having trouble getting along with his sainted brethren, she even urged him to consider joining her community as abbot. As its founder, she argued, he owed it to the nuns, who needed his counsel and protection.

Abelard replied warmly, even lovingly, but less ardently. Evidently alarmed by her expression of longings that he could never satisfy, and indeed that should never be satisfied despite her lack of vocation to the monastic life, he begged her to sublimate her passion, to offer her love and her sacrifice to Jesus. As for his joining the community, he naturally had misgivings, but in following letters they reached a compromise when he agreed to adapt the Benedictine rule—which was written for men—for women and specifically for her convent. To a great extent he simply formalized what she had written informally in her letters. They were of one mind on the subject of monastic reform.

Meanwhile, Abelard the obstreperous had been emerging from his uneasy diffidence into the polemic limelight once again. His writing and teaching cast such a cold, clear light on devoutly held doctrines that he attracted the attention of Bernard of Clairvaux, an extraordinarily gifted, anti-intellectual Cistercian monk and self-appointed defender of the faith. His attacks resulted in Abelard's condemnation by a council and then by the pope in 1141. He retreated, crestfallen, to the abbey at Cluny, headed by Peter the Venerable, a man of dispassionate wisdom and great tolerance. Somehow Peter managed to reconcile Bernard and Abelard and to persuade the pope to allow his guest to live out his life in peace at Cluny. The following year Abelard, aged sixty-two, died, and Peter brought his body to Paraclet for burial. He did this to honor a request that Abelard had made before his death, and to bring Héloïse some measure of consolation for the long years ahead. This man was, he told her affectionately, "your Abelard."

In the twenty-two years remaining to her, Héloïse and her nuns made their community a model of Christian monasticism. Its reputation for rectitude and for learning in what today we would call the humanities brought it not only the respect of intellectuals but also the admiration of the people at large. It became so esteemed by families with young women that Héloïse, before her death in 1164, had to establish six subcommunities, or "daughter houses," to accommodate the applicants. She was honored by abbots and bishops and popes. Abelard would have been very pleased with her indeed.

Lucrezia Borgia
and the
Prince of Salerno

Lucrezia Borgia was formally engaged to be married at the age of eleven, in 1491.

The Borgias were an intensely Spanish family living in an intensely Italian city, Rome. They were also newly rich social climbers whose family tree was dwarfed by the sequoias of the Spanish nobility. Lucrezia's father, Cardinal Rodrigo Borgia, always on the lookout for useful family connections, saw a splendid one in her betrothal to a young scion of a gratifyingly ancient Spanish line. Her status as the bastard daughter of a concubine was no impediment. All the cardinal's children were bastards, because of his theoretical celibacy, but this was no serious drawback in the high society of the times. The Spanish nobility might sniff at the Borgias' relatively dim ancestry but not at the chance for a family connection with the Vatican, however illegitimate.

Indeed, the cardinal was even able to do some picking and choos-

13

ing. Soon after Lucrezia's betrothal, he broke her engagement and had her married by proxy to another pubescent scion of a more prestigious Spanish family. But less than a year later, in 1492, he was elected pope. As Alexander VI, ruler of the papal states that spread across the calf of the Italian boot, he quickly grew more interested in Italian connections. Before the year was out, Lucrezia's proxy marriage was dissolved, and in June 1493 she was married to Giovanni Sforza, a widowed Italian nobleman of twenty-eight and count of the principality of Pesaro. (Italy was well behind the rest of Europe in the trend to nationalism.) Alexander needed the powerful Sforza family's military support in case the French landed in Naples to the south and thereby threatened the papal states.

What the pope did not know was that Giovanni, despite a proud bearing and harsh manner, was probably the least of the Sforzas in both power and character. He proved to be a thoroughly unreliable, treacherous ally. Partly as a result of the Sforzas' collaboration, French troops under Charles VIII were able to travel down the Italian boot, through the papal states (with Alexander's resentful but impotent concurrence), and into Naples as conquerors. There, besides acquiring from generous Neapolitan ladies an especially virulent brand of syphilis, brought by Columbus's crew from the New World and ironically fated to become known as "the French disease," they conducted themselves so offensively that Naples soon seethed with rebellion. As French health and morale waned, the young and rather callow Charles decided to stop playing Charlemagne and to return to the secure comforts of his homeland. He was encouraged in this decision by many of the Italian barons, who were inspired by the French leave-taking into prodding the dispirited visitors northward at every opportunity. They even engaged in a cooperative effort: Venice, Milan, and the papal states joined in a military league with the Spanish king and the German emperor, precariously throwing the rascals out by inviting some other rascals in. The last battle of the campaign, in July 1495, marked the end of the French visitation.

By this time Alexander had concluded that he had wasted Lucrezia on Giovanni Sforza and that he deserved another chance to use her more profitably. Through the powers of his office and a considerable transfer of ducats, he managed to have the marriage dissolved on the questionable grounds of Giovanni's impotence, thus leaving Lucrezia in a state of marketable virginity. In appearing before the papal commission that formalized her virgin status, she managed to conceal, under a voluminous gown, her sixth-month pregnancy, initiated apparently by an overly attentive papal chamberlain who had been conveniently eliminated before the hearing took place.

Alexander's touching faith in Lucrezia's marketability was rewarded when King Frederic of Naples made his nephew Alfonso the prince of Salerno and recommended him to the pope as a suitor for his daughter. Although Alexander surely recognized this as a good deal—Naples could offer weighty support in his quarrels with neighboring barons—he stalled for several months to get the best possible terms. Finally, in July 1498, Lucrezia and Alfonso, who was now also duke of Bisceglie and richer to the tune of a papal dowry of forty thousand ducats, were married in the Vatican amid the usual overpowering Renaissance splendor.

Lucrezia was no longer the passive, uncomprehending little girl that she had been in her previous marital and pseudomarital adventures in this totally male-dominated society. She was a young woman of eighteen now, a slender, accomplished, attractive blonde obviously ready for a husband more palatable than Giovanni Sforza, who among other things was fifteen years her senior. Since she was still acting strictly under orders, we can imagine her surprised delight on learning that Alfonso was her own age, beautifully educated, honest, diffident, courteous, and reputedly one of the best-looking lads ever to visit Rome.

She was probably somewhat nervous about her reputation and the effect it might have on Alfonso. Sforza, soon after signing the affidavit of impotence that permitted dissolving their marriage, began nursing his resentment against this aspersion on his Italian manhood into a towering rage. It was a rage undoubtedly fed by his suppressed recognition that his own greed for the payoff (he had been allowed to keep Lucrezia's dowry) had been used by the Borgias to lead him into his predicament. Rather than addressing the greed problem, he took the easier and more satisfying course of lashing out at the Borgias, spreading the rumor that they had conspired to get rid of him because the womanizing pope and his womanizing son, Cesare Cardinal Borgia, wanted the toothsome Lucrezia for their own bedtime calisthenics. This imputation of incest, encouraged by Alexander's obvious fondness for his daughter and his emotional dependence on her despite her chattel status, hovered about Lucrezia like a noisome vapor throughout most of her life.

Indeed, it has clung to her throughout history. Yet the unsavory aspects of her reputation, as celebrated for instance in the Hugo play and the Donizetti opera, seem to be calumnies planted in the fertile field of a gossip. The devious, conniving, lustful, and rapacious Borgia gentlemen had earned a horde of implacable enemies ever eager to blacken their reputations even beyond what they deserved, and if this required getting at them through the girl, so much the worse for Lucrezia. Against such questionable sources of information are the reports of people motivated to give an accurate account of her character and behavior—agents of the families of prospective husbands, for example, who wanted to take no trollop or viper to their collective bosom—and these reports are uniformly favorable. She had much of the addiction to creature comforts and clothing displays and social pleasures that characterized her time and place, but this was no debit in that time and place. Generally she was found to be a very pleasant young lady, spirited and fun-loving but discreet and considerate of others, a graceful dancer, a polished conversationalist, and generally a model of deportment.

Whatever her reputation among the gossipmongers, she certainly did not disappoint Alfonso, who was as delighted with her as she was with him. Their wedding night was evidently one of unalloyed bliss, at least if reports of their moonstruck behavior thereafter are to be credited. Lucrezia's opinion of marriage rose immeasurably. As they set up their elaborate Renaissance housekeeping in one of the Vatican palaces, Alexander observed her happiness and was overjoyed. His love for his daughter—doubtless a form of self-love—was deep and genuine, second only to his love of political maneuvering.

Therein, of course, lay the rub. He wished ardently to cement his relationship with King Frederic of Naples much further by marrying his son Cesare to Frederic's unmarried daughter (and Alfonso's sister). Frederic resisted, however. He was nervous enough about his present connections with the Borgias as it was—his daughter Sancia had been married for some time to one of Alexander's less consequential sons and was reputedly Cesare's mistress as well—and the thought of more cement dismayed him. In addition, he found the idea of his daughter's marrying a cardinal, or even an ex-cardinal, rather unsettling. And so he stalled, and stalled, until finally, in May 1499, during a visit to Paris, Cesare impulsively married a French princess. This broke the stalemate, but the French connection gave Alexander another and different sort of headache. The king of France, now Louis XII, claimed title to Naples, relegating Frederic to the status of interloper. So France and Naples were enemies, and Alexander found himself uncomfortably astraddle.

If it was an awkward position for him, it was all the more so for Alfonso, since eliminating him might be one way of solving the papal dilemma. And so in August 1499, after consulting with the Neapolitan ambassador, the young Italian took French leave, heading south to the protection of a nearby friendly castle. Alexander, upon learning of his abrupt departure, was furious with him for letting politics interfere with his love for Lucrezia. Papal troops set out at once to overtake the refugee and bring him back, but the best they could do was to intercept a letter to Lucrezia in which Alfonso explained his reason for leaving and begged her to join him. Since she never saw the letter, Lucrezia, now six months pregnant, was inconsolable over her beloved's apparently callous act of desertion. To distract her from her sorrow, Alexander sent her north to the beautiful town of Spoleto, which was under papal rule. To augment her distraction, he even appointed her governor of the town and its environs.

She acquitted herself quite well in this capacity, according to local chroniclers, who described her as a competent administrator and fair judge. Her stay in Spoleto was brief, however, because her doting father, always distraught over any absence of hers from his side, had managed to persuade Frederic to persuade Alfonso to return. The young man showed up in Spoleto in mid-September for a tearfully joyous reunion. After a four-day second honeymoon, the couple left Spoleto to join the pope in a town some twenty miles from Rome for another week or so of loving relaxation. In November, back at the Vatican, Lucrezia bore a son whom she named Rodrigo after her father. The ecstatic pope rewarded Alfonso by making him a commander in the papal army.

It was as a papal official, therefore, that Alfonso found himself riding out of Rome with other dignitaries in February 1500 to greet his brother-in-law Cesare, who was now returning from France after a number of French-supported victories over some northern Italian duchies. Alfonso could not have been very happy in this role, since Cesare was at best a friend and ally of Naples' foremost enemy. But Cesare's dazzling success as a warrior and his equally dazzling personality—despite both his conspicuous syphilis and his growing irritability—seemed to mesmerize his father and sister, as well as perhaps everyone else in Rome, and the young Neapolitan cooperated. Nevertheless, in the following months he seems to have shown some open resistance to the French influence at the Vatican, with comments which Cesare characteristically would have found offensive, if not flagrantly insulting. In addition, the situation might have been emotionally surcharged by the fact that Alfonso's sister Sancia joined in his resistance.

The climax came one evening in mid-July. Alfonso, after having a quiet supper with Alexander, Lucrezia and Sancia, was crossing the square when he was attacked by five armed ruffians. Severely wounded in head, shoulder, arm, and leg, he managed with some help to get back into the Vatican, where Lucrezia promptly fainted at the sight of him. Four days later both young people were still running a fever, until Lucrezia, perhaps through sheer will power, recovered enough to join Sancia in nursing her husband.

The two women, strongly suspecting that the assassination attempt had been an inside job and that somebody in the Vatican might want it completed, arranged that one of them would always be at the victim's bedside. They followed this procedure faithfully until one evening in mid-August when Alfonso, apparently on his way to recovery, was being visited in his room by some friends. A captain of Cesare's guard forced his way into the room and ordered all visitors to leave. When Lucrezia and Sancia protested angrily, he told them apologetically that he was simply following orders and if they wanted those orders countermanded they had better go to the pope. In their distress they forgot their pact and left together to find Alexander. When they returned with the papal countermand, the captain was still there and Alfonso was lying on the floor beside the bed. The captain explained that the wounded man had panicked, tried to get up, and, in falling, had struck his head on the floor. When the women rushed to him, they found him dead. Only much later was it revealed that he had been strangled.

There were no witnesses, of course. Alexander may have been helpless or, more likely, very reluctant to pursue any evidence that could lead to his favorite, and formidable, son. The best medicine he could think of for Lucrezia was to send the crushed young widow back to Nepi, where she had spent that happy week with Alfonso after his return. To keep her mind off the memories that the location would surely evoke, he appointed her governor of the area. She stayed there for the next four months, in deep mourning. Her sole consolation was her infant son, Rodrigo.

Within a month or so Alexander was already maneuvering to get her a new husband. This time he may have been motivated by concern for her welfare at least as much as by political profit. He was in his seventieth year now, and it was important that she marry before his death, after which she would otherwise become virtually a nonperson. She, of course, wanted to have nothing more to do with marriage. But with time and parental pressure she came around and in September 1501 was married to another Alfonso, the twenty-four-year-old heir of the Duke of Ferrara. No prince of Salerno, this Alfonso was cut from coarser cloth, a man more devoted to artillery than to the arts of love. But he was not an unkind man, and Lucrezia's life with him over the next eighteen years, though never touched by the passionate joy that she had known so briefly, brought her a measure of comfort and content. Despite a couple of extramarital affairs of the heart, evidently quite platonic, she did stand by him faithfully for better and for worse. After her death in 1519, this rough captain wrote a relative that he could not think of her without weeping over the loss of "such a dear, sweet companion."

Elizabeth I
and
Robert Dudley

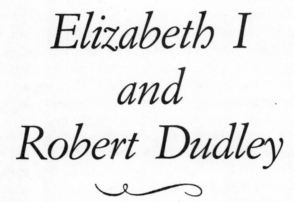

First and foremost, she was Queen of England. Indeed she *was* England, at least in the sense that none of the conniving nobles of the realm could command the wide popular support that she enjoyed, nor could they claim motivation much beyond their narrow personal ambitions. Elizabeth I was a politician first, a woman second, and if sex and romance could be useful in furthering her political aims, useful they would be. During most of her forty-five-year reign, for example, she regularly stalled ambassadors promoting princely suitors by advising them that she would have to marry a fellow Englishman, and just as regularly put off English suitors by informing them that, as queen, she really should marry a foreign prince.

Nevertheless, she was very much a woman, a woman who very much appreciated men. She was handsome, athletic, graceful, splendidly educated, intelligent, shrewd, witty, and flirtatious, and she was readily charmed by similar qualities in the men around her. During her long reign she flirted, at least, with Thomas Seymour, Admiral of the Fleet; Robert Dudley, Earl of Leicester; Sir William Pickering; Sir Christopher Hatton; François, Duke of Alençon; Sir Walter Raleigh; and of course Robert Devereaux, Earl of Essex, celebrated in Lytton Strachey's biography and Maxwell Anderson's play—in addition to countless other gallants of lesser repute. How far she carried her dedication to dalliance is not known. Her reputation at the time seems to have ranged from Virgin Queen to royal nymphomaniac. Surviving reports from ambassadors to their governments include everything from gossipy comment on her indiscretion ("The earl visits her regularly in her bedchamber") to results of more careful investigations suggesting that she was honorably undefiled. She herself on one occasion, after being upbraided by one of her ladies for causing scandal, protested that all her affairs were conducted in the unremitting presence of her solicitous retinue, so that she could hardly have consummated a love affair without the knowledge of the court. Furthermore, she added, no one would ever catch her making such a commitment to a man. And no one ever did. No nonparticipant, at least.

The man who brought her closest to making such a commitment, or perhaps even closer than that, was Robert Dudley. Their affair, which lasted through its ups and downs for more than thirty years, may have had its beginnings in the Tower of London, where they both were unwilling residents in the spring of 1554. Young Dudley, obedient son of the Duke of Northumberland, had been implicated in his ambitious father's plot against Elizabeth's older half sister, Queen Mary, and had been stowed away in the Tower for safekeeping. Elizabeth, though only a girl of twenty and no conspirator, provided a focal point for political discontent, especially Protestant discontent with the aggressively Catholic Mary, who felt more comfortable with her troublesome kitten mewed up. The Tower, however, proved as unsatisfactory for Mary as for Elizabeth, whose presence there made her too conspicuous a victim, and before long the young princess was transferred to a minor, run-down palace and kept there under house arrest. Robert also was released; having earlier acted under orders from his rather overwhelming father, he was now free to serve Queen Mary more reliably, which he did.

And so did Elizabeth, at least ostensibly. She could afford to wait quietly, even submissively. Mary was fortyish, frail, and feeble, suffering from delusions of pregnancy but much more likely to leave life than to give it. If Mary died soon, and childless, Elizabeth would soon be queen. When Mary brought her to live at the royal palace at Hampton Court, the heir apparent behaved herself there most pleasantly, especially toward Philip of Spain, who was Mary's consort and eleven years her junior. Both Elizabeth and Philip, very political animals that they were, recognized the mutual advantage in establishing amicable relations before ascending their respective thrones. When Philip left England for Spain in the summer of 1555, bitterly disappointed that Mary had failed either to make him the present king or to make a future king, he left behind strict orders that Elizabeth was to be treated with honor and solicitude.

During these years before Mary's death in 1558, Elizabeth found herself less able to control her emotions at the more personal, apolitical level. She fell in love, enthusiastically if not hopelessly, with the handsome, vital Robert Dudley, who was earning himself a solid reputation as both captain and courtier. He responded in kind, although he was never so able as Elizabeth to separate personal and political urges. Evidently he was very generous to her, even selling some precious land to help her out financially. When she became queen, one of her first acts was to appoint him as her Master of Horse, a post he was to fill for the next thirty years. She loved to ride.

The fact that he was married may have been all to the good from Elizabeth's point of view, since she could thus hold all the more easily to her resolve not to marry. But one day in September 1560 his wife was found dead, her neck broken, at the bottom of a long flight of stairs in their home. The London gossip cauldron at once bubbled furiously with rumors of uxoricide, although a more likely explanation was that a weakness in the poor woman's cancer-ridden body caused the fatal fall. Her death released Robert to pursue his political ambitions as well as Elizabeth herself, presenting Elizabeth with the dilemma of keeping his interest while resisting his proposals. Although he was a splendid dancer and enthralling romancer, she had reservations about his qualities as a husband, especially a husband with a head itching for a crown.

Robert's irresistible force had met its immovable object. His ceaseless efforts in his strenuous pursuit of the double prize ranged from the grandiose, as when he tried to negotiate for the support of Spain, to the frivolous, as when he suggested to Elizabeth at a party that a bishop in attendance would be glad to tie the binding knot on request. Elizabeth clearly enjoyed the fencing but was never so touched as to lose control; whenever the woman began to weaken into loving assent, the queen would forcibly assert herself, and Robert would lose yet another round. She continued to invite his company, to shower him with royal favors, to permit him to take liberties denied to others. In 1564 she made him Earl of Leicester. But she would not make him king.

Sometimes the bold Lord Robert would presume on their mutual affection rashly enough to invite a comeuppance. On one notable occasion one of his retainers went to the queen's private rooms for an audience but was stopped at the door by a gentleman charged with guarding her privacy. The earl's man returned to his master, who shortly appeared at the door and imperiously swept by the guardian gentleman. The gentleman, however, rushed ahead of him to Elizabeth and knelt before her with a plea cunningly designed to strike a royal spark. "Tell me," he begged her, "who wears the crown, the Earl of Leicester or Your Majesty?" The royal fire flared out at Robert. "I have wished you well," she told him, "but not to the exclusion of others. I will have here but one mistress and no master." Robert, thoroughly subdued, for some time thereafter (according to at least one chronicler) was a very model of loyal humility. Elizabeth, too, was eager to dispel any tension, and soon they were a loving couple again.

And so it went, on again, off again. In the fall of 1565 Elizabeth was greatly taken with an especially irresistible young stalwart of the court. Their flirting so annoyed Robert that he took up with a luscious lady of the court named Lettice Knollys. Although married, she returned his interest with interest, and now it was Elizabeth's turn to turn a little green. But after a period of reciprocal sulking and an angry scene of charge and countercharge, the two incorrigibles made up again and resumed their irrepressible dalliance. And Robert went right on hoping.

For another dozen tempestuous years, and then he gave up hope. In the summer of 1579 Elizabeth learned that he had been cozening her for nearly a year, having been secretly married the previous autumn to the widowed Lettice. True daughter of her father, she wanted to store him in the Tower, but the rule of English law prevailed, and the worst she could do was to keep him under house arrest for a while, and under orders to stay away from the court after that.

But not for long. She simply could not deny herself his company. His place in the court and in her affections was largely restored, so much so that John Lyly's play *Endymion* in 1585 portrayed him allegorically as the queen's lover. When he died in 1558 he owed her a fortune. His death sent her into a paroxysm of grief—undiminished by the news of the famous victory over the Spanish armada. She locked herself in her room and wept so long that her councilors, in alarm, finally forced their way through the door. Among her personal treasures found in a casket after her death fifteen years later was an affectionate note from Robert, labeled by Elizabeth in a trembling hand, "His last letter."

Deborah Read
and
Benjamin Franklin

~⁓~

It is engraved in American folklore now, the picture of the maiden standing in the door of her house and gently laughing at the young hero as, at the start of his adventurous life, he slogged down Market Street in Philadelphia, his pockets bulging with spare shirts and socks, his cheeks bulging with the large, puffy roll he was dispatching, his arms gripped to his sides to keep the other two rolls under them from falling. The girl, Benjamin Franklin remarked in his autobiography, clearly "thought I made, as I certainly did, a most awkward, ridiculous appearance."

He was a teen-aged fugitive from the close doctrinal confines of Puritan Boston, where his disputatious views on organized religion had garnered him a reputation as a smart-aleck atheist. He had fled now, in 1723, because he expected greater tolerance, or indifference, in Quaker Philadelphia (it would not disappoint him). And rolls cost only a third of what they cost in Boston.

Not long thereafter, having found a job with a local printer and having received his long-delayed luggage, he arranged room and board at a house nearby. The house, he was delighted to learn, was owned by a Mr. Read, whose daughter Deborah turned out to be the risible young lady of Market Street. This time, he felt, "I made a rather more respectable appearance" in her eyes. During the follow-ing months he found some opportunity, between his work and his insatiable reading, to cultivate her good opinion, as well as to form a very good opinion of her. "I had made some courtship during this time to Miss Read. I had a great respect and affection for her, and had some reason to believe she had the same for me; but, as I was about to take a long voyage, and we were both very young, only a little above eighteen, it was thought most prudent by her mother to prevent our going too far at present, as a marriage, if it was to take place, would be more convenient after my return, when I should be, as I expected, set up in my business. Perhaps, too, she [Mrs. Read] thought my expectations not so well founded as I imagined them to be."

The voyage was nothing less than a visit to London, and Deborah's wary mother was quite right about his overexpectations. Franklin had been gulled into making the trip by a character in touch with un-reality, if not an outright charlatan. He found himself in England without a job, without money, without connections, and without friends except a young man who had left his wife and children adrift in America and was more of a liability than an asset. Under these worrisome circumstances he wrote to Deborah only once in the nearly two years he was away, to let her know that he could not return as early as planned. Amid his various preoccupations during the following months, he came to forget her, as he put it in his auto-biography, "by degrees."

In the summer of 1726, promised a job in Philadelphia by a Quaker merchant, he returned home with renewed hope. But the merchant died almost immediately, as well as most inconsiderately, and again Franklin faced an impoverished present and a bleak future. If this was not enough to depress him, he could contemplate De-borah's situation. After months of nothing but silence from him, her mother and friends had begun giving her the you're-not-getting-any-younger treatment until, in despair, she had married a promising young man who proved to be little else. After he had frittered away her dowry, she discovered evidence of another wife waiting for him in England. On the strength of this she had left him and returned to her parents. Franklin's heart went out to her, for she could not now be reliably considered either married or marriageable, and this was a pitiable status for any American woman in the eighteenth century. He felt, if not guilty, at least largely responsible for her predicament, but his shrunken purse kept him from doing anything about it.

Over the next four years, amid dizzying ups and downs in his fortunes, he continued his renewed friendship with the Read family. They were not reproachful about his role in Deborah's misfortunes; Mrs. Read "was good enough to think the fault more her own than mine, as she had prevented our marrying before I went thither, and persuaded the other match in my absence." Yet "I pitied poor Miss Read's unfortunate situation, who was generally dejected and seldom cheerful, and avoided company. . . . Our mutual affection was revived, but there were now great objections to our union." Objections, to put it mildly. If Deborah's wastrel turned up after their marriage and could not be shown to have another wife, Ben and Deborah could be whipped and given life imprisonment for bigamy. Further, there could be no dowry, and there was a baby. Ben's reticence about the origin of his son William, who later became governor of New Jersey, has left historians to guess whether the baby was their son, or only his, or only hers. If only his, her willingness to raise the child as theirs would have greatly made up for the lack of dowry.

That possibility is related to another reason for Ben's wanting to settle down with a good woman. He was in his libidinous mid-twenties, and Pennsylvania law was quite high-minded and heavy-handed in matters of adultery and indiscriminate fornication. He had in the past "consorted with low women" and had considered himself very lucky to have escaped the pox (though not nearly so lucky as he really was). He was not eager to take such risks again. The risks involved in "our union" seemed less horrendous to him. Deborah was an attractive girl, and he was probably as much in love as a man of such varied intellectual talents and preoccupations could ever be. Nevertheless, he may have somewhat hedged his, or their, bet. When they were joined in September 1730, it was not in a formal marriage but in a common-law arrangement. Deborah simply began to be called Mrs. Franklin and came to live with Mr. Franklin. This procedure, whatever it might have been considered in Boston, was quite acceptable to the residents of Philadelphia and especially to the newly united Franklins.

Ben was a risk taker, as he was to prove much later when he signed the Declaration of Independence. He was lucky in that case, and he was in this. Deborah's prodigal husband reportedly was killed in a brawl in the West Indies; at any rate, he never returned. She was quite happy with Ben; although somewhat intimidated by his growing reputation, she was an "afeckshonet wife," as she signed herself in her letters to one of the most literate men in the colonies. Their relationship may have been more exclusive, as well as more romantic and passionate, than Ben was ever disposed to reveal in his letters. Much of his reputation for extramarital wandering in later years came from purse-lipped, professional disapprovers like John Adams. There is a good deal of difference between an openly flirtatious rogue and a dedicated lecher, a difference that John Adamses can easily overlook. What was more important, as Ben put it, was that the couple "mutually endeavored to make each other happy."

As partners, they also endeavored to make each other prosperous. On Market Street, only a couple of blocks from where she had first seen him wrapping himself around that roll, they opened a general store, which she managed, and a newspaper and print shop, which was chiefly his responsibility. Within two years he was out of debt, a happy emergence for which he gave her much of the credit. She might list the church sexton as the "seck stone," but she knew how to keep inventory—and how to work. They worked together constantly throughout each day without resort to hammer and tongs, eloquent testimony to their compatibility. He was lured from her side, and his work, only by his incorrigible reading of books and by the writing of *Poor Richard's Almanack*, which would set him on the road to fame and fortune. But he was by no means utterly distracted: In 1732 their son Francis Folger was born.

That son died of smallpox in 1736, and not until 1743 was their last child, Sara, born. By that time they had prospered mightily. Their investments in real estate, printing enterprises, and the like were enough to give them a comfortable income without noses to grindstone, and so Ben retired at the age of forty-two to devote himself to whatever struck his wide-ranging fancy, especially science and public affairs. This was also a turning point for Deborah, but a much less felicitous one. No more cozy partnership, no more togetherness at work. Her husband was, after all, the man who founded the world's first subscription library, established the Philadelphia fire department and reorganized the police, renovated the system of street maintenance, raised funds to set up a city hospital, helped found the University of Pennsylvania and the American Philosophical Society, improved the colonial postal service, did pioneering research in electricity which included the discovery of electricity in lightning and the invention of the lightning rod, developed the sturdily efficient Franklin stove, charted the Gulf Stream, urged the adoption of daylight saving time, invented bifocals, and proposed the use of lime to counter acidity in soils—among other things. How could any ordinary wife keep up with him? It was not enough to be afeckshonet.

To this occupational separation, in 1757, was added a geographical one when the Pennsylvania assembly sent Ben to London to represent it in a tax dispute with the proprietary Penn family. When he and son William left that summer, Deborah was heartsick but too afraid of the sea to go with him. She and Sara consoled themselves with the thought that their men would come back in about eighteen months, but in the event it was more like sixty-five.

He stayed home for two years after his return, although they were separated much of the time while he made long trips throughout the colonies on postal business. In October 1764 the assembly again dispatched him to England in the same tiring cause, for the Penn family were formidable and durable adversaries. This time Deborah was, according to Ben's testimony, his most valued correspondent. He looked forward to her letters, enjoyed them hugely, including their imaginative spelling, and was warmed by the admiring, solicitous love they brought him in his often uncomfortable isolation, especially during the turmoil brought on by the Stamp Act.

Yet his situation in England also offered many compensations— the stimulation of lively conversation, the respect and comradeship of fellow scientists, the entertainments—which took the edge off yearnings homeward. After June 1769, when Deborah suffered a stroke that dimmed her mind and memory, her letters diminished gradually in length and frequency. In September 1774 he complained, "It is now nine months since I received a line from my dear Debby." In December she was dead. The following February he finally came home.

Theirs was not the grandest, most spectacular passion in the history of love, but it was nonetheless an affair of the heart. A gentle one. In 1790, shortly before his death, Ben wrote to a French admirer in Paris (the wife of the chemist Lavoisier) to thank her for sending him a portrait that she had done of him. During the war, he wrote, the British had taken his portrait from his house, "leaving that of its companion, my wife, by itself, a kind of widow. You have replaced the husband and the lady seems to smile, as well pleased."

Abigail Smith
and
John Adams

‿❧

P hysically, neither of them was such as to inspire a deep romantic passion in the other. In 1762 Abigail Smith, although a willowy, pleasant-looking girl of eighteen, was certainly no voluptuous beauty. John Adams, a twenty-seven-year-old lawyer, short and stocky and on his way to rotund, was certainly no dashing cavalier. Shallow people may well have asked what they could see in each other. Yet the passionate and affectionate love between them survived long separations and intense political distractions for more than half a century.

Living their early lives in neighboring Massachusetts towns, they knew each other very casually for some years, and they were not impressed. But in 1762 John began visiting her home with a friend who was courting his sister, a friend whose charming good looks invited invidious comparison but apparently fazed neither John nor Abigail in the least. The sparks between them were conversational, the interaction of two very agile minds. This is what drew them together—as he once put it, like steel to magnet, feather to glass. As a mere woman in eighteenth-century New England, she naturally had had no formal education, but her affluent parson father had put his respectable library at her disposal and encouraged her to join in social gatherings with his literate friends, and her active and inquisitive mind took it from there. John, with a law degree from Harvard, was an aspiring young attorney with an interest in legal principles far beyond the grubby details of deeds and wills. Both were articulate, sometimes competitively talkative, eager to share knowledge, opinions, curiosity. When John's friend and Abigail's sister were married that November, John did not discontinue his visits. Three years earlier he had described Abigail in his diary in words of light dismissal. Now he wrote, "Tender feelings, sensible, friendly. A friend. Not an imprudent, not an indelicate, not a disagreeable word or action. Prudent, modest, delicate, soft, sensible, obligating, active." Soon they were discussing marriage.

John was ready, willing, and able, but Abigail was still considered too young to be ready or willing or able. In addition, her mother, as the wife of a parson of importance, felt that her daughter should be given some time to find something less disreputable than a lawyer, even one with a degree from Harvard. And indeed John had some misgivings about his ability to support a family, although his growing practice in Boston, combined with a house and some land he had inherited, constituted a comforting augury. Abigail, however, had no misgivings about anything and was very impatient with the few miles that separated them while he plied his trade in Boston, their togetherness limited to brief, if ardent, visits and longer, more ardent letters. The delay was lengthened when a smallpox epidemic broke out in Boston and he had himself inoculated—a precaution more uncomfortable, dangerous and time-consuming than it is today.

He continued to write while recovering from the inoculation, but his letters had to be smoked before leaving his house, to prevent contagion, and smoked again on receipt before being given to Abigail. In one of her letters she asked him if he had ever robbed a bird's nest and noticed "how the poor bird would fly around—just so they say I hover around Tom while he is smoking my letters." But gradually their wedding day grew more predictable, and in a letter worthy of much hovering John showed how he was looking forward to it. "Oh, my dear girl," he wrote (with eighteenth-century spelling and punctuation, updated here), "I thank heaven that another fortnight will restore you to me after so long a separation. My soul and body have both been thrown into disorder by your absence, and a month or two more would make me the most insufferable cynic in the world. . . . But you who have always softened and warmed my heart shall restore my benevolence as well as my health and tranquility of mind. You shall polish and refine my sentiments of life and manners, banish all the unsocial and ill-natured particles in my composition, and form me to that happy temper that can reconcile a quick discernment with a perfect candor." They were married in October 1764.

They settled in at John's house and small farm by the little town of Braintree just south of Boston, which they could see from nearby Penn's Hill when they went out walking together on a clear day. Since the house was large enough to include John's law office, they were together a great deal—no letters required. Their first child, Abigail, or "Nabby," was born in July 1765, and their second, John Quincy, almost exactly two years later. The children's upbringing, as well as the upkeep of the house and farm, became more and more Abigail's responsibility as John's practice increased and as he became involved in the intermittent rumblings of unrest over British policies in the colonies, particularly in the turmoil over the Stamp Act in 1766. He did some agonizing over the conflicting demands of home and family versus the law and politics but apparently convinced himself that they were not irreconcilable. In January 1768, with no little reluctance, he moved his family and office to Boston, where the legal and political action was.

This was fine with Abigail, who liked the big town of sixteen thousand and its bustling life, despite the noise and pollution. But she saw less of John now as his practice burgeoned. Many of his cases had political implications. He took on the defense of John Hancock, later of signature fame, against a charge of smuggling, and represented four sailors who had killed an officer of the Royal Navy in a struggle to decline his pressing invitation to join that venerable institution. When cases came to John involving an altercation between colony and crown, his sympathies were overwhelmingly colonial, but in his most celebrated case he defended a British captain and his men against a charge of murdering five colonists during the "Boston Massacre" in March 1770. He was the only lawyer in the vicinity of Boston willing to take the case, including pro-British lawyers. Although he and Abigail feared mob retaliation and expected his career to suffer permanent damage, they believed firmly in the right of the accused to counsel. Fortunately, the case did not come to trial until autumn, by which time the general fever had cooled down enough for reason to have a say in the matter. Only two of the soldiers were punished, receiving light sentences for manslaughter, while the captain and the other six men were acquitted. And John, far from becoming the butt of popular outrage, found his reputation for courage and conviction, and dedication to democratic processes, justifiably enhanced. Abigail, who shared in the applause, although not nearly so much as she should have, was proudly delighted.

She could, however, share in a goodly measure of his coffeehouse politics, since some of the gatherings were held in their home, where her intelligence and wit could gain her some entry into this male world. Among those attending such meetings were John's firebrand cousin, Sam Adams, and his wife. Although John was more conservative and cautious than Sam, the couples enjoyed their provocative conversations as well as an easy camaraderie. Abigail loved being with John on these and other similar occasions, and once in a while she even had time to go to court and watch him in action, but after he was elected to the Massachusetts legislature in June 1770, his absences from home during its sessions helped her understand the kind of sacrifice that might be demanded of her.

John's frantic pace caught up with him toward the end of 1770, when his health began to fail. In some alarm he and Abigail moved back with the family (four children now) to Braintree, where the air was purer and the demands on his time were less relentless. The next couple of years there, which included a good deal of circuit riding to keep up his law practice, did restore his health, and so they all returned to Boston in November 1772. Soon thereafter the Boston Tea Party, in which they were not involved, gave focus to the anti-British sentiment in the colony; and England's effort to blockade and otherwise isolate the city—though it proved a failure when the other colonies came to Boston's rescue—did nothing to lighten the Adamses' shared concern over America's future as well as their own.

Their concern was heightened in the autumn of 1774, when John was away for four months in Philadelphia as a delegate to the First Continental Congress. Not only did the calling of the Congress imply a trend toward rebellion, but there also was a chance that the British might round up the delegates and ship them to England for trial. The postal service offered John and Abigail little to nourish their love, but it was all they had. Letters could take two weeks to cover the three hundred miles between them. Further, John, suspicious of British surveillance of the post, usually sent his letters by private messenger. This and his feverish activity kept him from holding up his end of the correspondence to Abigail's satisfaction, faithful though he was. Their letters discussed management of the household and the farm at Braintree, financial crises, education of the children, his frustrations and satisfactions with the Congress, her worry over the still-simmering unrest in New England, and other social and political issues (such as slavery in the colonies, which especially distressed her in view of Americans' talk about freedom). Every so often their heartache over their separation would come to the surface, as when she wrote to her "Much Loved Friend, . . . I dare not express to you at 300 miles' distance how ardently I long for your return. . . . The idea plays about my heart, unnerves my hand whilst I write, awakens all the tender sentiments that years have increased and matured. . . . The whole collected stock of ten weeks' absence knows not how to brook any longer restraint, but will break forth and flow thru my pen."

It was not until three years later that it looked as though he might come home for good from his work with the Second Continental Congress, and then the couple were suddenly faced with his election by the Congress to join Benjamin Franklin and Arthur Lee in representing American interests in Europe. Again their need for each other yielded to their devotion to their fledgling country. In February 1778 John and ten-year-old John Quincy sailed for France, the latter being brought along to gain experience, learn French, and give his father some clerical help. Abigail encouraged them both to go, but not out of any selfish considerations. There she sat at home by the fire, she wrote in a rare moment of self-pity, "bereft of my better half, and added to that a limb lopped off to heighten the anguish." They reached France on March 30 and John immediately wrote to her, but she did not receive his letter until the end of June. By then she was near despair.

Over the next eighteen months John's letter were few, far between, and distressingly laconic. He was chronically, consumingly busy, and he was hesitant to express himself frankly in letters that might be intercepted, as indeed many were. After discovering that Franklin and Lee were more adversaries than compatriots, he decided that only one person should represent America in Paris and that it should be Franklin. He personally disapproved of Ben's suave rakishness but knew that it made him popular with the French. On his recommendation, the Congress appointed Franklin sole commissioner, and John came home in August 1779 to enjoy a second honeymoon with Abigail.

The honeymoon lasted through August and September. In October the Congress ordered John back to France as Minister Plenipotentiary to prepare for negotiations with Great Britain if and when the mother country's ministers showed themselves ready to come to terms. Abigail, despite her dismay, understood John's sense of duty and his love of being about the public business. She did not complain; indeed, she agreed that their sons, John Quincy and Charles, would profit immeasurably by making the trip with their father. And so off they sailed, in November.

Left behind with only two children and a farm now being run by tenants, Abigail unexpectedly had some time on her hands. By now totally convinced that John was, and would continue to be, far more interested in the public business than in his own, she took on a lifelong program of managing the family finances. She found that she was a good businesswoman, with a good sense of investment, and the activity gave her plenty to tell John in her letters. John cooperated by sending her articles which he could buy cheaply in Europe and she could sell dearly in America. The arrangement did not bring them luxury, but it did keep them safely out of the poorhouse despite the tax increases and painful inflation due to the war. Luxury never interested them, except in reverse: Abigail could grow quite agitated over the conspicuous luxuries being flaunted by Americans profiting from the war, and John, although attracted to the relative luxuriousness of French lifestyles, stoutly resisted it on principle.

By September 1783 they had been separated for four years by three thousand miles of formidable ocean, and both were reaching the limits of their endurance. It had always been possible for Abigail to risk the unpleasant crossing and join John in Europe, but her domestic and his political responsibilities, abetted by the feeling that he might come home at any time, kept them apart. That September, however, he was made one of the commissioners to negotiate a trade treaty with Britain (along with Franklin, John Jay, and later Thomas Jefferson). This appointment, and the increasing likelihood that he might afterward be named America's first ambassador to England, made it much less likely that he would be coming home any time soon. In his letters he began urging her to join him, together with their daughter Nabby. With considerable misgivings over the sea voyage and over her role as official wife and hostess in a strange environment, but with no doubts strong enough to keep her from John any longer, she made the necessary arrangements and, with Nabby, set sail from Boston in June 1784. After four weeks of seasickness, storms, and becalmings, they arrived in London, where John came to meet them. When he arrived at Abigail's lodgings, she was there alone. The couple were finally together after five interminable years, and the scene was of the kind over which, Abigail wrote later, even "poets and painters wisely draw a veil."

After three weeks in London, mostly as a tourist, she was severely disappointed in Paris, which she found comparatively small, dirty, and crowded. Because her French was inadequate, she was denied much conversation, and because her view of the French lifestyle was, even more than John's, the ant's view of the grasshopper's, she was rarely comfortable in company. In spite or perhaps because of their reunion, both John and Abigail began feeling homesick, although they took great delight in the continual visits of Thomas Jefferson. So it was with mixed emotions about Paris and Jefferson that they learned, in May 1785, that John, having been appointed Minister Plenipotentiary to Britain, was to leave forthwith for London— where, among other things, the people spoke a sensible language.

For this reason if for no other, the Adamses were happier in London than they had ever been in Paris. They were received courteously by royalty and nobility if not by all of the press, and they were able to make a number of good friends. But their happiness arose mostly from just being together. When Abigail was persuaded to visit Bath for a couple of weeks with some other Americans, they wrote each other almost every day. He wrote that he missed her keeping him warm at night, adding that if necessary he would take a "virgin" to bed with him for that purpose—"virgin" being a popular name for a hot water bottle. She responded to her "bedfellow" that no matter how much she missed him, she would not take up with an "abbe," reminding him that in France "they are so polite to the ladies as to accommodate them with an abbe when they give the gentlemen a nun." It was not a remark that she would have made to just anybody; doubtless she blushed as she wrote it.

By the end of 1787 John, having given up hope of negotiating a favorable trade treaty with Britain, asked that he be replaced and allowed to come home. They arrived in Boston in July 1788 to considerable public acclaim and for a long-awaited and satisfying reunion with family and friends. In March 1789, having finally gotten settled in their new home in Braintree, they learned that John had been elected George Washington's vice president and they would have to move the country's first capital city, New York. John had to leave immediately for political reasons, while Abigail had to stay behind for domestic ones. The next three months were filled with his letters importuning her to join him. She arrived in June, together with more than a hundred boxes of household goods. This time, because of her new official status, it took her somewhat longer to get settled, but she managed it before October 1790, when, courtesy of Congress, they had to move again, this time to the second capital, Philadelphia. They hated that city's miasmal environment—a yellow fever epidemic was a regular summer visitor—but luckily John had nothing much to do between sessions of Congress in his "insignificant office," as he quotably described it, so that they had to spend only their winters there.

This proved fortunate for them during John's second term, since they could not have taken four years of uninterrupted separation and since Abigail's health declined from recurrent bouts with malaria, draining her of the energy she needed to play the burdensome social role of the vice president's wife. She therefore stayed in Massachusetts while John traveled back and forth for his duties as president of the Senate. She missed him when he was away, but these intermittent separations she found much easier to take than the old protracted ones. Furthermore, her absence from Philadelphia relieved John of a great deal of entertaining which would have been expected of them as a couple and which they could not afford. In his first term such official frivolity had left the Adamses two thousand dollars in debt, a condition that they had always avoided assiduously. At the end of his second term they were ahead enough to put some money into their expanding farms. There may have been more method than malaise in Abigail's illness.

After John became President in March 1797, however, she felt much better about staying in Philadelphia and filling her role as First Lady. She enjoyed the deference shown to her almost as much as she enjoyed that shown to John, and this made the endless rounds of social functions more bearable. As her health improved, she even began to think of Philadelphia as an attractive city—at about the time that they had to move to the unfinished White House in the new unfinished capital, Washington, D.C. They made the move even though they expected that there were only a few months left of John's presidency, that he would serve only a single term. They recognized that John's successful efforts to avoid war with France had cost him the support of the hawkish wing of their own Federalist party led by Alexander Hamilton and that his support for the now notorious Alien and Sedition Acts had driven hordes of voters to Thomas Jefferson's new Republican party. John was so devastated by his defeat, which he considered a humiliating repudiation, that he left Washington surreptitiously early in the morning on Jefferson's inaugural day to avoid attending the ceremony and to hurry to Abigail, who had left for Massachusetts a few weeks earlier.

There they spent the rest of their lives together in reasonable comfort, surrounded by family and friends. Time healed the wound of John's defeat, for both of them. Their bitterness subsided, and before Jefferson left the White House, they began to develop republican—i.e., more democratic—viewpoints. As usual, they made the change together. When Abigail died in October 1818, John took her death hard, but not as hard as some expected. She was nearly seventy-four and he was nearly eighty-three, and he was confident of joining her soon. "The worthy President always appeared as the friend," a journalist wrote at the time, "who had lived himself into one with the wife of his bosom."

They had lived long enough to see John Quincy appointed Secretary of State by President Monroe. Abigail, unlike John, did not live to see their eldest son in the White House. Neither of them lived long enough to see his valiant fight, in the House of Representatives, against the crime of slavery. It would have made them proud.

Madame du Barry
and
Louis XV

"She pleases me," said King Louis XV of France. "She is pretty and she makes me happy. She makes me forget how soon I will be sixty." He was fifty-nine at the time.

In eighteenth-century France that was enough to give a luscious young doxy more political power than she could handle. Once she had been formally presented at court and awarded a title and a landed estate, once she had become the favorite of a king who ruled by a still awesome though precarious divine right, her influence was a factor to be weighed by both friends and enemies in the teeming cauldron of French politics.

Yet Jeanne Bécu, the Comtesse du Barry through a hastily arranged and quickly forgotten marriage, was a thoroughly apolitical person, unlike her predecessor in the king's affections, the notorious Madame de Pompadour, who had died five years before, in 1764. Like Pompadour, however, she had something special, even unique, that distinguished her from the ever-willing ladies on the royal satyr's interminable list. It was not merely her beauty, remarkable as that was. Although it may have been an outstanding talent for lovemaking, this seems unlikely in view of the oversupply of highly motivated competition. (This is not to suggest that her experience as a kind of call girl and as mistress to several aristocratic johnnies had not raised her above the level of basic training.) What does seem to distinguish her in the chronicles of the intrigue-laden court at Versailles has to do with her character, and more with what it lacked than with what it possessed. She was not inordinately self-seeking, ambitious, contentious, devious, waspish, underhanded, or vindictive amid a collection of courtiers and courtesans who were generally all such things and more. In the absence of such qualities, her affection for the king, who despite or because of his chronic debauchery was still an attractive man, may well have been quite genuine, as his clearly was for her.

Her rise (if that is the word) to the position of official royal mistress in 1769, while she was in her mid-twenties, resulted not from her scheming but from her being used by schemers. When she emerged, a toothsome sixteen, from her nine years in a convent school, no one could have dreamt where she would be less than ten years later. Her unmarried mother was a domestic servant, a cook, hardly a promising springboard for launching a daughter into the heady upper reaches of royal society. She did help Jeanne to get employment of sorts, first as a hairdresser and then as a companion to a dowager, but the girl's striking beauty stirred up trouble among suspicious relatives, resulting in her dismissal. A more stable job as a salesgirl in a millinery shop brought her a taste of that other world of careless luxury, as well as introductions to gentlemen eager to show her a pleasant and stimulating evening. During the next few years she attended many soirees, and it was apparently at one of these that she met the Comte Jean du Barry, an ambitious intriguer known widely in Paris as the *le Roué*. From 1764 until 1768 she was not merely his mistress but also the hostess at his salon, where she became acquainted with many of the Beautiful People of the time and quickly learned how to behave in such effervescent company. Her next stop was the palace at Versailles.

She went there in 1768 on business having to do with declining income from a government contract that the comte had signed over to her. But it was not business that kept her there, it was the king.

Somewhere along the palace's endless corridors she caught his eye, riveted his attention, and snared his heart. Shortly she was summoned to an interview, or audition, at which Louis was so thoroughly captivated that he commanded her continued presence. From the outset he seems to have fastened on her as his future official mistress. First he had to arrange for her to be formally presented at court, and the next few months were occupied with his attempts to do so over feverish opposition.

The opposition came, unsurprisingly, from the court establishment, the noble barnacles on the ship of state who felt their security threatened by the possibility that a former ribbon clerk and call girl, with maids and footmen in her family, could be raised to such prominence, so close to the throne. This anti-Barry faction, led by the formidably unscrupulous foreign minister, the Duc de Choiseul, and supported by the king's four spinster daughters, was powerful enough to give Louis himself pause. A devotee of indecision, he postponed Jeanne's formal presentation in the hope that the ruckus might die down or at least be neutralized by an opposing faction. As so often happens, indecision proved the best decision, at least from his viewpoint in this instance. The Comte du Barry, eager to promote a pseudofamily connection with the crown, hastily married Jeanne to his bachelor brother, who was then immediately dismissed into oblivion with a comfortable royal pension, supplied of course by cooperative Louis from behind the scenes. The marriage provided Jeanne with a somewhat dubious but usable title, creditable enough to eliminate her commoner status, which had been the greatest obstacle to her vertiginous promotion.

With that hurdle removed, support began building up rapidly, inspired far more by hatred of Choiseul than by any real interest in Jeanne's royal levitation. The duc had made many enemies during his decade of prominence in the French government, especially among the clergy and other conservatives. Now that there was a reasonable chance to assure his comeuppance and perhaps his retirement, the hostile forces suppressed their differences in the common cause. Their unity panicked the Choiseul camp, who overreacted with a flood of anti-Barry pamphlets so scurrilous, so salacious, so maniacally and obviously false as to hurt their cause beyond repair. Louis, whom they were meant to turn against his lady love, became more chivalrously devoted to her than ever. Madame du Barry was formally presented at court in April 1769, amid some vestigial muttering but also much open admiration, for in her bejeweled magnificence she was a sight for even jaded eyes.

Now firmly esconced in the royal favor, she was in a position to do considerable good or harm to others. Unlike her predecessor Pompadour, she was more inclined to good, to generosity and compassion. Her earliest acts of intercession with the king and his ministers, for example, saved a destitute girl whose child had been stillborn, and who had failed to notify the authorities of her pregnancy, from the death that the law required; spared from execution a soldier who had gone AWOL in a fit of homesickness; and rescued from the chopping block an aristocratic but penniless old couple who had stoutly resisted a creditor's seizure of the old homestead. Louis, delighted with the tenor of her requests, acceded to them warmly, thereby enhancing her reputation for kindness and for influence at court.

The old hostility at the court, however, still simmered beneath the surface, occasionally emerging in the form of snubs and thinly veiled insults. Louis, pained to see his beloved treated so and eager to provide some compensation, deeded over to her the beautifully situated and refurbished Chateau of Louveciennes as her home for the rest of her life. He showered her with jewelry and other finery, with servants, with whatever other comforts the age and his affluence could provide. Such loving attention did much to take away the sting of contempt and calumny.

The calumny and vituperation continued nonetheless from the pamphleteering minions of the implacable Choiseul. Yet these tactics, far from driving a wedge between king and favorite, inspired some schemers to form a cabal against the minister and enlist the comtesse's support. This proved largely unnecessary, however, because the frantic Choiseul finally dug his own grave late in 1770 by secretly committing France to help Spain in a war against England over, of all things, the Falkland Islands. The cabal did provide the shovel by informing the king of the minister's plans through the comtesse, knowing that Louis had given the strictest orders against any such commitment. In a fury he dismissed Choiseul, ordering him into a kind of house arrest. But the "house" was a luxurious chateau in which the duc pursued a lifestyle that quickly brought on a severe attack of bankruptcy. Desperately he applied to the king for relief, but Louis adamantly refused. Incredibly, through an intermediary Choiseul then begged the intercession of Madame du Barry, who, quite as incredibly, persuaded Louis to rescue him from his creditors and grant him a generous pension. Yet her reputation would never fully recover from the venom of Choiseul's pamphleteering.

The following year, 1771, was the year of the unspoken word. Louis had hoped that the departure of Choiseul would give him some rest from the defense of his lady love, for whom his infatuation was still a topic of court conversation. It was not to be. Early in 1770, Marie Antoinette had arrived from Austria to seal the Franco-Austrian alliance with her marriage to the Dauphin, the future Louis XVI. After the marriage in May she became, as Dauphine, the first lady of the court. She also came under the relentless influence of the king's harpy daughters, who welcomed her effusively, flattered her, and plied her for months on end with choice bits of nasty data on That Woman. Thoroughly cozened by their artful display of affection and solicitude, the fifteen-year-old princess, worldly-wise as a newborn kitten, swallowed everything they fed her. She would never, she determined, never, *never* speak to that awful woman as long as she lived.

This was a decision of enormous significance at the court of Versailles, as she soon learned. A most sacred rule of the pecking order stipulated that no one might speak a word to anyone of higher rank without first being spoken to. Thus the Dauphine's refusal to speak to the Comtesse du Barry was beyond any remedy by the latter. As it persisted through 1771, it became a topic of agitated conversation in the courts of Europe, as well as at Versailles, and threatened to disrupt the Franco-Austrian accord. Louis, acutely distressed, was too diffident, too embarrassed to confront the princess herself on the subject, but he did send court emissaries to remonstrate with her, including finally the ambassador from Austria, who inveigled her into a promise to speak a brief and casual word to the comtesse at an approaching reception. When the eagerly awaited moment arrived, however, just as she was about to keep her promise, the oldest and prickliest of the king's daughters raced up to her and swept her out of the room on the grounds that they were late for an appointment. This incident caused such tremors throughout Europe's upper crust that Frederick of Prussia, Catherine of Russia, and Maria Theresa of Austria (Marie Antoinette's mother), who were on the brink of a cooperative partition of Poland and wanted no trouble from France, grew concerned that Louis might try to upset their adventurous plans simply out of personal chagrin. And so it was that Maria Theresa sent her daughter a very strongly worded letter explaining the implications of her stubborn behavior. On New Year's Day, 1772, at a traditional social affair, the princess encountered the comtesse and commented, most laconically, on the large crowd of people at Versailles that day. No RSVP, of course. Thus an uneasy armistice was established, and Poland was soon thereafter carved.

This victory allowed the comtesse to enjoy a brief period of rest and relaxation. It also brought her the fawning attention of assorted toadies, and among these was the minister of finance, who sought to please her and thereby the king by giving her unrestricted access to the royal treasury. Virtually every morning she gave audience to clothiers, jewelers, and other merchants, who came to look on her as perhaps the most profitable market in Europe. Her uninhibited profligacy, fully supported by the king's slavish devotion and widely advertised among rich and poor alike, was to prove no small contribution to the eradication of the scintillating dungheap at Versailles in less than twenty years.

A goodly amount of unflattering comment continued to issue from the meretricious press, but without Choiseul to give it focus it lost much of its sting. A particularly salacious four-volume opus, written by a French scandalmonger living in England and entitled *The Secret Memoirs of a Prostitute, or the Adventures of the Comtesse du Barry from Her Cradle to the Bed of Honour*, might have finished off her reputation, but it was intercepted through the herculean efforts of the king and his agents to obtain the manuscript in a blackmail deal and burn it forthwith.

A much greater threat to Madame's security arose in the autumn of 1773: The sixty-three-year-old king, feeling his age, showed signs of growing awareness that he could die unexpectedly, suddenly, unshriven, locked in the mortal sin which his relationship with her entailed, ticketed for the lechers' corner of hell. The urgings of his youngest daughter, a nun, added to his trepidation. His fears emerged most vividly in his reactions to the sudden deaths of three courtiers in those months, all younger than he. But the final threat arrived in April 1774, when he contracted smallpox, and the royal physicians, for whom therapy consisted of draining the body of blood and nutrients, swiftly brought him to death's threshold. This meant the last rites, which meant absolution, and absolution meant the favorite's immediate dismissal.

Under these circumstances it would have well behooved the comtesse to take French leave. She did not. In a display of care and concern that may tell us something about the reasons for the king's devotion to her, she stayed with him as much as the doctors would permit, nursing him, comforting him in a sickroom noxious with one of the most contagious and terrifying diseases of the time. But on May 7, when he received absolution and the sacrament, she had to leave the palace for a friend's home some two miles away. Louis died on May 10. And the toadies turned like a school of fish toward the camp of her enemies.

For the next twelve months she was kept in a convent, where she became fast friends with the nuns, to their utter astonishment. Released in the spring of 1775 but forbidden to live within ten miles of Paris or Versailles, she bought an estate with funds from her still considerable wealth. There she lived quite luxuriously—and generously, according to testimony of the poor in the neighborhood—until November 1776, when she was permitted to return to Louveciennes.

There she stayed for the next sixteen years. There, too, she engaged in the second enduring love affair of her life, with a celebrated aristocrat, the Duc de Brissac. Both were destined to fall victim to the bloody frenzy of the Reign of Terror.

Marie Antoinette and Louis XVI

～୧～

They were married in May 1770. He was barely sixteen, she was only fourteen. Although Louis was Dauphin of France, grandson of Louis XV and heir to the throne, he was ill prepared to be either husband or king. Although Marie was an archduchess of Austria and his Dauphine, she was ill prepared to be either wife or queen.

At the wedding banquet the already corpulent Louis, a chronic trencherman, gulped and guzzled with such an all-consuming zeal that his grandfather warned him against stuffing himself on his wedding night. Louis, thoroughly puzzled by the advice, replied that he always slept more soundly after a hearty meal. That night, after being put to bed with his bride in the traditional public ceremony, he apparently fell sound asleep as soon as the curtains were closed. Growing up amid all the celebrated licentiousness of the French court at Versailles, he nevertheless had acquired neither the technical information nor the sensual inspiration needed for performing this royal duty. As for his bride, she had been brought up in the much stodgier Austrian court, daughter of a mother known for her ostentatious piety, and was quite unprepared to provide the requisite inspiration.

In the winter of 1776–77, two years after their coronation, Louis XVI and his queen were still childless, although by now they seem to have grown into a real affection for each other. Her mother, Maria Theresa of Austria, who had borne more children than she could readily count, was frantically embarrassed by her daughter's failure to provide France with an heir. In desperation she sent her son Josef to Paris to find out what in the world was wrong.

He arrived in April. As coruler of the Holy Roman Empire with his mother, he had some official functions to attend and some political fences to mend, but he did find time on a more personal level to have a little talk with his brother-in-law and to write out thirty pages of meticulous advice for his sister. Near the end of July, not long after his departure, she wrote her mother a pathetically exuberant letter that her marriage had been consummated. Louis told a spinster aunt, in effect, that he had finally tried it, and *liked* it; her reaction is not recorded. Nine months later Marie Antoinette gleefully complained to Louis about "one of your subjects who has been so rude as to give me a kick in the belly." Late that year she gave birth to a girl, but the couple kept trying, and in October 1781 a son and heir was born.

If they were ill prepared for their roles of husband and wife, they were certainly no better prepared to rule a kingdom, especially one headed for financial disaster and social upheaval. Louis was much more interested in casual reading and plebeian pursuits like ironworking than he was in statecraft. Although physically strong and brave, he was dilatory and phlegmatic to the point of lethargy. Although personally kind and compassionate, in the midst of the growing Enlightenment he firmly believed in his divine right to rule and to live like a king. As for his queen, Josef's advice to her had not been confined to bedroom tactics. As a monarch much influenced by the Enlightenment (he had spent his first few days in France disguised as a commoner), he upbraided her for her frivolous extravagance, her catastrophic gambling, her arrogant irresponsibility— although he may have recognized that much of her behavior could have resulted from sexual frustration. His advice, which deeply upset her, proved something of a turning point in her life—if by no means a

U-turn, at least a turn toward a more moderate, less flagrant lifestyle. Motherhood, too, had a rather sobering effect on her.

But the change was neither great enough nor obvious enough to affect her reputation, which had outgrown her girlish follies and now flourished in a compost heap of court intrigue and national prejudice. Ever since her arrival she had been the object of a venomous envy among courtiers who felt themselves threatened by her. In their vanguard was Louis's brother, the Duc d'Orleans, who had sons and who therefore had stood a chance of founding a dynasty of his own if Louis had died unmarried and childless. He and his untiring pamphleteers made the most of her Viennese origins, labeling her *l'Autrichienne*—with sly satisfaction, since *chienne* in French means "bitch"—and defaming her so unremittingly that she and Louis got to the point of being barely aware of all but the most vicious attacks. Louis was deeply distressed to see his wife so vilified but was much too gentle and passive a man to correct the situation forcibly.

Beyond the exaggerations of spendthrift habits and frivolous luxury were charges of sexual promiscuity and lesbianism. Curiously, her one love affair of record—an ardent but evidently quite platonic attachment to a Swedish count—was ignored by the scandalmongers, who of course were devoted to imaginative propagandizing, not to investigative reporting. She was in all likelihood a one-man woman (and surely a no-woman woman) if only because she was, as the phrase goes, a "devout" Catholic, not merely in the sense of engaging in the ritualistic amenities but also in accepting an ideology dedicated to celibacy as the ideal criterion of human behavior. She would not have been the first, or the last, person on earth to focus on the sexual aspect of her conduct to the neglect of many other aspects. In addition, a mutual affection grew between king and queen, especially in the 1780s. He apparently was entranced by his wife almost from the beginning; an eyewitness describes him at a dinner party ogling her in mesmerized infatuation, and this long before the tardy consummation. It took her much longer to adjust to his unprepossessing qualities—his sluggishness, his gluttony, his preoccupation with trivia, his incorrigible procrastination—and to appreciate his kindness and amiability (he reportedly never mistreated a servant, and he could be magnificently generous to victims of disasters), his personal courage, his tolerance of faults in others, his pride in and concern for his family. As he matured, the latter sort of qualities came to the fore, inviting from his queen a fondness that she probably had not felt earlier, when she herself was less mature. One of the many ironies in their situation was that, as royalty threatened with extinction by a bourgeoisie increasingly on the make, they were really a rather bourgeois couple.

A much heavier, more consequential irony appeared in what came to be called the Affair of the Diamond Necklace. In 1784 a Paris jeweler, who had made a lucrative career of catering to Marie Antoinette's taste for diamonds, came to her with a superb if ostentatious multitiered diamond necklace. He had spent several years collecting the stones for it, and now here it was—unique, and uniquely expensive. The queen, inhibited by her new sense of fiscal responsibility, declined the honor at such a price. (She knew that her earlier giddy profligacy had contributed to France's staggering national debt, although the *pièce de résistance* probably was Louis's ironic and very costly support of the American Revolution.) The jeweler went into a crying fit: He would be ruined, he would have to commit suicide. The queen reminded him that the king had already offered her the necklace as a gift, and she had declined it then. No jeweler should put all his diamonds in one basket. This one would have to make other arrangements, preferably short of suicide.

He did. A con man—or rather a con woman with a cooperative husband—heard of his predicament and gulled a cardinal, whose ambition was matched only by his credulity, into buying the necklace on the installment plan. The queen, they told him, wanted thus to acquire it without the king's knowledge; they even gave him a contract with a forged royal signature. But when the cardinal failed to make the first installment, the jeweler complained to the queen. It was then discovered that the artful couple had picked up the necklace for the cardinal, but the cardinal, upon inquiry, protested that he had never received it. The couple were discovered some time thereafter in London, living in conditions of conspicuous affluence.

Louis and Marie Antoinette apparently considered the affair an opportunity for vindication, since she was so obviously innocent of any wrongdoing. Convinced that the cardinal had the necklace, Louis had him arrested in public—indeed, on his way to the altar to say mass—and, under the queen's ever powerful but not always clever influence, arranged for the Parlement of Paris to try him for grand

theft. The cardinal spent many unhappy months in the Bastille awaiting trial.

The royal plan boomeranged. The cardinal's reputation was such
that he was accepted as a social climber and a rake, but not as a thief.
He became an object of popular sympathy, with suspicion falling on
the queen. The Parlement, made up mostly of petty nobility and
aggressive bourgeoisie, was an anything but impartial jury. The cardinal was acquitted in May 1786 in a verdict so worded as to suggest
that the queen knew more than she had admitted. In a rare fury at
this treatment of his wife, Louis discharged the cardinal from all his
offices and sent him to an abbey, thus alienating everyone.

When the con woman was caught, the Parlement sentenced her to
be branded and sent to prison for life. After a year in prison,
however, she escaped to London, where she spent the rest of her life
publishing interminable memoirs accusing the queen of an assortment of crimes and aberrations and, according to some historians,
giving her reputation its *coup de grâce.*

Early in 1787 Louis's comptroller-general persuaded him that,
with the country on the verge of financial collapse, an "Assembly of
Notables" should be called to impose land taxes on the nobility and
clergy, who had never before been subject to direct taxation. The
king complied, but the Assembly consisted of various grades of
nobility and clergy, so that any such tax scheme obviously was dead
before it was even proposed. The public discussion of the national
debt and the country's dreadful predicament, due so largely to the
more exalted nobility's arrogantly conspicuous consumption, and
coming as it did so soon after the diamond-necklace caper, sparked a
wildfire of seething resentment throughout the city and into the
provinces, especially among the bourgeoisie and peasants, who were
paying for all this highfalutin extravagance. And since such feeling
needs focus for high intensity, the queen was more than ever the
center of spiteful attention. The Assembly, after spending a month
achieving this objective but no other, adjourned.

Marie Antoinette's influence with Louis remained undiminished.
A courtier in attendance during these difficult times described the
king's face lighting up, when the queen spoke to him, "with a love
and enthusiasm that even the most beloved mistress could hardly
hope to inspire." She used this influence now to introduce some

severe economies at Versailles, but, seen against the background of the accumulated debt, they were pitifully little, and pitifully late. In July 1787 the Parlement of Paris curtly informed Louis, in effect, that the power to tax lay not with the king but with the presumed representatives of the people in the Estates General. Louis, supported by the queen, dismissed the Parlement, summarily banishing its members from the city, which was immediately seized by a paroxysm of rioting—which in turn caused the royal vacillator to recall the Parlement for another futile session. It repeated the first session's rejection of taxation of nobility and clergy, called for the election of a tricameral Estates General representing the clergy, nobility, and commons, and then adjourned. Meanwhile the national debt continued to grow.

The Estates General did not meet until May 1789. The glacial pace of the election might have been expected, since it was the first to be held in 175 years. The meetings were held not in Paris but at Versailles, with the king and queen in attendance amid much pomp and circumstance. Thomas Jefferson, who was there, described the proceedings as impressive "as an opera," although he did not specify the opera. What he did not know was that the royal couple's somber dignity was due in part to their anxiety over the illness of their eldest son, who was thought to be dying. He did indeed die, early in June, and within months Marie Antoinette's hair turned completely white. She was only thirty-four.

Later that month Louis, typically, ordered royal troops to surround Paris and Versailles but also ordered that they were not to shed a drop of their countrymen's blood. Thus he managed to infuriate the already simmering populace while preventing the soldiers from protecting the palace against the fury. He also managed to undercut any remaining forces for moderation, which were now swept aside by the most disreputable, violent, bloodthirsty elements in the city. On July 14 they gave the Revolution its character when they stormed the Bastille, tore its governor to pieces, and paraded through the street with his head on a pike. The royal troops withdrew, falling back to Versailles, where Marie Antoinette was burning secret state documents and packing her jewelry into a single casket.

She was, after all, the woman who had been credited, inaccurately but not unjustifiably, with the celebrated remark that if the people had no bread, let them eat cake. In October a mob of nearly six thousand frenzied women—fishwives, laundresses, domestic servants, whores, all half-crazed by hunger and by the sight of starving children, and armed with such weapons at hand as pitchforks, sickles, knives, and broomsticks—marched to Versailles, forced their way into the palace, and were prevented from achieving a bloody assassination only by the drawn bayonets of the palace guard. They remained crowded around the palace, however, screaming threats and insults and insisting that the royal family leave Versailles for the Tuileries, in Paris. When Louis promised to do so, they drifted away. He and his family left that day, never to see Versailles again.

All this turmoil was being viewed with considerable concern by the crowned heads of Europe, to whom class was more important than country. For some time Marie Antoinette had been appealing to them for help, especially to Austria of course, in the hope that they would feel threatened enough to invade France and restore what she doubtless thought of as "law and order." The treason, she felt, was in the revolution against divinely appointed royalty, which should be rescued by other divinely appointed royalty. It was an opinion that would do her in.

It was also impractical. That other royalty was made up not so much of rescuing eagles as of vultures awaiting their opportunity. By June 1791, despairing of rescue and alarmed at the unceasing uproar in Paris, she and Louis tried to leave the country, incognito, with their family—not in a light, fast carriage, but in a berlin, a ponderous nine-passenger coach for which today's equivalent might be a motor home. Their leisurely flight was interrupted and they were brought back to Paris. Their attempt at French leave was not the most popular thing they could have done. The streets around the Tuileries rang with curses day and night. With so much unemployment, countless people had nothing much else to do.

Nor did Marie Antoinette's appeals abroad, when they became known, attract much sympathetic consideration from the perpetually howling mobs. She continued her campaign, however, as secretly as the general environment of espionage would allow. To give her fellow royalty more time to rouse themselves, she influenced the king to veto important measures passed by the Estates General and its successor, the National Assembly, further alienating crown and country. In June 1792 another crowd of noisome rabble, this time mostly male, invaded the Tuileries and did not stop until they were actually confronting the king—who, when attacked by a very large ruffian in the vanguard, calmly but unhesitatingly threw him out of a window. But then, in an effort at conciliation, he accepted a revolutionary red cap, put it on his head, and showed himself on a balcony to the crowd outside. In that crowd was a nonparticipating observer, a young lieutenant-colonel named Napoleon Bonaparte, who remarked to a companion (he wrote later) that "if the poor driveler had only cut down five or six hundred with his cannon, the rest of them would still be running." Louis instead suggested a tour of the palace, which so bemused his visitors that they dispersed quietly before nightfall.

By now France was technically at war. In August 1791 Prussia and Austria had issued a declaration that European royalty should come to the rescue of the French throne, and the French revolutionary leaders, hoping to unify the country behind them, declared war on both powers in April 1792. That August foreign troops invaded, and that August the royal family was imprisoned.

The revolutionary forces became surprisingly unified and effective against the intruders, who never did reach Paris. In January 1793 Louis was tried, convicted, and sent to the guillotine by the latest version of the legislature, the National Convention. In April a group of loyal conspirators planned an escape for Marie Antoinette on a false passport but were inadvertently foiled by the Commune when it suspended all passports. In October, after she had been tried and condemned, other conspirators plotted to rescue her on her way to the guillotine, but the plot was discovered by the police. On the scaffold she seemed quiet, even serene. In walking across the platform she inadvertently stepped on the executioner's foot. Her last words were, "I beg pardon, monsieur. I did not do it on purpose."

Catherine the Great
and
Grigory Potemkin

◄∾◦❯►

By her own count, Grigory Aleksandrovich Potemkin was the Empress Catherine's fifth lover. The fifteenth, he once angrily charged in a jealous moment. No, she tersely replied, the fifth.

After some youthful flirtations, she evidently had her first serious affair in 1752, when she was the grand duchess. Eight years earlier, as a minor German princess chosen by the Empress Elizabeth, she had married Elizabeth's nephew Peter, the grand duke, or crown prince, of Russia. The marriage was a political one, of course, arranged between Elizabeth and Frederick of Prussia. Peter was sixteen, she fifteen, and neither was particularly interested in the other. They were, in fact, quite incompatible, becoming more so as they matured.

The marriage may never have been consummated. Peter may have been impotent for the first eight years, until he underwent a minor operation that corrected his inadequacy, and after this he seemed less interested in Catherine than in extramarital targets of opportunity.

Whatever the reason, their marriage was childless until September 1754, when Paul, an eventual heir to the throne, was born. At the time, Catherine had been involved in her first serious affair, with a young court chamberlain, for a couple of years.

He was spectacularly handsome, at least in her eyes, and at least in contrast with the smallpox-marked, ungainly Peter, for whom her initial distaste had blossomed into a mild but durable repulsion. During those eight loveless years she had read ravenously, especially the works of French rationalists like Voltaire and Diderot, while Peter occupied his time rather listlessly with mindless macho interests such as military exercises and hunting and drinking, as well as with intolerable but interminable fiddle playing. This courtier, though no genius, was apparently better equipped to respond to Catherine's ready wit and to tolerate her inquisitive intelligence. And far better equipped to satisfy her waxing sensuality.

But in 1755 his fervor began to cool. On diplomatic visits to Sweden and some German principalities, his temperature dropped precipitously amid the soothing flattery of foreign ladies while she, confined to palace routine in St. Petersburg, remained as feverish as ever. In this early affair as in others to follow, Catherine showed a natural talent for loving not so much wisely as much too well. Her love for him was her preoccupation, her obsession. When word came to her that he was making their love a topic of light conversation at parties in foreign capitals, she broke with him sadly, bitterly, and finally. But not vindictively, cad though he was.

Her grief, however genuine, proved assuageable. A Polish Adonis named Count Stanislaw Poniatowski, whose family had lived for some years as exiles in England, arrived in the spring of 1755 as an aide to the new British ambassador. The ambassador, a man of graceful middle age, suave sophistication, great personal charm, and formidable diplomatic skill, fully recognized the importance of personal relationships, including very personal relationships, in the conduct of diplomacy. On arriving in St. Petersburg, he had to abandon such designs as he had on the empress's bedchamber because of her poor health and political preoccupations. Catherine seemed a promising alternative, but, since she was young enough to be his daughter, he circumspectly, regretfully opted for introducing her to the more compatible Poniatowski. And for lending her money.

The young count proved compatible indeed. Slightly younger than

Catherine, he was a good-looking, personable, attractive, cultivated fellow who fell irretrievably in love with Catherine without delay, thoroughly fascinated by her comeliness, her "mouth that seemed to ask for kisses," her agile mind and gay wit. Before long the feeling was mutual. One evening, when a resourceful friend of both managed to lead the unsuspecting (or barely suspecting) Poniatowski into Catherine's boudoir and abandon him there shortly before her arrival, the evening climaxed in a consummation devoutly to be wished by all concerned.

The affair was ardent, remaining so for the four or five years that it lasted. It might well have lasted much longer but for the interference of the Empress Elizabeth, who could not stomach Poniatowski's Roman Catholicism. Aware of Peter's unsatisfactory performance in the role of husband and of her own amorous indiscretions, she was willing to tolerate Catherine's search for loving comfort in arms other than her husband's. But not in Poniatowski's. The count was packed off to Poland in 1761—where, through the machinations of Catherine with Frederick of Prussia, he became king in 1764.

Meanwhile, back in the palace, life grew more difficult for Catherine. Elizabeth died in January 1762 and was replaced by Peter, who was enjoying a warm and durable intimacy with a young lady of the court. Catherine, although crowned empress consort, was neglected and even treated rudely in public by the new emperor, whose personal and political behavior—including a slavish adoration of Frederick of Prussia, a return to his irrepressible Lutheranism, and an alarming military adventurism conducted for his personal aggrandizement—rapidly alienated many important people. Rumors grew rife that Catherine would soon be divorced, replaced with Peter's ladylove, and generally relegated to the status of nonperson. Factions began to gather in her support, some wishing to put her son Paul on the throne, with her as regent, others wishing to make her empress. Among the latter groups was her latest lover, Grigory Orlov, and his four brothers, especially one named Alexis.

The Orlovs were a patriotic, politically powerful family strongly opposed to Peter's Prussianizing influence. The five brothers, all professional soldiers and officers in the Imperial Guard, could count on a great deal of army backing in a palace coup. They were bold, colorful characters, devoted to the kind of macho tradition established by their grandfather, who, when he was about to be beheaded in a mass execution of rebels against Peter the Great, kicked aside the severed head of the preceding victim with the remark that he had to make room for his own. (Peter, who was present, was so impressed with his panache that he reprieved him and returned him to the army.) Of the five, Grigory was probably the most colorful; he was recklessly daring on the battlefield and irresistibly so in the bedroom. He and Catherine, five years his senior, met in the summer of 1759. It was mutual enthrallment at first sight. It was also the beginning of a decade-long love affair, as well as of a successful political alliance. (And eventually of a child, a boy, born in April 1762.)

And so it was that, very early one morning in the summer of 1762, only six months after Elizabeth's death and Peter's coronation, Alexis Orlov arrived at Catherine's summer residence not far from St. Petersburg. The time had come for action, he told her. Peter reportedly was getting suspicious that something was afoot, and, for all his dilatory nature, might take some preventive measures. Grigory was waiting for them just outside the city with several regiments. Catherine's response was immediate. Within a few hours, in the church in which she had been married and in the presence of the Orlovs and some fourteen thousand troops, she was proclaimed empress of Russia by a compliant bishop, with the Grand Duke Paul declared to be her natural successor.

On the next day Peter was urgently persuaded to abdicate, and in less than a week he was dead. He had been given into the custody of Alexis Orlov, who may have murdered him but who could have merely stepped aside to allow any of countless volunteers the opportunity to do so. Catherine later was accused of complicity, but without any proof. She was not heartbroken over Peter's convenient elimination, of course, but neither was she bloodthirsty. Claimants to the throne under the czars and czarinas were a kopek a dozen, and she must have feared that murdering Peter would be only the beginning. Some of her supporters, obviously, disagreed.

Her love for Grigory Orlov, and his for her, flourished after her accession. She wanted to marry him but was stymied by her political advisers, who insisted that she should either marry a foreign prince or, like Elizabeth of England before her, remain tantalizingly unmarried. In compensation she kept Grigory at her side, intermittently but day and night, at ceremonies of state and in the privacy of her boudoir. She consulted him, appointed him to high-sounding administrative jobs and military commands, lavished great estates and multitudinous serfs on him to keep the wolf from his door. She kept him at the palace, living in luxurious apartments connected to her own by an inconspicuous staircase.

But he grew restless. The administrative jobs were bureaucratic and the military commands were supernumerary. Soon after her coronation, uneasy over the prospect of becoming a court hanger-on, he had suggested an amicable parting of their ways. She had insisted, or begged, that he stay beside her. Yet with the passage of time and her inevitable absorption in her time-consuming efforts to haul Russia out of its feudal quagmire, the soldier in him became ever more impatient. To add to his discomfort, he became the butt of deep hostility and some ridicule from those who resented his role of unanointed consort. At one point he announced that he was leaving, escaping the vanities of court life to take refuge in a remote rural retreat, and that he had invited none other than Jean-Jacques Rousseau to join him there. But when the Swiss Thoreau declined his invitation, his plan collapsed.

He found some comfort in irascibility, and then in extraimperial sex. Catherine displayed great sympathetic patience during his relentless parade of amours, continuing to show confidence in him. He fully justified that confidence in 1771, when she put him in charge of efforts to prevent an attack of plague from decimating the population of Moscow; he was so successful that an arch was erected there honoring "him who rescued Moscow from the plague." This, however, proved only a brief interruption of his devotion to dalliance. When he told Catherine in 1772 that he was in love with his thirteen-year-old cousin and intended to marry her (having already seduced her), she sent him to the Balkans on a diplomatic mission and turned to a young cavalry officer, fifteen years her junior, for consolation. As for Grigory, his consolation on his return was to receive the title of prince, with lavishly appropriate emoluments. But never again her affection.

The cavalry officer lasted only a couple of years. Despite his physical charms and good intentions, he was never more than a stopgap whom she later described as a random selection born of desperation. In the end she found him an intolerable bore, and he was packed off to live in luxury on a vast estate deeded to him as a gratuity for services rendered.

Her next selection seemed quite as random, if not downright perverse. She had known Grigory Potemkin for a dozen years, ever since he had ridden in her company during the coup d'état that had put her on the throne. He had distinguished himself, and she had rewarded him with the customary promotions and land grants. In those days he had been a very attractive fellow, ten years younger than she, a strapping giant with the kind of vital, forceful, rollicking personality that she greatly admired of men. (At one palace party he had dared to mimic her German accent to her face—and to a tee— and she had been much amused.) He was quite a man, but she had been too wrapped up in Grigory Orlov to give Potemkin or anyone else a second romantic thought. Now, in 1774, he was in his mid-thirties, rough with hard military service, heavy with overeating, much blemished from wining and wenching. His face also was marred by the loss of his left eye—due to a brawl, an accident, or an infection; the stories differed, and he did not discuss it, but the loss so depressed him at the time that the moody giant retreated to a monastery and stayed there for more than a year, returning only after Catherine offered him some political posts worthy of his ability, intelligence, and overwhelming energy.

To this impressive wreck Catherine now became irresistibly attracted; with this impressive wreck she fell girlishly in love. (Her terms of endearment in her letters—pigeon, peacock, doll, toy, marble beauty, jungle lion—are indicative.) And he reciprocated, ardently, passionately. It was love at thousandth sight, the love of her life and his. In late 1774, historians now believe, they were secretly married.

Yet the erotic element in their mutual devotion came to an end after only a couple of years, victim at least partly to foreign policy, particularly their shared concern with "the Greek project," the drive south to establish Russian suzerainty in the Ukraine and the Crimea and Russian naval control of the Black Sea, where the Turks held a weakening sway. Unlike her previous lovers, Potemkin was a man of great determination fueled by vast ambition and gently channeled by Catherine's broader experience in statecraft, and he was only too happy to take charge of Russian imperial expansion. Catherine was only too happy to have him to do so, given her intense interest in such expansion. But this meant that he would be in the southern regions, away from her in St. Petersburg, almost without interruption. Their solution to this problem, apparently arrived at through mutual consent, resulted in an arrangement unusual even in royal liaisons.

Although their mutual devotion and affection remained undiminished, and although Potemkin had previously shown signs of being a very jealous lover, Catherine now embarked on a program of dalliance with young lovers that was to make her the talk of Europe, or at least of the salons. At first the court at St. Petersburg was astonished at what seemed to be Potemkin's precipitous fall from power. The astonishment gradually turned into catatonic amazement as it became clear that he was still utterly secure in Catherine's esteem and affection, that their feelings were mutual, that he was politically as powerful as ever, and that each young lover was chosen with at least his concurrence, and usually according to his preference. The arrangement made their separation more bearable, since the sauce for the goose was also sauce for the gander, and since the southern campaign was generally proving a great success. During the first six months of 1787, Catherine made a spectacular trip through her newly acquired southern territories in a procession led by her lavishly appointed three-room sleigh drawn by thirty horses. At Kiev the procession transferred to a fleet of enormous, elaborately furnished barges for their round-trip tour on the Dnieper River. The triumphant Potemkin, after giving her an elaborately royal reception, was rewarded with a royal title, Prince of Tauris (the ancient name for the Crimean peninsula), before the empress and her unwieldy retinue returned to the capital. And their paradoxical relationship, a kind of arm's-length embrace, continued.

But it became strained in 1789, when word reached Potemkin that the sixty-year-old Catherine's latest lover, a twenty-five-year-old guardsman whom he had *not* chosen or approved, was alienating the court with his naively arrogant behavior. Potemkin hurried to St. Petersburg and remonstrated strongly with Catherine, even giving her much pain by saying that her infatuation with this young wippersnapper had lessened his love for her. She tried to mollify him with praise for how well he looked (and how *good* he looked) and what great things he had achieved, but she would not agree to part with her lovely guardsman. Potemkin stormed out, retreating to his own palace nearby to contemplate his next move.

That move was to give a party for Catherine that he hoped would make her forget everyone but him. For the two thousand guests, he provided a string of stage plays and ballet performances, with music provided by a new, gargantuan pipe organ, a large choir, and a three-hundred-piece orchestra. Preparations, including rehearsals, went on for weeks until the evening late in April 1791 when Catherine arrived at seven to be greeted by her gorgeously appareled host in the enormous ballroom of his palace, which was festooned for the occasion with 20,000 candles inside and 140,000 lanterns outside. After some fancy dancing, and some theater and ballet, dinner was announced by a Persian beating a drum while riding into the room on a gem-encrusted, spring-powered mechanical elephant. After a dinner fit for more than a king, Catherine was escorted to the palace's winter garden, where, amid the fountains and exotic flowers and trees, the prince brought her to an obelisk of agate decorated with a jeweled C. Among other things. (The Revolution was more than a century away.)

But he did not understand. Catherine, if she did not fear death, at least desperately wanted to live as close to forever as possible, and her guardsman, young enough to be her grandson, symbolized a kind of eternal youth for her. When she left Potemkin's incredible party that evening, she significantly failed to promise, or even to let him infer, that there would be any change in her love life. He accepted her obstinacy with good grace. In July they had their last dinner together before he headed south again, this time to discuss peace terms with the Turks. In September he fell grievously ill, and before mid-October he was dead.

When Catherine was given the news, she, too, fell ill and for several days could not hold back the tears at the thought of never seeing him again. Her need for him did not end with his departure, nor could it be dealt with by any guardsman. "My idol, the Prince Potemkin," she wrote a friend some time afterward, "has died in Moldavia." Five years later she, too, would be no more.

Josephine
de Beauharnais
and
Napoleon Bonaparte

"**I** await you, am filled with you. The thought of you and that rapturous evening have my senses in a ferment. Sweet, matchless Josephine, what have you done to my heart?"

Thus General Napoleon Bonaparte to Josephine de Beauharnais, in one of countless ardent letters. She was not the only love in his life, by any means; not even his only wife. Yet his love for her was central and enduring, unquenchably surviving the more casual, briefer amorous encounters that provided him with occasional escape from his feverish role as conqueror of Europe. During his lifetime women swarmed about him, seeking an exchange of favors, for he was known to be a ridiculously generous lover as well as an unaccountably attractive man. His name was linked by tireless rumor with the names of dozens of eager aspirants, ranging from nubile young fledglings to relatively wise old birds, and credibly linked with a dozen or so. But his name has been linked by history with that of Josephine.

She was older than he when they met, and more experienced. In that Paris spring of 1795 she was the thirty-one-year-old mother of a fourteen-year-old boy and a twelve-year-old girl, as well as the more or less securely ensconced mistress of Paul-François Barras, then a first among equals in France's political turmoil. Napoleon at twenty-five was a newly appointed general recently poverty-stricken but now enjoying a precarious triumph from his squelching of a Paris rebellion against the Revolution, a young man whose love life had evidently been limited to a brief romantic idyll with a provincial damsel and an even briefer evening with a Paris tart.

Josephine's father had been a genteel beachcomber on the island of Martinique in the West Indies, raising her in carefree poverty until a family-arranged marriage brought her to Paris in 1779. Her aristocratic husband, Vicomte Alexandre de Beauharnais, gave her the two children but little attention, seeking distraction elsewhere, especially among the more sophisticated belles of the city's salon society. The Creole country girl from Martinique, deeply hurt, spent a great deal of her time in tears—she had a penchant for crying jags throughout her life, to Napoleon's continual dismay—until she recognized that Paris was deep in an age of dalliance to which she had better adjust.

She adjusted splendidly, but only after her husband arranged a formal separation so that he could live more conveniently with a mistress to whom he had grown obsessively attached. Josephine was given custody of the children and a comfortable, reliable allowance. Then, during a year spent in an abbey with other similarly abandoned women of title, she proved herself a quick study, emerging with a very useful supply of worldly wisdom, grace and poise, and a beautiful taste in clothes and other furnishings that one day would be the admiring talk of Paris if not all of France. She was not a classic beauty but was rather a handsome woman who could use even defects to good purpose. Since she did not have dazzling teeth, for instance, she developed a habit of smiling demurely with mouth closed and head lowered somewhat, but with her eyes lifted to her partner most attractively.

Her newly acquired skills gained her entree into society in time for her aristocratic connections to get her thrown into prison in 1794.

Her husband was already there (he had supported the Revolution but was guilty of moderation), and it was chiefly her frenzied efforts to get him released that brought them together again. He fell victim to the guillotine toward the end of June, and Josephine doubtless would have shared his fate soon thereafter if the bloody Terror had not been abruptly ended, largely by Barras, a few weeks later. Suddenly she was a free woman again, but without any income now and with two children to support.

Her mother was able to give her a little money, but Josephine needed more than a little money to indulge the expensive tastes which she had begun to acquire and was eager to develop. She had been quite friendly with a General Hoche in the loosely supervised environment of the prison and now took the opportunity to nurture that friendship after his release. This earned her a modest, not very reliable income until she was given title to some of her husband's property. But it brought her also, more significantly for her future, an introduction to Barras, whose mistress she soon openly became as Hoche faded into the background.

Barras was Napoleon's patron. He had been impressed by the young artillery officer's stellar performance at the siege of Toulon in December 1793. In October 1795, when he and the rest of the national government were imperiled by a rebellion led by a formidable array of national guardsmen, he remembered Napoleon, recalled him from impoverished obscurity, had him appointed as his assistant, and put him in charge of the loyal artillery. After squashing the rebellion with a few (and now legendary) "whiffs of grapeshot," Napoleon, suddenly a popular hero, was given command of the Army of the Interior. As such he issued a long-overdue order calling in all arms held by civilians, and it was this order that brought him Josephine. Apparently feeling that a more or less official mistress of Barrass should set an example, she turned in her late husband's sword, but her (and his) young son Eugène pluckily marched to the commander's headquarters, talking his way into Napoleon's office, and pleaded for the return of his father's sword. Napoleon, struck by the boy's spunk and panache, ordered the sword returned to him. He hardly had time to get back to weightier matters before receiving a visit from Josephine to thank him for his kindness. Weightier matters lost their urgency while he stole a moment to fall precipitously, irresistibly, inextricably in love.

Returning her visit a day or so later, he introduced her to an intensity of passionate wooing such as she had never known before. It alarmed her. Although she appreciated his reputation for personal bravery and his perceptive intelligence, his importunate ardor and seeming possessiveness made her uneasy. But then so did the attitude of the dissolute Barras, who seemed increasingly interested in Napoleon's suit and decreasingly interested in her charms. Within a few weeks she was Napoleon's mistress and, doubtless to her surprise, an object of marriage. Barras, to allay her misgivings, promised to give husband Napoleon command of the French army in Italy. After the marriage, a simple civil ceremony in March 1796, he kept his promise.

Napoleon was two hours late for the wedding, perhaps because he had been busy obtaining a forged birth certificate showing that he had been born in Paris rather than in humble Corsica. He gave his age as twenty-eight and she gave hers as twenty-nine, thus narrowing their six-year difference. After a honeymoon of about thirty-six hours, rather spoiled for Napoleon by the unremitting presence of Josephine's pet poodle and a long visit with her children, the new commander of the Italian campaign left hastily to assume his duties. From inns and other stopping places along his way, and then from his headquarters, came a steady stream of love letters begging her to join him in Italy as soon as possible. She kept putting him off, on one occasion even pleading pregnancy as an excuse. But by June her husband had led his decimated, demoralized, stagnated French army through eight victories against great odds and established his control in northern Italy. In Paris the news of his triumphs made him the greatest little hero since Joan of Arc, and his wife, a modest person but very gregarious, enjoyed basking in his limelight. Finally her resistance crumbled under the pressure of his letters, and perhaps of the growing rumors that she did not return his now celebrated love. In July she joined him in Milan.

They were not together very much in Italy. He had to leave Milan continually for the fighting required to protect his rear from Austrian attacks and to extend his control throughout the Italian boot. For a while Josephine accompanied him on some of these campaigns, but roughing it with an army on the move was not her favorite lifestyle. When she came under fire one day, she decided that she much preferred Milan and returned there posthaste. During the following year or so Napoleon resumed his voluminous correspondence, complaining frequently over her lack of response. When he did finally get to Milan, it was to dress her down for creating a scandal, however unjustified, with a young adjutant, and for accepting vast quantities of gifts from solicitous Italians with bribery on their minds. Josephine cried a good deal, eventually persuading her still-adoring husband to let her keep the gifts if she promised not to accept any more—and thereafter, for years, explaining each new gift (each one he asked about) as part of the original horde.

In the fall of 1797, having conquered all of Italy, Napoleon returned to Paris. Since Josephine now decided that this was the ideal time for her to tour Italy, he returned without her, waiting impatiently until she rejoined him about a month later. They entered on a round of dinners, parties, balls, and other social affairs which she thoroughly enjoyed—fortunately for Napoleon and for the social life of Paris, since he would not go anywhere without her. This was due only partly to his romantic attachment. He still loved her, was still in love with her, but he had begun to recognize the extent and intensity of the muted opposition growing up about him, and he sensed that the support of this graceful, amiable, admired, and influential woman might prove invaluable.

In one vital respect, however, she had utterly failed him. Since the notion of dynasty, of hereditary rule, was still strong to European politics, he needed a son, an heir to fulfill his fondest daydreams. Josephine had not given him one and now, despite her recent claim of pregnancy, was probably past her childbearing years. But this was not as pressing as his need to weaken his most implacable enemy, England, and to this end he now began planning a campaign in the Middle East designed to cut off some of Albion's vital supply lines. Government leaders encouraged him, delighted at the thought of his leaving Paris and perhaps being killed in battle or at least becoming hopelessly bogged down in a military quagmire.

He and his troops sailed for Egypt in July 1798. He wanted Josephine with him, of course, but decided to spare her the heady pressures of roughing it in the desert, although she did go as far as Toulon to wave goodbye. Within a few weeks after his landing, Napoleon was master of Egypt, although an English fleet under Lord Nelson effectively destroyed French naval power at the Nile delta on August 1, thus isolating Napoleon and his troops from their homeland. The news of this naval disaster, however, shook Napoleon less than a letter received from an informant in France reporting that Josephine had bought a large suburban estate, curiously named Malmaison, and had installed her adjutant of Italian fame to enjoy the large house with her in cozy cohabitation. The letter and its transmittal may have been inspired by one or more members of Napoleon's multitudinous family, who were perpetually livid over Josephine's deportment, for, besides making him a notorious cuckold, she was using his hard-earned credit to buy the estate, its lavish furnishings, and just about everything else within her reach. Napoleon wrote his brother Joseph a rather pathetic letter begging him to get control of the situation. Doubtless recognizing that Joseph would have about as much influence over Josephine as over Lord Nelson, and tiring of his role of disdained lover, he decided to have a taste of the sauce for the goose. He even had some harem beauties conscripted for his inspection and appraisal, an operation that proved quite fruitless for him but not for some of his aides. He needed not so much an erotic release as a touch of romance to provide some distraction from his maps and battle plans and from his constant fear of assassination at the hands of some conquered malcontent. Before long he found it in the coquettish personality of a young lieutenant's wife, who, after her enraged husband made her his ex-wife, became Napoleon's steady mistress for the rest of his Mideast sojourn.

That sojourn ended rather abruptly in the fall of 1799. Napoleon, after extending his sway as far as Syria, was forced back into Egypt by the British, with help from the Turks. Thoroughly stymied, he determined to take French leave. He and a few loyal aides furtively crossed the Mediterranean, narrowly missing capture by Nelson's ubiquitous cruisers, and reached Paris early in November. There they staged their famous coup d'état that made Napoleon virtual dictator of France. As for the lieutenant's ex-wife, he did not see her again, although he sent her lavish gifts and arranged a very satisfactory marriage for her. Throughout his life he proved a splendid after-the-interlude matchmaker.

If she had provided him with an heir, she might well have taken Josephine's place at his side. But she had not, and Josephine regained her place by overwhelming his dikes of resistance with an irresistible flood of tears, to his family's intense chagrin. Clearly he was still in love with her—although his passion had cooled, their relationship hereafter was by no means wholly platonic—but he also had a political reason for the reconciliation. Since much of his support came from the relatively conservative and respectable bourgeoisie, urban and rural, his new preeminence required behavior more conventional than that expected of a soldier in the field. In Paris he could not parade a mistress about as openly as he had in Cairo. And so he swallowed hard, settled her monstrous collection of debts, including the mortgage on Malmaison, dismissed her lover (but took no revenge on him), and welcomed her back into his embrace, quite literally, without recrimination. The chastened Josephine reportedly never took another lover. Responding to his genuine affection, she became a surprisingly solicitous wife.

She apparently had come to appreciate the extraordinary soldier-statesman that he was, as well as the indulgent husband that he also was. As he underwrote her habitual extravagance, so she overlooked his casual affairs as more or less occupational hazards. For the next four or five years (1799–1804) they enjoyed a fairly serene life together, marred for Josephine chiefly by the guerrilla warfare incessantly waged by her in-laws, and by her barrenness, which she knew made her vulnerable, even dispensable.

To the in-laws' utter consternation and grinding of teeth, Napoleon stuck by her after a vote of the French senate gave him the title of emperor in May 1804. That December he was crowned emperor, and she empress, in the same coronation ceremony. As the couple emerged from the Notre Dame cathedral afterward, the Paris crowds cheered for her as lustily as for him. She was reportedly a wonder to behold that day, radiantly coifed, radiantly gowned, radiantly bejeweled, radiantly shod, and radiantly happy.

During the next five years she was reasonably if not always so radiantly happy, reveling in the perks and pleasures of her Olympian social position while her husband busied himself with invigorating hostilities against the English, Swedes, Austrians, Russians, Italians, Spaniards, and Portuguese, who variously, and sometimes concertedly, opposed him. But something occurred that threatened her position more than all the anti-Napoleonic coalitions put together: Napoleon, who had never fathered a child and had long been anxious over his ability to do so, finally did so (beyond reasonable doubt) in a moment of dalliance. This clearly indicated to him that he could produce a royal heir if he could marry a suitably royal partner. An imperial research project revealed that the Archduchess Marie Louise, daughter of Emperor Francis I of Austria, not only contained flawlessly royal blood but also sprang from a long line of philoprogenitive women. In November 1809 he made the excruciating decision and informed Josephine that they would be divorced. Although there was a great deal of weeping and swooning and carrying on, the copious tears seemed partly crocodilian, since she had long expected the news and was utterly confident that she would be splendidly provided for at Malmaison. In this respect he was indeed as generous as ever, but in April 1810 he and Marie Louise were married. And Napoleon's male heir, one of history's most futile gestures, was born the following March.

The marriage was a contented one. In his early forties Napoleon's energy level was diminishing, approaching that of four or five men instead of a dozen or so. Marie Louise was only eighteen, a virgin, but Napoleon found her quite mature and unexpectedly sensual, yet placid and undemanding enough to conserve his flagging resources. Unlike Josephine, she was not bright enough for any conversation on politics or statecraft, but this deficiency doubtless made her company all the more relaxing. She was not a Josephine—nor a Marie Walewska, the lovely Polish countess who had surrendered to Napoleon first as a patriot and then as a loving and much beloved mistress, and who had borne his first, reassuring son a year earlier. But Marie Louise was a respectful empress, a dutiful wife, and a pleasant surprise. And her son was for Napoleon a treasure of rare delight.

The marriage was a total failure politically. Before it was two years old, the Austrian connection that it was supposed to have welded tight was broken after Napoleon's disastrous Russian adventure, when Marie Louise's father joined her husband's enemies with a hundred thousand Austrian troops. After his final defeat and abdication in April 1814, Napoleon never saw his wife or son again. Or at least not *that* son: He would see his son by Marie Walewska when she visited him briefly during his exile on the island of Elba.

Meanwhile, Josephine had been spending the years since the divorce holding unofficial court at Malmaison, continuing to enjoy the company of the rich and powerful, including quite a few platonic but solicitous visits from Napoleon himself. After the abdication she fled from her home in panic but soon learned that she had nothing to fear. Quite the contrary, on her return she was honored by many visits from an impressive assortment of conquerors, especially Czar Alexander, paying homage to her still-powerful attractions. But she was not to enjoy this form of adulation for long. She contracted diphtheria and by May 29 she was dead.

A year later her daughter Hortense (the mother of Napoleon III) was with Napoleon during his final retreat from Paris. He had escaped from Elba and had virtually reconquered France before his astonished enemies could react, with overwhelming force, to drive him from Paris and, ultimately, to his second exile, on St. Helena. Before his departure he took Hortense with him for a last brief visit to Malmaison. Furniture, drapes, carpets, everything reminded them of Josephine's grace, her elegance, her love of beautiful things. When they came to the room where she had died, he asked to enter it alone. After a few minutes he came out, and Hortense noticed that there were tears in his eyes.

Emma Lyon
and
Lord Nelson

〜◦〜

In August 1798, Rear Admiral Horatio Nelson was the toast of Naples, where the wife of the British ambassador, Sir William Hamilton, was the former Emma Lyon, a woman of low birth but exalted beauty. Early in that month Nelson's fleet had virtually destroyed the French fleet in the Bay of Aboukir, ending Napoleon's hopes for a conquest of Egypt and leaving the Little Corporal temporarily stranded in northern Africa. For this victory the admiral had received a large grant of solid English pounds and the title of Baron of the Nile. When he repaired with his fleet to Naples for rest and recreation, he was greeted there by admiring multitudes as conquering hero, first class. No Francophiles allowed.

In the greeting vanguard came Lady Hamilton, who embraced the hero with more ardor than protocol demanded. One story has it that she swooned with fervor, but the tale probably was invented by a romantic committed to love at first sight. In fact, this was their second encounter. Five years before, she had rendered Captain Nelson a great service. He had brought his warship to Naples with a request from his government for some troops to support British tactics in southern France. The Queen of Naples (which was not merely a city but also a state occupying a goodly slice of the Italian boot) was Maria Carolina, a sister of the late Marie Antoinette and an intimate friend of Emma Hamilton, who had been a great comfort to her since the rather unnerving demise of the French monarchy. The two women not only were good friends and strong characters, but they also had bemused husbands. King Ferdinand chronically neglected affairs of state to pursue such manly hobbies as pigsticking and wenching, while Sir William, though a conscientious ambassador, was much more absorbed and imaginative as a vulcanologist and antiquarian. Thus Maria Carolina practically ruled the political roost and Emma the diplomatic one. So when Nelson came to Naples, it was chiefly Emma who put him up at the embassy and who saw to it that he was given his troops.

Their interest in each other remained on this level throughout his stay at the embassy, at least to all appearances and doubtless in fact. He wrote to his wife of Emma's amiability and her kindness to their son (actually, his stepson), who was serving as his aide. The captain and the lady did not see each other again for the next five years, which Nelson spent at sea almost without interruption and in battle to the edge of exhaustion. In a fight on shore in Corsica later in 1793 he lost much of the sight in his right eye, and during an assault on the Canary Islands in 1797 his right elbow was so badly shattered that his entire right arm had to be amputated—in a small boat pitching about in the surf. In Aboukir Bay, too, he had been severely wounded, his forehead gashed deeply above his right eye. On his arrival in Naples that day in 1798, therefore, he was a wreck of a man, at forty old before his time, prematurely grizzled, shrunken in the face because of front teeth lost to naval cuisine, older than Emma by seven years as well as shorter by perhaps a couple of inches. But in those five years something must have happened to Emma, too, as she followed his spectacular career, his victories and injuries. When she appeared on the deck of his flagship, she took one look at him, burst into tears, and ran over to embrace him. He returned the embrace with his single arm, and together they repaired to the embassy, where she devoted herself to nursing him with much tender, loving care.

They made no effort to conceal their growing mutual attachment. Her husband was sixty-eight at a time when the average life expectancy was less than fifty. He was rheumatic, suffered from respiratory and liver problems, and seemed to grow more weary with life every day; and he had a very high threshold of jealousy. Nelson's wife was quite a satisfactory one by all conventional standards, but their marriage, never a very passionate affair, had been cooled for years by the intervening sea. Emma and Nelson were pulled together by chemistry and pushed together by circumstances. She was quite open in her affection and admiration for him, and he responded in kind. Months before they actually became lovers, they were depicted as such by wags and wits, gadflies and gossips. Sir William Hamilton, for as long as he lived, received Nelson as an honored guest in his house, in Naples and later in England. He kept his suspicions, if any, to himself, and his wife and her lover reciprocated by being so discreet that their relationship was never common knowledge, despite widespread conjecture.

Lady Hamilton was not promiscuous. Daughter of an illiterate blacksmith in rural northern England, who died when she was only a year old, she had little to offer as a young woman other than her beauty and her warm, witty companionship. She was wise enough to offer these commodities not injudiciously but selectively, to one man at a time, as Sir William might later have testified. Her first patron was a country squire, her second was a young nobleman, and her third was Hamilton, the young nobleman's elderly uncle. Since she was deeply in love with the young man, she was also deeply hurt when he packed her off to his uncle in Naples. But Hamilton, a widower, was kind and generous, and proud of her as well, and soon she grew comfortable in the relaxed Neapolitan atmosphere, especially after becoming acquainted with the queen—who, after the goatish king had made a clumsy pass at Emma, suggested delicately to Sir William that a Lady Hamilton as personable as Emma would be a very welcome addition to the social affairs at court. Delighted by this prompting, which he felt sure would elicit King George III's permission, the ambassador proposed to Emma, and they were married during a visit to England in 1791.

As both mistress and wife, Emma was as decorous as she was decorative. She was no libertine. Now, as Her Excellency the Ambassadress (as the queen addressed her on formal occasions), she was respectable enough for Mrs. Grundy. It is easy to believe that in her encounter with Nelson in 1793 her behavior was quite proper and her motives simply patriotic. By 1798, however, after living with a preoccupied man in his ailing sixties for seven years, she may have been suffering from a form of neglect that could make a woman susceptible to the radiance of a star of Nelson's magnitude, especially when the star proved badly in need of some female refurbishing. The surprise may be that she lowered the gate so deliberately.

As for Nelson, if his flagship had not needed repair even more than he, he may well have only stayed overnight in the embassy, bidding Emma a friendly, but only friendly, farewell the next day. But the ship repairs took four days, at the end of which he was irrevocably hooked, as was she. Their close association, furthermore, continued beyond this time because the French Revolution abruptly found its way to Naples. The king and queen and assorted courtiers quickly concluded that departure would be the better part of valor, and the Nelson-Hamiltons threesome helped them escape to Sicily. Emma's loyalty and daring in this episode, her practical approach to the problems involved in spiriting royalty through a turbulent sea of egalitarian hostiles, must have raised her to new and giddy heights in Nelson's admiration and affections. In any case, when the court and the embassy returned to Naples after the city was recaptured and Sir William (who had lost priceless art treasures to the sea during the escape) decided that he had had enough of the ambassador business to last the rest of his life, the friendly threesome returned to England together. Emma was unmistakably, though not conspicuously, pregnant. Most observers thought she had gained some weight.

About three months later, toward the end of January 1801, Emma came down with an extraordinarily severe cold and took to her bed. The child was born. A daughter, Horatia. With the help of her own devoted mother, who incidentally must rank as one of the sturdiest supporting characters in history, she managed to bear the child and transmit her to the care of a Mrs. Gibson of Little Titchfield Street without Sir William's knowledge, or at least without his interference. And Mrs. Gibson thereafter proved as discreet as she was conscientious. When Nelson, who was then on duty in the Channel, received word of the birth from Emma (in an elaborately coded letter), he was ecstatic. Henceforth Emma would have a rival in the doting department.

Inspired perhaps by the blessed event, Nelson began to think in terms of domesticity. Since his sea duty offered limited opportunities for house hunting, he asked Emma to find him a house in the country, not too far from London, and to furnish it for him. She did so with gusto, buying a rather unprepossessing home in Surrey, some six miles from the city, and transforming it into a model of early-nineteenth-century suburban living. She included provisions for her husband's comfortable and almost continual presence (a stream ran through the property, and she had a bridge built, for instance, to provide for his obsessive fishing), thus justifying *her* almost continual presence. The place proved a delicious haven for Nelson, who could enjoy some taste of home life with his beloved Emma—and occasionally with Horatia, especially during Sir William's infrequent absences.

Early in 1803 Sir William went home to die. Emma and Nelson stayed at the bedside until the end, after which he discreetly moved to a nearby hotel, leaving her in the care of a female relative. Almost immediately after the funeral he was ordered to sea again, and he did not return until August 1805.

His visit then was almost idyllic; he basked in the daily companionship of the woman and the child whom he loved beyond all else. But it was also a short visit. For almost two years he had been chasing the French fleet, trying to corner it into a decisive fight, and now an opportunity arose to catch it off the Spanish coast, near Cape Trafalgar. He yearned for domestic tranquillity, but the call of duty and the exciting prospect of a final battle against his lifelong enemy were irresistible. And it was, of course, a final battle, not only for the French fleet but also for him. When Emma received the news of his death, she screamed and fainted.

It is hard not to draw a veil over the rest of the story. Although Emma had never lived frugally as Lady Hamilton, she had lived within her ample means. But from the time of buying the house in Surrey, she became uncontrollably extravagant, partly because she was uncontrollably generous. Sir William's estate had been left mostly to his nephew and heir, with a comfortable but not lavish annuity for Emma; Nelson, who had to provide for his wife, also left an annuity for Emma, but it soon proved to be based on unreliable investments. For the rest of her life Emma was pursued by creditors, quite literally, as she moved from one address to another and finally to France. She wrote an endless series of pleading letters to the government, to friends and relatives, begging for help, but nothing came from the government and very little from anywhere else. Horatia, like her sturdy grandmother before her, stuck with Emma till the end—in this case, Emma's end, in squalid poverty, in Calais.

Her funeral was a rather squalid affair, too—except that every chief officer from every English ship in the Calais harbor came ashore in dress uniform and followed her coffin to the cemetery.

As for Horatia, she returned to England, where she enjoyed a happy married life and lived to the age of eighty.

George Sand
and
Frédéric Chopin

~⌒~

If evidence is needed that George Sand and Frédéric Chopin were in love, surely that celebrated time that they spent together on the Mediterranean island of Majorca provides it. The wonder is that they emerged from the experience still speaking to each other.

It sometimes seems that they spent years there, but actually the visit lasted only three months. They arrived in November 1838, two years after they had first met in Paris at a party arranged by Franz Liszt at her request. Chopin played that November evening in 1836. She listened, intently. She also chain-smoked cigars as she lounged by the fire with her head wrapped in a scarlet bandana and her legs encased in trousers of purple velour, all very Turkish. The incipiently tubercular Chopin did not at all appreciate the cigars, and the rather sober, conventional Chopin was not particularly fond of her ostentatious getup. She was thirty-two, renowned for flouting convention in her novels and her conduct. He was twenty-six, less renowned though much lionized. He wrote his family that he had met "an important celebrity, Madame Dudevant, known as George Sand," adding that he had found her rather unattractive. Perhaps this aloofness piqued Sand's curiosity or challenged her self-image, for at the next party that they both attended, in December, she arrived dressed in red and white, the colors of Chopin's beloved Poland. Soon after this she asked him to her country home, but Chopin declined the invitation.

She pursued him. He was good-looking, self-possessed, courteous, alluringly unwell, and capable of creating music that mesmerized her. Perhaps he could bring her the perfection that she had sought and never found in other lovers. The possibility intrigued her; hope springs eternal in even the most sophisticated breasts. She arranged casual meetings at casual parties on casual occasions. Whenever and wherever he played, almost invariably she was there, conspicuously, if sincerely, absorbed. Eventually Chopin discovered that she was much more attractive than he had realized—then companionable, then desirable, then eagerly available. By the spring of 1838 they were lovers. By summer they were both deeply in love.

That fall they decided to spend the winter together in the sun. The Spanish consul in Paris recommended Majorca for its magnificent climate and serene environment. They arrived in the capital city of Palma in mid-November with her fifteen-year-old son and ten-year-old daughter, glad to escape the cold, wet northern winter, eagerly anticipating the warm, bright, health-restoring days and softly lustrous nights. In a lyrically joyous letter, Chopin wrote to a friend of the turquoise sky, the lapis-lazuli sea, the emerald mountains, the heavenly air—"life is wonderful!"

That was the first week. The second week brought spectacularly stormy weather, with sheets of rain driven by galelike winds. Chopin was caught out in it, returning to their small villa with a deep, relentless cough. Then it grew cold—more painfully cold than anything she had ever known before, Sand wrote later. And damp, so damp that everything felt and tasted soggy. Since the rented house boasted neither stove nor fireplace, Sand tried to make do with coals in a heavy pan, which created so much smoke that Chopin's cough grew alarmingly worse. The French consul, in response to her desperate

plea, sent three doctors to the house. Chopin reported their diagnoses in a letter: One said he was dead, another that he was dying,
and the third that he was going to die.

This may have been very nearly true. A rumor spread through
Palma that he was dying of tuberculosis, and the fear of contagion
pressured the owner of their house to evict them quite unceremoniously, as well as to bill them for the fumigating and refurbishing of
the house as required by Spanish hygienic regulations. After a brief
stay with the indomitable French consul, they moved to an abandoned monastery on the rocky crest of a nearby hill, bag and baggage
in a mule cart (including a small piano rented for the occasion). In
mid-December Sand wrote a friend (she wrote nineteen thousand
letters in her lifetime) that Chopin was very ill.

The former monastery was a medieval disaster. With its great stone
bulk thrust up into the merciless wind and rain from nearby mountains, with its vast and drafty interior providing the minimum in
clammy shelter, it was less than an ideal environment for a man af-
flicted with a racking cough and bloody sputum. The weather also
provided frequent isolation, since the rain-soaked roads leading into
Palma were often impassable. Yet this was not an unmixed blessing,
since Sand hated to have any dealings with the people there, whom
she considered a rude and thieving lot. She was kept very busy running the primitive household, devotedly nursing Chopin and con-
scientiously tutoring the children, son Maurice in Greek history and
daughter Solange in French grammar. Somehow she also managed to
do a great deal of writing on her novel *Spiridion*. As for Chopin,
whom she described in a letter as very weak and in pain, he completed twenty-four preludes, a scherzo, and a polonaise. If we are
inclined to dismiss their stubborn adherence to their vacation plans
(despite all the meteorological travail) as a refusal of incorrigible
romantics to face reality, we might consider whether we could be so
productive under such duress. And so irrepressibly loving.

By February, although the weather had turned fine again, they
decided that Chopin would have to return to France without delay,
for medical treatment. Most of the trip was a nightmare, but after
they arrived in Marseilles, found a competent doctor, and settled
down for some serious resting, Chopin recovered quickly, to Sand's
intense relief. She continued her self-sacrificial nursing, worried quite

literally that he was too good for this world, too exquisitely perfect (as she put it from the depths of her adoration), and might be taken from it for that reason if for no other. He responded with loving gratitude, and by recovering.

That spring in Marseilles did much to make up for the winter in Majorca. The weather was pleasant, they were able to avoid autograph-hunting types, and they were very much alone together. In the summer of 1839 they moved to Nohant, Sand's inherited property far south of Paris, to which she had a first-rate grand piano delivered. Here the couple lived with the children each winter for the next seven years, spending their summers in Paris, both living artistically productive lives. Occasionally they would be separated by their work—she to oversee production of a play, for instance, he to give a rare concert (he loathed performing)—but more often they were united by it, especially since she was utterly fascinated by and dedicated to his genius. At Nohant she could give him, among other things, the solitude that he needed for his composing and indeed for his composure. And when he needed distraction and reaction, she could invite the kind of people—Liszt, Balzac, Flaubert, Turgenev— who could furnish, rather than demand, entertainment. She even arranged for a physician, an old friend, to take Chopin under his therapeutic wing, treating the acutely sensitive artist psychologically as well as medicinally.

But this also was the doctor who advised her in the early 1840s, according to her own not very reliable testimony, to break away from Chopin, gradually and gently but resolutely. She had allowed her feelings for her lover to grow, gradually though by no means resolutely, more maternal than was good for the relationship. When she was in Paris alone, her letters home often were addressed to "my three dear children." Under these circumstances it is hardly surprising that the first thing to go in the couple's mutual attachment was physical desire. Chopin's precarious health doubtless contributed to its decline. (Though a passionate romantic, he was never the sexually overheated type.) By 1843 daughter Solange, now a precocious fifteen, was dryly referring to him as asexual, and by 1845 Sand, on the dubious grounds that sexual activity could kill him, began seeking relief from tension elsewhere. In 1846 she wrote *Lucrezia Floriani*, one of her less memorable novels, which described the deterioration of a love affair resembling theirs closely enough to cause some of their mutual friends embarrassment, although Chopin ostensibly admired it.

The affair continued in this emotional twilight, sustained by residual affection and concern as well as by vestigial habit. It could not withstand the severe strain put upon it by the marriage of Solange to a misguided fortune-hunter in the spring of 1847. Sand, who had favored the marriage, quickly changed her attitude as she watched her son-in-law voraciously consuming the dowry. She vented most of her resentment against Solange, with whom she had never been really close. Chopin was in Paris at the time, hurt that Sand had told him nothing about the marriage and had not invited him to the wedding. In the ensuring brouhaha between mother and daughter, he took the daughter's side. He had long felt a romantically paternal affection for the girl, and now that she was in Paris he gladly took on the role of protector. This endeared him to Sand not at all. In July 1847, after an exchange of nasty letters, the break was complete.

With one exception, they never saw each other again. In the spring of 1848 they met in Paris, in the vestibule of the home of a mutual friend. He was leaving, she arriving. He asked whether she had heard from Solange lately. When she replied that she had heard no news for a week, he politely informed her that she was now a grandmother. After telling her, briefly, what he could about mother and child, he left.

Eighteen months later he was dead. Her own report that she was ill for days after hearing of his death can be ascribed to her taste for self-dramatization as easily as to genuine emotion. The news may have done no more than stir the ashes. Certainly his absence did not affect her productivity. In the twenty-seven years remaining to her, she wrote at least as much as she had written in the preceding quarter-century. Somewhat the same thing can be said of her succession of lovers. As for her last days, one can read through many accounts of them without finding any mention of Frédéric Chopin.

Queen Victoria
and
Prince Albert

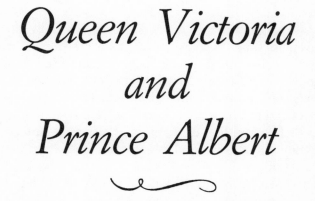

Can an "arranged" marriage bring happiness? Few marriages have been so thoroughly arranged as was that between Queen Victoria of Great Britain and Prince Albert, a son of the House of Coburg in German Saxony. From about the age of five Albert was aimed like an arrow at the young woman who, because of royal mishaps and sterilities, was expected to succeed her ailing uncle William IV on the English throne. Victoria and Albert shared an uncle, King Leopold I of Belgium, who did most of the aiming, his hand guided by a suave, self-effacing, effective private secretary named Baron Stockmar. It was chiefly Stockmar who supervised Albert's education in Germany and his training in the social graces in Italy, all designed to prepare him for marriage with Victoria—or at least, if the plan went awry, with one of the consolation prizes available from the chaotic collection of duchies and principalities jostling about in the Germany of the early nineteenth century.

Young Albert was a hard-to-aim arrow. He much preferred the idea of becoming a naturalist. He had no interest in politics, power, or perks. He was only vaguely interested in marriage; as a youth he was stoutly unprepossessing, hardly a cynosure of predatory female eyes. But he was a very serious lad who had developed, perhaps in reaction to his parents' extramarital shenanigans and scandalous divorce, a prodigious sense of duty. When Leopold and Stockmar laid out the neglected boy's course for him, he accepted it obediently as his lot in life.

He was only one arrow of many. Victoria, especially after she became queen in June 1837, was visited by a spate of princelings, dukelings, and other noble aspirants, more than she could reasonably keep properly sorted out. Matchmakers cropped up everywhere, placing their bets on such candidates as the Grand Duke Alexander of Russia, of whom Victoria was very fond, and even her prime minister, Lord Melbourne, fifty-eight, of whom Victoria, at eighteen, was also very fond but not *that* fond. Many if not most of the bettors were putting their money on Prince Albert, perhaps because of King Leopold's widely recognized motivation and clout (he was by far Victoria's favorite uncle). What they did not know was that the new queen, who was at least as strong-willed and hardheaded as Leopold, remembered Albert in 1839 as that pudgy sixteen-year-old she had met some three years earlier, a clumsy boy who seemed to suffer from some sort of sleeping sickness. By the prospect of marriage with such a creep, as we might put it today, she was not amused.

But, oh, how Albert changed between May 1836 and October 1839. Tall, broad-shouldered, tanned from his exposure to the Italian sun, he was now as fine a figure of a man as might be found in all Europe, with a splendid head of hair (with wigs out of fashion, male coiffure was all the rage) and eyes of compelling blue. After the first day of this latest visit, Victoria confided to her diary, "It was with some emotion that I beheld Albert, who is *beautiful*." She was indeed quite smitten. She was also delighted that her romantic yearnings did not conflict with political realities: Albert seemed a very likely choice for the role of prince consort. He was not so tall as to make her seem a pygmy in public appearances. His reserve and sobriety offered assurance that, unlike some of his relatives (and hers), he would not disgrace the crown. Yet he was socially graceful and, like Victoria, enjoyed dancing and music. Finally, since he disliked politics, he could be expected to avoid meddling in the government of the realm. Or so she and her advisers thought.

Albert also had been less than eager to pursue his destiny. Although he considered Victoria tolerably pretty and vivaciously attractive, he had learned enough about her headstrong behavior to give him pause. When he learned early in 1839 that Uncle Leopold had received a letter from the queen that a marriage "could not take place till two or three years hence," if at all, he reacted with quiet anger. Very well, he concluded to himself, if my uncle insists on my visiting the queen, my first words with her will inform her that I am tired of the delay and hereby (as he wrote of it later) "withdraw entirely from the affair." On his arrival in October, however, these proposed first words to Victoria were preempted by Victoria's first sight of the beautiful new Albert, and they were never spoken. Victoria was instantly, obviously, and quite understandably no longer interested in delay.

Nor was he. But he could not propose to her for reasons of protocol, and she could not propose to him for reasons of maidenly modesty. She overcame this obstacle easily enough, assigning her favorite lady attendant the task of informing his favorite gentleman attendant that the queen was mightily impressed with the prince. Back came the answer, through the intermediaries, that the prince was ready, willing, and able. This volleying continued, somehow, for five days. On the sixth they met. He could make her very happy, murmured Victoria, now utterly entranced, by making her fondest wish come true. This would make him equally happy, he replied, as sincerely if not so fervidly. They embraced. Victoria's diary for the next three months suggests that their primary activity was embracing and kissing as often as the other, more public aspects of their relationship would permit.

Among these more public aspects was the controversy over Albert's status as consort. The mesmerized Victoria wanted him to be nothing less than king, but Melbourne eventually persuaded her that this wish was not only impractical but also unwise. It would take an act of Parliament to make Albert king, he pointed out; even if Parliament were so disposed, it should not be encouraged to make kings, since it might then be all too ready to unmake them as well. Very well, then, she countered, at least he should be a member of the royal peerage, first in rank after the queen. Not a chance of it, came the reply, from Melbourne and others: The lords of the realm would never allow a foreigner to precede them in the royal succession. In the end she had to settle for assorted perks and privileges of a much less imposing and more obscure character, such as an army field marshalcy, the Garter, and "the right of quartering his arms with those of the queen." Her marriage, like every other affair of state, was bound to meet with some opposition, even vehement opposition. When this took the form of Parliament's reducing Albert's expected allowance of fifty thousand pounds a year to thirty thousand (the country was in an economic recession), an angry prince and King Leopold might well have opted out if they had not been so inextricably opted in. And if Albert had not been so genuinely in love.

As for Victoria, she was beside herself with impotent rage, calling those dreadful Tories all the unpleasant names she could dredge from her limited Victorian vocabulary. Yet she herself gave Albert a rather hard time over his choices for his personal staff, apparently at the instance of that favorite lady attendant, who, having been Princess Victoria's governess for many years, was reluctant to see her considerable influence diluted by the influx of a lot of foreigners. After the wedding in February 1840, in the Chapel Royal at St. James's Palace, the happy couple and a mob of attendants repaired to Windsor Castle for an evening of festive hyperactivity. When Victoria and Albert went to inspect the commodious suite of rooms they were to share, he discovered that the ex-governess's bedroom opened onto the queen's dressing room. It would take him two years to ease the lady into retirement and, by this time with Victoria's willing consent, start bringing in a few foreigners to join Stockmar.

The next few years were surely the most formative years in Victoria's life. Under Albert's loving, gentle, but persistent tutelage, she changed from a generally gay, pert, uninhibited, and unconventional girl into the staid and proper matron who gave her name to an at least ostensibly staid and proper age. It was not Victoria who was Victorian, but Albert. Indeed, for many years some of her critics described her reign as Albertine. Yet she was not playing Trilby to his Svengali, and certainly not Ingrid Bergman to his Charles Boyer in *Gaslight*. He loved her too much simply to manipulate her, to use her for his own purposes. Perhaps *she* loved *him* too much, for she so idolized him that she became almost a distaff version of her husband without either of them fully realizing it. Oh, he doubtless noticed a considerable improvement, but only with time.

It is to his credit that he never disillusioned her. This was not a case of a woman's slowly emerging from her first fine careless rapture to gaze glumly at her beloved's feet of clay. On the contrary, although Victoria the woman was quite rapturously in love from the outset, early in the marriage Victoria the queen displayed strong reservations over giving Albert any role in government. Only gradually, with the passage of time, and after Lord Melbourne assured her that there could be no harm in letting Albert see official papers, did the queen succumb to her consort's powerful personality, dismaying energy, and formidable competence. Especially after she began bearing their nine children, she became housewife and mother and he became king. This could not be legally and literally the case, of course, but when Napoleon III came to London in 1855, Albert joined with him and assorted panjandrums in councils of state while Victoria had a nice chat with the Empress Eugénie in a drawing room. It was, then even more than now, a man's world.

And Victoria was a man's woman, the kind of woman who needs a man. For three years after her accession Lord Melbourne filled that need with sage political advice and affectionate personal counseling, as well as with witty observations, amusing anecdotes, and spicy gossip. But in an August 1841 election he and his Whig party were voted out of office, to Victoria's tearful and fearful chagrin. Although the two of them corresponded faithfully thereafter, Melbourne was no longer available as father figure, and his departure immeasurably deepened Victoria's dependence on Albert (and, interestingly, on Albert's mentor, Stockmar, who had become quite a fixture at court). The prince proved invaluable during the transition period, chiefly in making Sir Robert Peel, the new and not so friendly Tory prime minister for whom Victoria had an abiding distaste, feel reasonably comfortable in his new relationship with the crown, a relationship that eventually grew quite warm and trusting. (Albert is generally credited with strengthening the British monarchy by placing it "above party.") Victoria as queen had to make more adjustments to reality than she ever had as princess. Albert, who had been making difficult adjustments almost since birth, was enormously helpful in showing her how.

But not in one major respect. Victoria resented having to bear his children. Her pregnancies and deliveries were usually not especially complicated or painful, but she simply did not like children all that much. Infants in particular were rather nasty little things. She was a queen, after all, whose job was to rule the land, not populate it. Yet Albert, whose sexual activity was focused exclusively on his wife, kept her very busy in the family production department while he kept himself busy in the state planning department. Although she could hardly say that she did not ask for the assignment (she was passionately fond of what she called "fun in bed"), Albert's willingness to put up with her procreative discomforts and inconveniences was never one of the things that brought them closer together. Not even his solicitude when she was pregnant could diminish her frustration.

With the departure of Melbourne, however, and the induced retirement of her ex-governess in September 1842, Victoria seemed to relinquish the scepter if not the crown to Albert. This created some problems with the politicians and the governmental bureaucracy, since neither Albert nor Stockmar yet had a very tight grip on the British notion of constitutional monarchy. Both men were fussbudgets addicted to the formal memorandum. Their sometimes rather imperious communications were a source of chronic irritation to those favored with them in the upper levels of British officialdom, especially since the memos so often displayed a dispassionate clarity of thought. There is no reliable evidence that Victoria ever said the famous line, "We are not amused," but there is good reason to believe that many British politicians did. Frequently.

They might have been better off, on balance, if they had been more receptive to his meddlesome advice. Lord Palmerston, as foreign minister from 1846 to 1851, continually repulsed Albert's attempts to moderate his aggressive foreign policy, but as prime minister after 1855, and after Albert's interfering had proved of obvious value in the success of the Great International Exhibition of 1851 and in the conduct of British participation in the Crimean War in 1853–56, the doughty old gentleman joined a growing group of statesmen who now actually sought Albert's counsel and administrative assistance. Victoria was delighted with her husband's new popularity and influence, of course, although she worried about what overwork and nervous tension might do to his health. Never robust, he began a slow decline in health during the 1850s. Revolutionary unrest on the Continent, the plight and neglect of England's industrial poor, constant sniping among the unregenerate English nobility against "that German fella," antagonism and ridicule from the press, boredom with aristocratic bores at unavoidable social functions, and now heavier governmental responsibilities, all were taking their toll.

Toward the close of the decade, Victoria could sense the beginning of the end. Albert would come alive only during their rare holidays in Scotland, at Balmoral Castle, where they could indulge, alone, their mutual love of murmuring forests and mountain lakes and streams. On their return to London she could almost see the energy draining from him, the light going out of his eyes, the burdens now resumed bowing his shoulders and slowing his step. This was the case on their return in November 1861, when they received word of the notorious affair between "Bertie," the Prince of Wales, and the actress Nellie Clifden. For Albert, who had raised his son most strictly, no doubt too strictly, and who considered sex outside marriage an abomination, this was the blow that killed him. Or so Victoria believed, so strongly that, when Albert died that December, she refused to be the one to call Bertie to the bedside.

Not until two "dreadful years of loneliness" had passed did the stricken queen emerge from mourning. For almost forty years thereafter she ruled England in the way that she felt Albert would have wished. His hand was still on the scepter.

Mary Todd
and
Abraham Lincoln

 ~

The story of their first meeting is a famous one, at least as she told it later. It was at a ball being held in the winter of 1839 to mark the moving of the state capital from Vandalia, Illinois, to Springfield. Mary Todd had come to Springfield in search of a husband. (She lived there with a married sister.) Abraham Lincoln had come to Springfield in search of a career. But the young lawyer, having lost a legendary love to malaria in one instance and having been rejected in another, was also looking for a wife. When he saw Mary in her silk dress, he wasted no time in getting her name and approaching her: "Miss Todd, I want to dance with you in the worst way." And that, she reported, was exactly what he did.

She, it turned out, had more to her than a pretty dress and the pretty neck and shoulders that it left uncovered. She had a head on those shoulders, and he soon found that it was by no means an empty one. She was bright, literate, articulate, well educated in literature, music, and French, which she spoke fluently. She soon discovered that this lanky giant was at least as intellectually agile as she, that he liked to discuss poetry and politics as much as she did. Used to shallow men, she was fascinated by the depth and variety of his personality, his sinuous mind and changing moods, as he was enthralled by her effervescent vitality, her sparkling intelligence, her resilience, her enjoyment of life. They saw a lot of each other during the weeks following the ball.

Mary spent the winter deciding. Should she accept his proposal of marriage or concentrate on James Shields, the Democratic state auditor, or on Stephen A. Douglas, Abe's political rival-to-be? To the consternation of her Kentucky-aristocrat family, and over their immediate vocal objections, she decided on Abe, who at the age of thirty (she was twenty-one) was formally uneducated, embarrassingly impoverished, and generally quite unpromising. Having thus chosen, she was crushed to learn that *he* was backing away. In one of his moods of blackest melancholy, he told her that he had so little hope of supporting her in the style that she and her family enjoyed, or anything approaching it, that he wanted her to release him from his promise. When she burst into tears, of indignation as much as shocked sorrow, his resolve melted, he took her in his arms, and he renewed his proposal. Yet his doubts remained, and the passing of time brought on quarrels until, on New Year's Day 1841, they agreed not to see each other anymore.

Evidently this was more her decision than his. She had a temper and could distress him mightily by displaying it. After their separation he was described as going "crazy as a loon." A friend wrote that "he was confined a week, but though he now appears again he is reduced and emaciated in appearance and seems scarcely to possess the strength to speak above a whisper. His case at present is truly deplorable but what prospect there may be for ultimate relief I can not pretend to say. I doubt not but he can declare 'That loving is a painful thrill. And not to love more painful still.' " He tried to get help from doctors. He tried to obtain a job as a consul in South America. A year later he was still despondent, but the successful marriage of a good friend heartened him enough to begin seeing Mary again—a rueful Mary who was delightedly eager to resume their friendship.

That friendship took a political turn when Mary and a woman

friend, with Abe's knowledge if not help, began writing anonymous and acidly satirical letters to the *Sangamo Journal* against Auditor Shields, who responded by demanding the letter writer's name. The *Journal*'s editor gave him Lincoln's name, and Abe, after gallantly accepting responsibility, found himself challenged to a duel. Part of the story is that, since he had the choice of weapons, he ungallantly proposed cow pies at five paces—an unlikely filigree, though not entirely out of character. The actual weapons were gross enough—broadswords, to be wielded on a sandbar in the Mississippi River, where the Illinois law against dueling did not apply. But Abe tired of the nonsense before a blow was struck and offered to publish a statement that the satire in the letters was meant to be political, not personal. Shields accepted this, and the farce concluded on a note of guarded amity.

Mary's family remained firmly opposed to her association with this disreputable oaf, while she as firmly opposed their opposition. But her sister and brother-in-law, once they were convinced that the wedding was inevitable, were generous enough to offer their spacious parlor for the ceremony, which took place in November 1842. That was the last that she would see of gracious living for the next few years. From a life of easy luxury she entered upon one of assiduous budgeting. The couple enjoyed no honeymoon, moving immediately to a boarding house, the Globe Tavern, where Robert Todd Lincoln was born in August 1843. The tavern environment being a cut below Mary's wildest dreams and less than ideal for a baby, Abe managed to rent a somewhat more respectable three-room cottage for the following winter. In the spring of 1844 he was earning enough to buy the larger, more comfortable house that they would call their own until their final departure for Washington, D.C. The second of their four sons was born there in March 1846. (Only Robert would live beyond his teens.)

The greatest strain on their marriage was Abe's absence for six months out of every year, when he "rode the circuit" throughout central Illinois with other lawyers and the circuit judge, trying cases that cropped up along the way. Mary's discontent with this arrangement was aggravated by the conspicuous pleasure that Abe took in his circuit riding, which gave him daily opportunities not only to indulge the sporadically gregarious side of his nature but also to accumulate a great variety of legal experience. Like it or not, it was the only practical way to bring home enough money to provide food and warm shelter and to satisfy, to some extent, Mary's taste for pretty clothes and "nice things," at least until he could build up an adequate practice in town.

Her interest in conventional possessions and amenities and his disregard for them were among their many chronic incompatibilities. The most obvious of these at first sight was their spectacular physical disparity: she was fourteen inches short of his six feet four, a difference she found so embarrassing that she would never allow a photograph to be taken of them together. Where she was used to the dress and deportment of a pretentious Southern upper crust, he, for all his innate warmth and dignity, was more scarecrow than clotheshorse and could be downright vulgar in manner and speech. She was usually, and unusually, alert and sensitive to whatever was going on about her; he was often abstracted, preoccupied, moodily introspective. When she was exuberantly talkative, he was frequently taciturn. When she wanted the stimulation of a rousing argument, he would withdraw from the field and into himself, inaccessible. And with Billy Herndon, Abe's law partner and close friend, she quarreled bitterly throughout her life. Yet she and Abe loved *and* admired each other, and she was acutely aware of the truth behind a remark made by a relative, "Mary, if I had a husband with a mind such as yours has, I wouldn't care what he did."

Among the things they shared was ambition. They were both overjoyed when Abe's hobnobbing about the state paid off with his election in 1846 to a term in the House of Representatives starting in October 1847. She was especially happy about their trip to Washington, which included a stopover in her native Lexington, Kentucky, to impress her now-reconciled family with her newly prominent husband and their two healthy boys. But life for her in Washington was a letdown. A congressman's wife was much less important there than in Lexington, Abe was busily away from home most of the time, and the boys were actively underfoot all of the time. In the spring of 1848, therefore, she returned to Lexington, where the slaves that her husband would free (with, then, her zealous approval) could make her life more comfortable. Abe apparently was relieved at first to see her go, but any feeling of relief was soon replaced by loneliness for her. "When you were here," he wrote in April, "I thought you hindered me some in attending to business; but now, having nothing but business—no variety—it has grown exceedingly tasteless to me. . . . I hate to stay in this old room by myself." To which she replied, "How much, I wish instead of writing, *we* were together this evening, I feel very sad away from you. . . ."

Although Abe's performance in Congress was less than historic—only his nervy, loud opposition to the Mexican war has been remembered—he returned to Springfield to find his standing in the Whig party considerably enhanced. He was asked to stump New England for Zachary Taylor, making Mary proud of his burgeoning reputation as an orator. She was proud, too, after her father's death, when her family asked Abe to come to Lexington and defend them against a challenge to the will. Wife and husband had become a very married couple, and this helped them maintain their equilibrium after their young Eddy's death from diphtheria early in 1850. They had nursed him together for nearly eight weeks, and now they turned to each other for solace. To give Mary comfort, Abe took up formal religion for the first time, renting a family pew at the First Presbyterian Church, which they kept throughout the 1850s, and even attending services with her from time to time. He brightened her life, too, with their sons Willie, born in December 1850, and Tad, born in April 1853. Perhaps because of their experience with Eddy, as parents they loved their boys not so much wisely as too well, indulging them often to the exasperation of their sometimes irritated guests.

Their income and social position rose most respectably during the early 1850s, although Abe seemed politically becalmed. In May 1854 the passage of Senator Stephen Douglas's Kansas-Nebraska Bill, which sought to permit the extension of slavery by popular referendum in newly admitted states, spurred Abe into lobbying the Illinois legislature the next February to elect him to the U.S. Senate, but in an inconclusive three-way race, although he had the largest plurality, he threw his weight to the opponent who was also against the Douglas bill. Soon thereafter he left the dying Whig party and joined the new Republican party, which condemned the extension of slavery. Although the move troubled Mary, she defended him loyally against criticism from relatives and friends.

Thus it was the Republicans who nominated him in 1858 to run against the Democrat Douglas for the U.S. Senate, to engage the little senator in the famous debates, and, although he lost the gerrymandered election, to earn for himself a national reputation. This last was not so clear then as it is now, and he was desperately dejected by the result, feeling that his political career was at an end. Mary also was crestfallen, having been totally confident that his victory would be a stepping-stone to the White House, something she did not expect his defeat to be. But in May 1860, after two busy years of traveling with her husband on what today we call the rubber-chicken circuit, she could sit back with satisfaction at the Republican National Convention in Chicago and watch him being nominated the party's candidate for President of the United States.

During the campaign her always lively interest in politics was heightened, deepened, widened. Abe, to avoid getting involved in the sectional disputes dividing the country, stayed at home during the campaign but was visited daily by a stream of visitors—party leaders, supporters, campaign advisers, reporters, cartoonists, well-wishers. This gave Mary plenty of rehearsal experience as hostess and VIP-greeter, as well as tactful bouncer of undesirables. Abe's manifest respect for her bolstered her ego and gave her confidence in what seemed pretty heady company. She was in her element. The year 1860, probably the happiest in her life, saw its climax for her, for them both, on election night. She stayed home, anxiously, while her husband walked to the telegraph office to check on the returns. When New York clinched his victory, his immediate reaction was to say that he would have to go home and "tell Mary about it." He did so, and she found the news delicious.

The next year was not so happy. While Abe was being spurned by the South, Mary was being snubbed by the snobs, the parochial pooh-bahs of Washington society, who considered her a backwoods upstart. Congress gave her an opportunity for a kind of retaliation when it appropriated a large sum of money for refurbishing the White House. She spent (indeed, somewhat overspent) the money splendidly, converting the mansion from its appalling run-down condition into a richly fashionable home and magnificent setting for the care and feeding of the most highfalutin visitors, foreign and domestic. But her personal extravagance in wartime, her meddling in political appointments (she was surely the most political First Lady in history), and the imperious manner that sometimes concealed, sometimes compensated for her acute sensitivity to slights, all invited criticism and even hostility from the Washington establishment.

As a Kentuckian born and bred (unlike Abe, who was a Kentuckian born but not bred), she shared some of the soft Southern racism expressed in the hackneyed assertion that "dear ol' Mammy is practically one of the family." Some of her relatives sided with the Confederacy. Like her native state, she was on the borderline until opting, clearly, for the Northern cause. As a result, rabid Southerners accused her of being a turncoat, and rabid Northerners accused her of being a Confederate sympathizer. The controversy became so heated that a congressional investigating committee began an inquiry into her loyalty. To forestall this absurdity, Abe walked over to the Capitol and read a statement to the committee: "I, Abraham Lincoln, President of the United States, appear of my own volition before this committee of the Senate to say that I, of my own knowledge, know that it is untrue that any member of my family hold treasonable communication with the enemy." He said it with such conviction and sincerity, as well as dignity, that no official notice was ever taken again of the rumors against Mary's loyalty.

One thing that the war did for her, for them, was to keep Abe at home. They were together most evenings and even took daily rides, side by side, in the presidential carriage, often to visit the wounded in military hospitals. Abe never showed any serious interest in another woman, partly because Mary could be embarrassingly jealous, but mostly because he just was not interested. At a White House reception he remarked to a reporter standing beside him, as his eyes lit on Mary talking easily with some guests, "My wife is as handsome as when she was a girl and I a poor nobody then fell in love with her, and what is more, I have never fallen out."

On that tragic evening at Ford's Theater in April 1865, while John Wilkes Booth was making his way to the presidential box, Mary and Abe were sitting there together, sharing their enjoyment of the play, and holding hands.

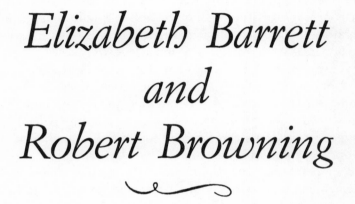

Elizabeth Barrett
and
Robert Browning

In January 1845 Elizabeth Barrett was nearly thirty-nine years old, a spinster confined by tuberculosis to a sofa in one room of her father's commodious and now famous house at No. 50 Wimpole Street in London. Her widowed father, a classic Victorian patriarch, loved his dozen children generously and affectionately but so possessively that he despotically opposed any move, by any of them, to leave the fold for any such disreputable project as marriage. This restriction applied especially to Elizabeth, who had always been his pet and whose growing public reputation as a poet brought him immense pride and satisfaction. His firm grasp on her gave her no problem, for she loved him deeply and, since the death of her favorite brother five years earlier, neither enjoyed nor expected any rival for her affection. She calmly assumed that she would live out her few remaining years in her sickness.

She had published a large collection of poems the year before, and in one of them she had paid brief tribute to some of her contemporary fellow poets, among them Robert Browning. In January 1845 the author of *Paracelsus* and *Pippa Passes*, at thirty-two, was in a valley of despair, of critical neglect and public indifference, which depressed even his normally buoyant spirit. When a friend gave him a copy of Elizabeth's poems, therefore, he was touched and greatly bucked up by her reference to him. So moved, he read the whole collection, and in that destiny-laden month he wrote her a note that included a straightforward account of his reaction: "I love your verses with all my heart, dear Miss Barrett . . . and I love you too."

That last seems a bit premature, but perhaps he really did, incipiently. Not only was he enchanted by the active, perceptive mind and warm heart that he detected in her writing, but he also had for many months been hearing her praises sung by a mutual friend, a self-appointed Cupid, a matchmaker and cousin to Elizabeth named John Kenyon. Kenyon was a contemporary of her father; he was also a friend of her father but would not have been if that formidable gentleman had known that he was drumming up suitors and, among other things, had occasionally arranged for Robert to pay Elizabeth a visit, only to be turned away each time by the excuse of her illness. The Wimpole Street house was a bastion guarded by an unassailable butler and a large, determined family headed by a swain-eating ogre. Despite the growth of her reputation and the lengthening list of would-be callers, she was not at home to anyone but very close friends and one or two irresistibly puissant gate-crashers.

This was her preference as much as her father's. Her brother's death had so crushed her spirit—she was laden with guilt because he had stayed with her at her urging during a visit to the seashore for her health and had been drowned during a storm—that she really cared to see no one but her closest friends. Her only therapy, her only relief, was to bury herself in her poetry, to "work, work, work," as she put it. When Robert's frequent letters to her, straying from topics like Greece, Rome, the Renaissance and literature in general, began pleading for permission to visit her, she put him off. It was still January, and winters "shut me up as they do dormouse's eyes; in the spring, *we shall see*: and I am so much better that I seem to be turning to the outward world again." Indeed she was much better. For five years her rate of improvement had been barely perceptible to those who loved her, but Robert's attentions brought her a sudden, powerful tonic. In a very real sense, he swept her on her feet.

But then she had swept him off his. For both of them it was a case of love before first sight. They fell in love with each other's work, with each other's learning, with each other's love of beauty and poetry, and finally with each other. In May of 1840 Robert at joyous last gained entry to the inner sanctum. She was deathly afraid that he would be disappointed, but it was already too late for that. He declared his love immediately and so impetuously that she recoiled— no, she was too ill, she could not love, could not marry—he must never speak of it again.

He did speak of it again, gently but stubbornly. He wrote about it in the unceasing letters that filled the gaps between their too infrequent meetings. (Mr. Barrett tolerated these visits from a fellow poet, but the lovers thought a low profile the better part of valor.) Her protests grew weaker as she grew stronger. She walked about her room, then about the house, then about the neighborhood. She began going out for drives. In early September, when her beloved spaniel Flush was stolen and held for ransom, she actually sought out the thieves and negotiated for the dog's return. And by then she had agreed with Robert's insistence that they must get married and run away to live in the healthful climate of sunny Italy.

He had a plan: marry first, secretly (so that in an unexpected showdown the ogre would be legally powerless to prevent Elizabeth from joining her husband), then leave for Italy as soon as they could do so without causing an earthquake in London. He was forced to put the plan into operation sooner than he had anticipated, for within a week Mr. Barrett abruptly dispatched one of his sons to "the country" to rent a house. The family, he announced with his customary grace, must move forthwith to permit the refurbishing of the Wimpole Street stronghold. Both lovers were alarmed. Another winter in sooty London—the mere thought chilled Elizabeth to the marrow, yet she found it hard to make the big decision. "It seems quite too soon and too sudden," she wrote Robert hesitantly, "for us to set out on our Italian adventure now." His excited reply came within hours, reminding her that a delay now could mean another year of waiting. "You see what we have gained by waiting. We must be *married directly* and go to Italy. I will go for a license today and we can be married on Saturday."

That was Thursday, September 10. Late Saturday morning they were married, respectably if hurriedly, at St. Marylebone's Church, with her loyal maid and his sympathetic cousin as witnesses. After the unceremonious ceremony, they separated and went home lest a long absence arouse suspicions at the stronghold. In her room Elizabeth settled down to a mixture of happily anticipating her departure and dismally dreading the effect on Papa. Her wait was brief. On Wednesday Papa announced that moving day would be next Monday, and Robert immediately arranged for her and her maid to meet him at a bookshop Saturday afternoon. By mid-October they were ensconced in an apartment he had rented in Pisa, where the mild winters were considered just the thing for weak English lungs. In the spring of 1847 they moved on to that gem of the world's cities, Florence, which was to be their home, though intermittently, for the rest of their married life.

Back in London, Mr. Barrett, astonished that she had deceived him, retreated into a shell of bitter outrage. None of her letters to him was ever answered. He spoke of her rarely, and then only as if she were dead. But Elizabeth could correspond with others in her family. Among other things, she wrote to one sister that she had suffered a miscarriage in Pisa, marveling at how easily she had survived it. "Everyone wonders to see me recovering my strength now by handfuls, or heartfuls." By March 1849 she was strong enough to give birth to their son in a normal delivery. That summer, to escape the heat and mosquitoes, they stayed in what she called an "eagle's nest" in the mountains between Florence and Pisa, where they would "go out and lose ourselves in the woods and mountains, and sit by waterfalls on the starry and moonlit nights." She was even well enough to ride a horse five miles into the mountains on a picnic trip. "We dined with the goats, and baby lay on my shawl rolling and laughing."

It was there, in that year, that she first showed him the forty-four sonnets destined to rank among the most celebrated love poems in the language. (It is the forty-third that starts, "How do I love thee? Let me count the ways.") He found them exhilarating, moving, almost intimidating. They were too private to be published (she maintained) yet (he insisted) too exquisite not to be published. The dilemma suggested a stratagem. He had often called her his "little Portuguese" because of her slightly dark complexion, and so the poems were published, in 1850, as though addressed to the Portuguese poet Camoëns by his mistress, and under the double-meaningful title of *Sonnets from the Portuguese* in a volume of poetry by Elizabeth Barrett Browning.

In 1851, the Brownings visited London. Celebrities now, they were kept busy by "callers," including his charming parents and her brother George, whose reflective disapproval of their behavior quickly melted in the warmth of Robert's welcome, the vision of his happy sister, and the winning ways of his new nephew. But from the ogre the couple received only a bitterly censorious, abusive letter and a parcel containing all of Elizabeth's letters to him, unopened. London's air had already begun to affect her health, and Robert feared the damage that despair over her father might do to her. They returned to the Continent without further delay.

Yet they returned to London the next year. After spending about eight months in Paris, including a good deal of time with George Sand, her idol (but not his), Elizabeth had recovered her health enough for them to go back for a visit before returning to Italy to spend the winter in Rome and Florence. There, in the sun, they both set to work, he on his *Men and Women*, she on her verse novel, *Aurora Leigh*. They did their writing quite separately and not at all competitively, each considering the other the superior artist. Doubtless she was thinking of their situation when she wrote the lines that Romney addresses to Aurora, "Beloved, let us love so well, / Our work shall be the better for our love, / And still our love be sweeter for our work." They had their disagreements, inevitably. On social and political questions they held similar opinions, of a kind that today we call liberal, but her idealism led her into more radical views than his skepticism could abide. On spiritualism, so popular in their time, her ready acceptance clashed sharply with his almost cynical rejection, so sharply that they wisely called a truce and banished the subject to the region of the taboo.

In 1857 Elizabeth, especially after the death of her father aggravated her latent feeling of guilt, began coughing more often. Even in Rome and then in Florence her lungs seemed to grow more congested, very slowly and erratically but unmistakably. She became too weak to make the trip to the mountains for the summer, and the hot humidity of the cities made her gasp—more painfully for Robert than for her. She was quite weak during most of June 1861, and on the last day of that month she died, peacefully, in her husband's arms. The next evening he wrote his sister that "the future is nothing to me now, except inasmuch as it confines and realizes the past. . . . How she looks now—how perfectly beautiful."

He was to outlive her by twenty-eight years. He wore her gold ring conspicuously on his watch chain for the rest of his life.

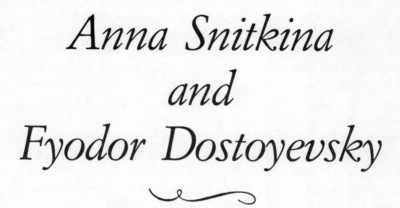

Anna Snitkina
and
Fyodor Dostoyevsky

W hen Anna Snitkina and Fyodor Dostoyevsky met in 1866 in St. Petersburg, she was twenty and he was forty-four. He had been a struggling, indigent writer longer than she had been alive. Although his first novel, *Poor Folk*, had received some mild plaudits after its publication in 1843, his work since then had elicited critical reactions ranging from disparagement up to indifference. In his youth, after a last-minute reprieve from a sentence of death for political conspiracy, he had spent four years at hard labor in Siberia and then another four wretched years as a forlorn private in the Russian army. After his release he had spent a dozen or so miserable years plugging away at his writing in spite of ceaseless sleeve-tugging by relatives in even worse shape, fraudulent treatment by conscienceless publishers, relentless badgering by a host of creditors, and his own inability to hold on to money—all complicated by the unpredictable attacks of his chronic epilepsy.

Yet these obstacles to productive writing and untroubled living were minor compared to his pathological addiction to gambling, depicted in his depressingly autobiographical novella, *The Gambler*. He was neither skillful nor lucky, losing far more than he won, yet in the vicinity of a roulette table, or any similarly enticing equivalent, he would lose all self-control. Since the disease came from deep within his character, from some innate defect, he had no hope of curing himself. He needed help from someone else, someone loving enough to give him patient sympathy and also to give his terrible problem the practical consideration that it deserved.

Crime and Punishment was published in 1866 but brought him little praise or money for many years. His situation was so desperate that year that he had to sign a humiliating contract which stipulated that, if he did not come up with a new novel by November 1, the publisher would have all rights to everything that he had written, was writing, or would write. The situation was complicated in September, when he paid a visit to an oculist and was told that he had a choice between cutting down on his writing or going blind. Stop writing out your manuscripts in longhand, the doctor advised, and dictate them instead. In the vicinity, luckily, was a shorthand college, and the director had just the person that Dostoyevsky needed. She was his outstanding pupil, Anna Snitkina.

She was a lucky, lucky choice. Her father (who had died shortly before) and her mother apparently had been omnivorous readers and had been so fond of Fyodor Dostoyevsky's stories that they had given their daughter the nickname Netochka after a character in one of them. Anna herself, a longtime devoted fan, was ecstatic over this opportunity to be of help to her idol. But at their initial session Fyodor, still suffering from the effects of an epileptic seizure the night before, was ill and highly irascible. He dictated imperiously, requiring her to read everything back to him, criticizing her as slow and error-prone, and finally dismissing her quite tersely. On sudden second thought, however, he told her to come back for more the following day. Anna returned home furious, determined never to see that intolerable despot again. But she softened the next morning, heeded her conscience, screwed up her courage, and did go back for more.

The second day was not nearly as bad, and over the next few weeks the new team apparently produced enough to fulfill the Stelovsky contract—at least quantitatively, which is all the law can require. Meanwhile a personal relationship had been developing. Fyodor had shown Anna how personable he could be in his better moods, and a romantic affection was bringing them ever closer together. Anna, quite spellbound by Fyodor's unpredictable genius, had fallen hopelessly in love with him. She told her sister, who warned her that it was indeed a hopeless match: He was twenty-four years older than she, poverty-stricken, burdened by debt, sick, and all in all very undependable. Neither sister was aware that he had proposed marriage to four other women since the death of his first wife, a termagant, about thirty months before. Such awareness, however, would have been as inconsequential to Anna as her sister's reservations were. She impatiently looked for signs of Fyodor's feelings for her. When he one day subtly, allegorically, proposed marriage by remarking that he had discovered a diamond hidden among his papers, she rapturously accepted. They were married in February 1867.

During the first few weeks of marriage, Anna suffered some mistreatment from Fyodor's stepson and sister-in-law, who seemed distressingly like Cinderella's older sisters. Anna's mother, observing this at a distance, but anxiously, recommended that Anna persuade her husband to take her on a tour outside the country, so that they could be alone together during these critical weeks of their marriage. It would be expensive, but she could make a contribution, and Anna could sell or pawn some of her clothing and furniture and other things. With the money securely in pocket, Anna suggested the trip to Fyodor, who was very reserved in agreeing to the trip, pointing out that it could not be for more than two or three months. They departed shortly after Easter, little suspecting that they would not be back for more than four years.

The first four months they hit bottom. Fyodor wrote not a line. Anna nervously kept up her shorthand by using it for her diary (which was to prove a mine of information to her husband's biographers). During a brief stay in Dresden, the couple were separated when Fyodor left for a four-day visit to Hamburg, where he expected to win enough money (he told Anna) to take care of all his debts and let them tour Europe in comfort. Anxious as this announcement made her, she made no protest. This was his dream, she told her diary; to resist it, if not futile, could be devastating for him.

Seven or eight days later she had a letter from him reporting that he had lost the money he had taken to Hamburg and needed some that he had left behind—in order, of course, to recoup those losses. Despite her misery at being alone in an unfamiliar city, she sent along the money with a note that he need not hurry back. Eleven days later he returned, penniless. Not only had he lost the additional money at the tables, but he also had pawned his watch and lost that money too. Anna was nonetheless rapturous over his reappearance.

With a little more help from her mother they got by until Fyodor received an advance, surprising as it was exhilarating, from a publisher named Katkov, to whom he had promised a book. The 84 gold napoleons were accompanied by a note warning that this was the last advance. The couple settled their bills and took off for Baden-Baden. It was a full day's trip on a hot, filthy train, particularly difficult for Anna, who was in the throes of morning sickness. Whey they arrived, on Thursday evening, July 4, they possessed 65 napoleons. And Baden-Baden had about as many roulette tables as it had inhabitants.

It was too late to do any serious gambling that night, but the next morning found Fyodor in a casino near their hotel. Soon he was back, confessing to Anna that he had lost all 15 napoleons that he had taken with him. Since she controlled the family purse, in theory, she extracted an agreement that he would not go to the casino more often than once a day. But that afternoon, when he begged her to let him show her the casino, she went with him, and he lost another 5 napoleons.

When she felt unwell the next morning, he promised to stay home and care for her but soon afterward left for a very brief visit to the casino. He came home about eleven that evening, utterly crestfallen, to report that he had lost another 20 napoleons. When she felt better the next day, Sunday the 7th, he made five compulsive visits to the casino. That evening, when she audited the family finances, she discovered that they had only a dozen napoleons left.

Then suddenly his luck turned from catastrophic to tolerable. The fair wind blew through Monday and Tuesday, when the couple counted a fortune of 166 napoleons. But in a compulsive situation, nothing feeds on itself like success. By Wednesday evening the fortune had shrunk to 20 napoleons. On Thursday he lost 19 but scrounged another 6 by pawning a set of earrings and a brooch that he had presented to Anna after their wedding. Losing the 6 left him with 1. On Friday, the nineteenth, he disappeared with the last napoleon and all their change, pawned their wedding rings, ran a winning streak up to 180 francs (no more napoleons), lost 177, then ran another streak up to 180 francs again, and returned with the rings and his winnings to Anna in triumph. She paid the rent.

And so it continued. By late July the couple were penniless again and expecting eviction momentarily for nonpayment of rent. One day he had sold her fur coat for 8 francs and had given her 2 francs for dinner. He lost the 6 francs at the casino, then came back for the 2 francs, which he also lost at the tables. On another day he had peddled a couple of her dresses and quickly gambled away the 30 francs they had bought. August continued this sort of routine, although her compassionate mother and sister sent her some money—with a note that Anna's pawned belongings back home were soon to be sold by the pawnbroker. Fyodor took the money to the casino, never to see it again. He seemed quite unconcerned about the loss of Anna's things. After three more wretched weeks on the financial tightrope, she somehow persuaded him to leave Baden-Baden for Switzerland on August 23. They arrived in Geneva with 18 francs. But there, to her happy surprise, he began working on a new novel, *The Idiot.*

And there she had an idea. Suspecting that the severe disapproval and opposition that was visited on his gambling had probably aggravated his addiction, she asked herself a radical question. If someone encouraged him to gamble, would he lose interest? And maybe stop?

She knew that there were roulette tables at nearby Aix-les-Bains. Why don't you try your luck, she asked him. And because you cannot expect to win over the long haul, take only a certain amount and stop when you have lost it. He was willing to make the attempt—this was *her* gamble, after all. He did, and he found it worked. He came back home satisfied and resumed work on his writing.

They were now happy parents of a small daughter. When the girl died in 1868, he went back to his compulsion, but only briefly. He continued writing while they resumed their touring and his restrained gambling. In April 1871, just before their return to Russia, she suggested his trying the tables at Wiesbaden. He did, and he lost a little money, but he seemed uninterested, preoccupied. Indeed, he was preoccupied—with the characters for his immortal *The Brothers Karamazov.*

He never gambled again.

Lord Alfred Douglas
and
Oscar Wilde

Oscar Wilde was a wittily entertaining writer of British comedy whose life was a Greek tragedy. He was something of a larger-than-life hero, at least in certain respects, and a flaw in his character led inexorably to his downfall. That flaw was a kind of egocentric fatalism that brought on his self-inflicted ruin.

He set the stage by being aggressively anti-Victorian in a society gripped by the prurient prudery of the Victorian establishment. He arrived in England from his native Ireland in October 1874, at the age of twenty, for his final college year at Oxford, and he soon embarked on a campaign to earn himself fame or notoriety,whichever came first. At a time when most art was widely considered as vaguely immoral, he became the most conspicuous of London's dissenting aesthetes through extravagant foppery, going to parties in knee breeches, a velvet coat, and a cavalier's shirt with a cascading green tie, and on occasion carrying an impertinent sunflower or lily in his languid grip. He was well over six feet and prodigiously strong—strong enough, for instance, to throw four large, drunken ruffians out of his rooms at Oxford as easily as if he were emptying wastebaskets, and thereby to garner for himself a campus reputation for something besides affectation—yet he infused his public character with an air of effeminacy as provocative (in both senses, depending on the beholder) as it was intentional. In the late 1870s and the early 1880s, he made a career of this public character, displaying it especially on a publicity tour of America in 1882 to drum up interest in D'Oyly Carte's production of Gilbert and Sullivan's comic opera *Patience*.

He also wrote provocative poetry with sentimentally pederastic lines like "A fair slim boy not made for this world's pain," later changed to "A lily-girl, not made . . ." in honor of Lillie Langtry. But his poetry attracted not nearly as much attention as his posing and his one-liners—"The only way to get rid of a temptation is to yield to it." In the late 1880s he took a brief turn at fairy tales, which proved largely innocuous, and in 1891 he published his novel, *The Picture of Dorian Gray*, a morality tale branded as immoral by most critics because of what he called its purple passages (barely lavender, needless to add, by today's standards). Some considered it well written and suitable for themselves but too well written and quite improper for others. Oscar reveled in the controversy, which he stimulated at every opportunity out of the joy of battle and increasing sales. That same year he wrote a politically radical magazine article which earned him a reputation as a socialist as well as a libertine among establishment types. And after returning home from Paris, where he had written his play *Salomé* only to have it banned in London, he took to habitually wearing the green carnation boutonniere that French homosexuals then used for identification.

It was also in 1891 that he met the twenty-one-year-old Lord Alfred Douglas, then in his second year at Oxford. Alfred was enchantingly beautiful, stunningly aristocratic (being one of *the* Scottish Douglases), enthusiastically gay, and soulfully poetic. This last quality irresistibly attracted Oscar, without totally eclipsing the first. "My Own Boy," he wrote upon receiving one of Alfred's poems about a year later, after they had gotten to know each other better, "Your sonnet is quite lovely, and it is a marvel that those red rose-leaf lips of yours should have been made no less for music of song than for madness of kisses. Your slim gilt soul walks between passion and poetry."

By this time the bisexual Oscar had a family: his loving and increasingly neglected wife Constance and two young sons. For a while after the marriage in 1884, he had been a model of domestic solicitude, but his extracurricular interests, professional and gaily otherwise, had drawn him away from the happy hearth. (Constance, fortunately, had an income of her own.) As his professional reputation grew—as a playwright, now, with the acclaimed and profitable productions of *Lady Windemere's Fan* and *A Woman of No Importance*—so did his reputation as a gay voluptuary. His sudden success seems to have given him an idea that celebrity has no ceiling, that he had grown out of reach of the society he flouted. Instead of following up his two stage hits with another, he spent most of 1893 and 1894 cultivating his intimate, if recurrently stormy, relationship with Alfred—"You are the divine thing I want, the thing of grace and beauty"—cultivating it so assiduously and openly that friends like Max Beerbohm became ever more anxious that he was provoking the establishment into a battle that he could not possibly win.

The battle was brought to him early in 1894 by Alfred's father, the Marquis of Queensberry, who had invented the famous rules for boxing a quarter of a century earlier. Although he had lunched with Oscar and Alfred six months before and had reportedly been charmed by his son's witty friend, the charm now had been considerably eroded by the persistent rumors of gay hanky-panky. As one of the most irascible men in history, he was particularly incensed when a popular novel appeared which, entitled *The Green Carnation*, presented as central characters two mutually affectionate gentlemen named Esmé Amarinth and Lord Reginald Hastings, aesthetes to the tips of their manicures. The objects of the satire were not very hard to identify, and for Queensberry, a paragon of macho rectitude who manfully mistreated his wives and children and could brook no trace of effeminacy within scenting distance, this was more than he could stand. Off went a letter to his son insisting that he immediately break all connection with "this man Wilde. . . . With my own two eyes I saw you both [in a restaurant] in the most loathsome and disgusting relationship as expressed by your manner and expression. Never in my experience have I seen such a sight as that in your horrible features. No wonder people are talking as they are. Also I now hear . . . that his wife is petitioning to divorce him for sodomy and other crimes." This last suggestion was quite untrue, but Queensberry, like many another establishment figure, could work himself into a foaming lather over moral aberrations which were not among those to which he was addicted. He was not greatly mollified by Alfred's laconic reply, "What a funny little man you are."

Nor was he particularly gratified to learn that his son had immediately thereafter left with Oscar for a two-week vacation in Algiers. Then in early 1895 the success of Oscar's *An Ideal Husband* and the even greater triumph of *The Importance of Being Earnest* poured a large helping of salt on his wounds, with an extra helping provided when he was refused admittance to the theater on *Earnest*'s opening night. (He had brought a large bouquet of vegetables to throw at Oscar during the curtain calls.) A few days afterward he left a visiting card for Oscar at the latter's club, on the back of which he had written, "To Oscar Wilde, posing as a somdomite," the misspelling probably due to blind fury. When next the "somdomite" visited his club, the hall porter gave him the card enclosed in an envelope, explaining that only he had seen it, and he did not understand it. Oscar, instead of simply tearing it up and discarding it, filed suit for libel.

Why he did so no one knows. Alfred may have egged him on just to get at the old man, but Oscar was never quite that maneuverable. Queensberry had threatened dire physical violence during a brief meeting with Oscar in mid-1894, and Oscar may have decided now that a cowardly bully so bent on vengeance could be hazardous to his health and should be neutralized. Or he may merely have decided to get rid of this pest without giving any thought to his own vulnerability or the assiduous hostility of his adversary. He was so absurdly overconfident of victory that his choice of lawyer was not Sir George Lewis, an expert on the law as it pertained to homosexuality, but Sir Edward Clarke, a barrister with a splendid reputation but without the necessary expertise.

The contrast between his self-assurance and the anxiety of his friends is highly visible in a description by Bernard Shaw of a luncheon meeting that he attended with Oscar, Alfred, and Frank

Harris, whom Oscar had asked to testify to *Dorian Gray*'s underlying moral excellence:

"For God's sake, man [answered Harris], put everything on that plane out of your head. You don't realize what is going to happen to you. It is not going to be a matter of clever talk about your books. They are going to bring up a string of witnesses that will put art and literature out of the question. Clarke will throw up his brief. He will carry the case to a certain point; and then, when he sees the avalanche coming, he will back out and leave you in the dock. What you have to do is cross to France tonight. Leave a letter saying that you cannot face the squalor and horror of a law case; that you are an artist and unfitted for such things. Don't stay here clutching at straws like testimonials to *Dorian Gray*. I tell you I know. I know what is going to happen. I know Clarke's sort. I know what evidence they have got. You must go." It was no use. Wilde was in a curious double temper. He made no pretense either of innocence or questioning the folly of his proceedings against Queensberry. But he had an infatuate haughtiness as to the impossibility of his retreating. . . . Douglas sat in silence, a haughty indignant silence, copying Wilde's attitude as all Wilde's admirers did, but quite possibly influencing Wilde. . . . Oscar finally rose with a mixture of impatience and his grand air, and walked out with the remark that he had now found out who were his real friends; and Douglas followed him, absurdly smaller, and imitating his walk, like a curate following an archbishop.

Oscar's casual response to this and other urgent pleas that he flee to the Continent was that he had been there often and recently, and "One can't keep going abroad unless one is a missionary, or what comes to the same thing, a commercial traveler."

The first day of the trial, April 4, consisted almost entirely of a protracted exchange between Queensberry's attorney and witness Oscar on art and morality, especially as exemplified in *Dorian Gray*. Oscar held up his end wittily and persuasively, but on April 5, the lawyer began mentioning names of disreputable young men with whom Oscar had been associated (Queensberry had spent his pretrial days in research) and threatening to put a knowledgeable and talkative witness on the stand. Oscar, now as alarmed as he should have been all along, withdrew his libel suit on Clarke's recommendation. His alarm was more than justified, for Queensberry's defense counsel immediately submitted a record of the trial, as well as depositions from Oscar's young associates, to the Director of Public Prosecutions. Oscar, after waiting fatalistically the rest of the day for his arrest, which came in the late afternoon, spent that night confined in the Bow Street Police Station.

He spent the next six weeks, through most of April and May, in court and in jail. He was released for a while on outrageous bail (supplied partly by one of Alfred's father-loathing brothers, partly by a clergyman shocked at the treatment of Wilde by the British press and public) and stayed with a compassionate family because he could not find a hotel that would admit him. Despite a prejudicial judge, his first trial ended in a hung jury, but his second concluded with a verdict of guilty of violating a section of the criminal code enacted "for the protection of the young," some of the young men having been under 18. The judge gave him the maximum sentence, two years at hard labor, expressing regret that he could not throw away the key.

Before the trials Alfred had visited him in jail faithfully, every day, but during them he went to France on counsel's advice. Although he wanted desperately to testify, he agreed more realistically that his appearance in court, even his presence in London, might be an indiscretion. But his absence was hard on Oscar, who wrote him between trials with dramatic intensity, "My dearest boy, This is to assure you of my immortal, my eternal love for you. . . . If prison and dishonour be my destiny, think that my love for you and this idea, this still more divine belief, that you love me in return will sustain me in my unhappiness and will make me capable, I hope, of bearing my grief most patiently. . . . Oh! may I live to touch your hair and your hands. . . . Dearest boy, sweetest of all young men, most loved and most lovable. Oh! wait for me! wait for me! I am now, as ever since the day we met, yours devotedly and with an immortal love." The letter would not have greatly strengthened his defense in court.

Oscar's first year in prison, at the Warnsworth and then at the Reading jail, made him the victim of two successive wardens notable for righteous cruelty. He was steeped in a deep, unceasing misery. As he put it in *The Ballad of Reading Gaol*, "In Reading gaol by Reading town / There is a pit of shame, / And in it lies a wretched man / Eaten by teeth of flame. . . ." His misery brought on a splenetic bitterness against Alfred, revealed later in his *De Profundis* (in its final, 1961 edition). Conditions improved considerably during his second year, thanks to a new and less moralistic warden at Reading, but the improvement, for someone like Oscar, was never much better than a little air-conditioning in hell.

By the time of his release in May 1897, Constance, whom Oscar described as always gentle and good, had obtained a legal separation and was living with the children in Italy under the name of Holland. He, too, took another name, Sebastian Melmoth, under which he lived in Paris, with occasional trips to Italy and Switzerland. One trip to Italy, that September, he made with Alfred; the old mutual attraction was more than either could resist, despite vigorous protests and objections from relatives and friends. Alfred, wrote Oscar in a letter, "offered me love, and . . . in my loneliness and disgrace I, after three months' struggle against a hideous Philistine world, turned naturally to him. Of course I shall often be unhappy, but I still love him. . . ." Yet in the event it proved no longer the all-consuming love that they had known in the past. Prodded by Alfred's mother, and seduced by her offer of money, the lovers parted, this time for good. "He has been sweet and gentle and will always remain to me as a type of what a gentleman and friend should be," Alfred wrote, "but I have lost that supreme desire for his society which I had before, and which had made a sort of aching void within me."

In November 1900 Oscar, having spent his last three years dodging creditors, sponging on friends, and insatiably picking up pretty boys, died in Paris of an ear infection caused by an injury incurred at Reading. He was a deathbed convert to Catholicism, a religion to which he had long been attracted for its colorful and artistic ritual if not for its moral restrictions. Otherwise he seems to have remained unchanged to the end. One of his last remarks concerned the wallpaper in his bedroom. He simply could not stand it, he complained, and one of them would have to go.

Alfred came to Oscar's funeral, and paid all the expenses.

Marie Sklodowska
and
Pierre Curie

Not every girl is likely to find her name in the dedication of a paper on "Symmetry in an Electric and Magnetic Field." Not every girl would revel in the experience. But in April 1894 Manya Sklodowska was thrilled by that dedication, even though it was only a handwritten note from its author, at the top of her copy. After all, a short time earlier she had achieved first place in the physics examination at the Sorbonne, and second place in mathematics. She could appreciate the quality of Pierre Curie's paper, as well as of his scientific work in general.

She also appreciated him as a person, increasingly. They had met only a few weeks before. He was thirty-five, already a man of some repute as an experimenter and a teacher; she was twenty-seven, a Polish student living in the bohemian Latin Quarter that had sprung up about the University of Paris. She was still a bit uncomfortable with the French language and customs, having left her native Warsaw only three years earlier. (It was at about this time that she changed her name to the French form, Marie.) Yet the two of them had gravitated to each other as though seeking a shared symmetry in a magnetic field. Pierre was almost as quiet and reserved as she was, but soon he was visiting her in her sixth-floor garret, pouring out to her his dedication to science and his hopes for a worthwhile career. On this subject he could be very articulate, and she was just the girl to be swept up by his eloquence.

Not so much so, however, as to yield to his suggestion that they rent an apartment together on the Rue Mouffetard to save on living expenses, despite his fervent though dubious assurance of separate bedrooms. Nor did she agree when he asked her to give up her plans to spend the summer of 1894 in Warsaw. Indeed, she even brought him to the edge of panic by hinting in her letters from there that she might not return at all. Yet return she did, and in the fall he took her to a Paris suburb to meet his parents. That visit proved pleasant for all concerned. Marie was to become especially attached to Pierre's father, a physician whose competence and professional integrity she greatly admired. She and Pierre were married, in a modest civil ceremony, in July 1875, after which she was entirely willing to share a small apartment with him.

The life that they now shared together was not much different from the life that they had shared separately. His teaching at the School of Physics and Chemistry gave her daily opportunities to help him prepare for his classes and thereby to learn rapidly, efficiently, and very pleasantly. Her own work, a study of the magnetic characteristics of various grades of steel, resulted in her first scientific paper, published in the fall of 1897. Although lacking succinctness and originality, it demonstrated a dogged thoroughness that would serve her—and Pierre—splendidly in their future work.

The major innovation in their married life was that newfangled contraption, the bicycle, which had been introduced to footsore society less than ten years before. Among their wedding presents was a gift of money for two of these wonderful machines, which were still regularly frightening horses but were also delighting a fast-growing multitude of both men and women. Since Marie had no patience with blue-nosed shock at the unmaidenly straddling involved, she and Pierre found their new toys pleasantly useful not only for local transportation but also for occasional vacations spent wandering inexpensively about France. They could take the bikes on trains to mountains and lakes and seashores, reveling in the easy mobility furnished by applied science and in the easy happiness furnished by romantic love.

These idylls were, of course, only infrequent interruptions of their work routine. A more serious interruption was her difficult pregnancy, which ended in September 1897 with the birth of Irène. Yet Marie continued doggedly with her work not only through the pregnancy but also through all the time- and energy-consuming problems of raising her young daughter. In a small, damp, cramped room at the school, without adequate equipment and without enough money for more, she feverishly devoted every spare moment to a series of experiments designed to test the effects of various metals, especially uranium, on the electrical conductivity of the surrounding air. The investigation was a fashionable one, since radioactivity—or at least what we now call radioactivity—was a new discovery and all the rage in scientific circles. More important, Pierre, who had invented a very sensitive electrometer, had an extra unit available for her experiments. With this device and a lot of patience, she could, she hoped, accumulate enough data for publication and for her doctorate.

She discovered that uranium and thorium made air conductive, and that the intensity of this effect depended solely on the amount of the element in the sample, regardless of the sample's condition. This suggested that the emanations affecting the air might be atomic in origin rather than molecular, since molecular changes in the samples ought to be readily observable. She also found that pitchblende, left over after the extraction of uranium, gave off emanations four times as strong as those of uranium. It must, she decided, have within it a substance much more energetic than uranium.

In April 1898 she published her first paper on radiation, reporting the radioactivity of thorium, only to find that a similar report had been published in Germany a couple of months earlier. Although her paper contained a brief comment on the pitchblende phenomenon, it attracted little notice. Pierre, however, became so excited by her discovery that he decided to pursue the investigation with her, temporarily forsaking his own work on crystals. That same April they began working on their first sample of pitchblende in their effort to reduce it to the intensely radioactive substance that it contained. What they did not know was how enormously radioactive that substance was and how infinitesimal were the amounts present. Their first sample of pitchblende weighed only a few ounces. Soon they were to graduate to pounds, and eventually to tons.

For four laborious years the couple spent their days grinding, pulverizing, sifting, heating, and cooling shovelfuls from the great pyramids of discarded pitchblende that they had managed to have delivered from a nearby uranium mill. The process was a grueling one of refining the products of successive refinements, so that the final product would be the residue of a residue of a residue, almost literally *ad nauseam*. Marie, an early feminist with the courage of her convictions, did more than her share of the exhausting physical labor; a visiting scientist once spoke of her, admiringly if condescendingly, as working "like a man." The environment aggravated the difficulty of the work, which had to be done, in heat of summer and cold of winter, either outside or in a rickety, drafty shed grudgingly provided by the school. Another visiting scientist wrote of their laboratory that, if he had not seen the chemical reduction equipment on the tables, he would have thought it all a practical joke of some kind.

The results were no joke. Marie was to remember the years in that "wretched shed" as the happiest years of their life together. Pierre not only loved her devotedly but also admired her as a fellow scientist. He appreciated her relentless thoroughness and shared her growing sense of achievement as bottles of their refined product, in the dark shed at the end of each long and labor-laden day, glowed silently but somehow triumphantly on the rude shelves about them. They knew, from spectroscopic tests run by a friend, that the bottles contained a spectacular new element, which they named radium, and their joy in discovering it was undimmed by the mysterious aches and pains, the weariness even after rest, which troubled them increasingly.

Of less importance to them was their growing fame. Their primitive laboratory and, later, their house on Boulevard Kellerman became meccas for noted physicists and chemists. Although the French scientific establishment never gave them the recognition they deserved, they were given teaching jobs that kept them going financially—Pierre at the Sorbonne and Marie at a "normal" school for girls. They both published articles on their work—an imperishable necessity then as now—and in June 1903, on the strength of a thesis describing the brief history of radium, Marie was awarded her doctorate in physical science, *très honorable*, by the University of Paris.

Among those attending the celebration party that evening was the Canadian physicist Ernest Rutherford, whose theories and experiments on the nature of radioactivity had already brought him worldwide fame. This was his first meeting with the Curies, and he was charmed. He was also alarmed. For when Pierre, toward the end of the evening, held out a tube with its zinc-oxide inner coating gleaming from the radium solution that it contained, Rutherford noticed for the first time that the hands holding it looked very red, as though terribly, terribly chapped. Just holding the tube seemed to cause Pierre some pain. Marie's hands, too, though not so startling at first sight, looked much the same.

Three months earlier a friend had implored the couple, in a ten-page letter, to take better care of their health. He ascribed their chronic fatigue, rheumatic pains, and other symptoms to overwork and careless eating habits. What he did not know was that they were working in an environment many times more radioactive than is considered tolerable for workers in the atomic-energy industry today. They did not know this either, and Marie was genuinely perplexed when, in August, she gave birth prematurely and the child, a little girl, died soon after the delivery. She was not only perplexed but deeply disappointed, as was Pierre.

Their disappointment was severely aggravated the following year by, of all things, the consequences of their receiving the Nobel Prize in physics in November (sharing it with Henri Becquerel). The seventy thousand francs that came with the award greatly eased their money worries, but the change from modest renown to worldwide, popular celebrity brought them unwelcome attention from badgering reporters and photographers, autograph hunters, social butterflies, professional alms-seekers, and various other parasites. To their teaching load and laboratory work were now added such time-consuming activities as giving interviews and answering avalanches of letters. They found themselves looking back wistfully at those lonely days in the shed. In this sense, according to Marie's later testimony, their receiving the Nobel Prize proved almost disastrous.

Yet in other respects it was a blessing. It brought Pierre some long-delayed recognition from the French academic establishment, especially in the form of a professorship at the Sorbonne, including a laboratory and a small group of assistants supervised by Marie. (Despite Pierre's diffidence, it was the male half of the team who predominantly got the recognition.) In 1905 Marie resumed her teaching, twice a week at the girls' school, where she broke ground by training her students in experimental as well as theoretical physics. (Nice young girls were expected to learn solely from books.) She also took time out to give birth to her second daughter, Eve, and was overjoyed by the baby's perfection. As the Nobel hubbub gradually quieted down, she was able to spend some time with her two daughters, to her invariable delight.

Meanwhile, Pierre pursued his work with radium. In 1904 he published a paper, with two of his colleagues, describing the effects of extended exposure to radioactivity in experimental rodents: The animals suffered from congestion of the lungs, for instance, and from a form of leukemia. Yet neither he nor Marie extrapolated such data into the human—and particularly his own—experience. He continued to work in a radium-centered environment and to carry samples of the deadly stuff in his pockets.

Yet it was not radium that killed him. Early one rainy afternoon in April 1906 he left a scientific meeting in a hotel on the Left Bank, stopped for a moment at his publisher's office (in vain, since it was closed by a strike), and, with his umbrella open and obscuring his vision, began to cross a busy street. Within seconds he was dead.

He had collided with a team of two horses pulling a heavy cart. While the driver tried desperately to stop, Pierre slipped under one of the horses, and a wheel of the cart rolled over his head, shattering the back of his skull into more than a dozen pieces. The cart driver was not arrested; he was clearly not at fault. In a way, it was probably radium that killed Pierre: Doubtless he was absorbed in thinking about it in his characteristically absentminded fashion, and blundered into the horses. At any rate, his swift, if premature, death surely saved him a great deal of suffering.

But not Marie. For days she mourned almost uncontrollably, wandering about the house in a daze, fondling things that Pierre had valued, hovering on the brink of nervous prostration. What finally saved her, as might be expected, was her work. Not only did she return to the laboratory, but she also accepted the Sorbonne's offer of Pierre's professorship, becoming France's first woman to hold such a post. She bought a house, half an hour away by commuter train, where her aging father-in-law, now a widower, happily watched over the children. In November the superphilanthropist Andrew Carnegie, impressed by her history of sturdy independence, set up a scholarship fund for students staffing her laboratory, making her thereby more independent than ever.

But independence of spirit is not a universally admired quality, especially in women. In 1910 Marie made the mistake of seeking election to the Academy of Sciences in competition with a less celebrated but male scientist. Their rivalry for the honor became daily fare in the press, which included a cheering and jeering section of rabidly male chauvinists. (Marie was not only a woman but also a *foreigner!*) She lost the election narrowly but unmistakably, in June 1911, and never again solicited an honor of any kind.

Yet this loss was instrumental in bringing her an unsolicited honor in the fall of 1911, the Nobel Prize in chemistry, ostensibly for the isolation of radium as a metallic element. Her shabby treatment by French academicians—and far shabbier treatment by the French press in stirring up a steamy scandal over her affectionate relationship with a former student of Pierre's, the respected physicist Paul Langevin—aroused widespread sympathy for her in the international scientific community. This feeling doubtless contributed to the human aspect of her selection, which not only recognized her own independent achievement but also made her the first person, male or female, to receive a second Nobel Prize. In accepting it at the formal ceremony in December, she thanked the committee for herself and for Pierre.

During World War I, with the help of daughter Irène, she organized a fleet of two hundred "radiological cars," or vans, to provide X-ray diagnoses at the front. During the last two years of the war, such diagnoses were conducted for more than a million wounded soldiers. After the war she toured the United States as a twenty-four carat celebrity, receiving from President Harding a precious gram of radium for use in the Radium Institute which the French government had belatedly established for her. In 1929 she paid the States a second visit, on a spectacularly successful fund-raising tour, sailing home just three days before the great market crash that could have made the tour a failure.

For the rest of her life she remained a very busy woman, especially in her laboratory, surrounded by her family of students and researchers. She took great pride in the achievements of daughter Irène and son-in-law Frédéric Joliot, including the discovery of artificially induced radioactivity that was to bring them a Nobel Prize in 1935.

She was not to live to see them accept it. Although publicly she tended to dismiss news stories of radium's health hazards, and although she herself had proved unusually resistant to its effects into her sixties, privately she confessed to a fear that it was responsible for, at least, the sores on her hands and her troublesome cataracts. When she died, in the summer of 1934, she was suffering from pernicious anemia.

Shortly before her death she destroyed her personal files, with a notable exception. She could not bring herself to burn Pierre's love letters from forty years before.

Charlotte
Payne-Townshend
and
George Bernard Shaw

~ꝰ

"A s a lady and gentleman were out driving in Henrietta St., Covent Garden, yesterday, a heavy shower drove them to take shelter in the office of the Superintendent Registrar there, and in the confusion of the moment he married them. The lady was an Irish lady named Miss Payne-Townshend, and the gentleman was George Bernard Shaw." Thus Shaw's notice of his marriage, sent to a London newspaper for its edition of June 2, 1898.

He was a confirmed bachelor of forty-two, she a confirmed spinster of forty-one. Or perhaps "determined" would be a more accurate word in each case, for both had childhood memories unpleasant enough to turn them from any thought of marriage. In 1875 his mother, leaving his witty but often besotted father in their native

Ireland, took off with his sisters to England, where she supported herself as a music teacher. Bernard (who detested the name George) joined them the following year and lived with them for the next twenty years in a household so unkempt as to border on the squalid. Although his mother was chiefly responsible for his love and knowledge of music, she was a slovenly housekeeper who inspired his blithe carelessness about his personal appearance and surroundings; in any case he was hardly the product of an ideal nuclear family. Charlotte's parents did not separate, but her mother was a relentless shrew who nagged her gentle father into an early grave and made her childhood, as she later described it to T. E. Lawrence, "perfectly hellish." When the mother died in 1891, Charlotte was in her mid-thirties and still defiantly unmarried. She was also, as a rich heiress, the target of many suitors, threadbare and otherwise, eager to share her lifestyle, but their imprecations only hardened her further against any such entanglement.

As for Bernard, his resolution against marriage was based less on principle than on preference. He knew that marriage could occasionally be idyllic, as in the case of his socialist friends Beatrice and Sidney Webb, who were a love-welded model of utter compatibility emotionally, intellectually, politically, irrevocably. But he was unwilling to take a chance, to make the necessary commitment. He enjoyed playing the field, with occasional conquests to make the game worthwhile, yet always returning to life with mother. This was the Bernard Shaw who could write to a touring Charlotte, some six months after he met her, "Only for Ellen Terry, who is quite angelically consolatory, and Nelly Heath, who is painting my portrait, and Lottie Fairchild, who makes me read my plays to her, and Ailsa Craig, who chaperones Lottie, I should be utterly lonely without you."

He seems to have been a philanderer without enough sexual drive to be a lecher. His greatest love was Bernard Shaw in any role, including that of Don Juan, whom he played as a kind of amorous chatterbox. He loved writing love letters much more than the women to whom he wrote them, and he loved hearing himself talk on any subject, including love. On one occasion, after paying a visit to a very ill Mrs. Patrick Campbell, he received a short note from her apologizing for not being more responsive to his extended remarks. "Oh dear me," she wrote, "it's too late to do anything but accept you and love you—but when you were quite a little boy somebody ought to have said 'hush' just once!"

But in 1896 Mrs. Pat the celebrated actress was some fifteen years away in his future, and Charlotte was now the prime object of his romantic affections. From the standpoint of their resolution against marriage, they met rather inopportunely, for they were both under the spell of the Webbs' blissful union. The Webbs, indeed, had brought them together and were delighted to see their interest in each other, since the Webbs' Fabian coterie of nonviolent socialist propagandists, for whom Bernard was a tireless spokesman, could use the support of a compassionate woman burdened with more money than she could spend on herself.

Her money surplus, in fact, often pricked her with serious feelings of guilt, and she was attracted by the Fabian Society's theory that the remedy for social injustice lay not in continuing personal charity or in fomenting class struggle but in changing social values through reasoned argument. She was also attracted by the members of the society, whose interests and conversation immeasurably transcended the gossipy chitchat that polluted the gatherings of her social set. Her interest in such extraordinary subjects as history and comparative religion and social justice had given her a reputation—splendid woman, y'know, and good company, but rather eccentric at times in her conversation. Among the Fabians she felt quite comfortable, for they were at least as eccentric as she was in conversation and more eccentric in seriousness of purpose.

She soon learned that Bernard Shaw was the star of their meetings. Already an established musical and dramatic critic and a budding playwright, he was inexhaustibly articulate, fluent, and witty. His monologues sparkled like a polished fencing sword in action. He loved, as he put it, to "coruscate." He was a slender six feet, good-looking, athletic, personable, brimming with Irish blarney at its scintillating best—among other things, a walking, talking invitation to female infatuation. Charlotte perceived the invitation readily enough but resisted any impulse to accept it on general principles. Yet she was vulnerable. Recently, after rejecting so many suitors, she herself had been gently but unmistakably rejected by a remarkable Swedish doctor whom she had met in Rome. They had fallen in love and her resolution against entanglements had begun to crumble; but his similar resolution was stronger than hers, and the affair had ended with neither consummation nor confrontation.

Thus she was on the rebound when she joined Shaw's audience. Before long he was making her an audience of one, at first occasionally and then more often, for he felt drawn to this Irishwoman who, though not beautiful, was handsome, with rich brown hair and eyes of shining green to match his of piercing blue. He enjoyed talking to her, and even with her, as his intellectual equal, which she probably was in most respects, and she reveled in this treatment. They saw much of each other over the next two years. When Charlotte was away—visiting relatives in Ireland or pursuing her addiction for touring Europe—he wrote her reams of romantic letters. (He was undoubtedly incapable of writing a genuine love letter, except perhaps to himself.) Amid all his female companionship, he insisted, he was desolate without her. Of course, he had not asked her to marry him.

Although Charlotte was mature enough to be on guard against this overgrown imp, she admired him enormously. This was, she felt surer each day, what people called a "great" man. She realized that she was not only falling in love with him but also beginning to think that the care and feeding of such a man might be worth a permanent entanglement. Yet nothing might have come of this attachment if he had not got himself into a predicament that seemed to demand some urgent care and feeding. Besides working himself nearly to prostration, he failed to treat an injured foot properly and was approaching basket-case status when Charlotte arrived in London from her incessant traveling. One visit to his room at his mother's was enough to convince her that he had to come away with her to the country, where she would hire nurses to take care of him. He was weak enough for her to convince him. And for him to ask her to marry him.

He explained his turnabout in his typically elfin way, in a letter to Beatrice Webb:

It was planned I must go away to the country the moment I could be moved, and that somebody must seriously take in hand the job of looking after me. Equally plain, of course, that Charlotte was the inevitable and predestined agent, appointed by Destiny. To have let her do this in any other character than that of my wife would (in the absence of your chaperonage) have involved our whole circle and its interests in a scandal. . . . I found that my objection to my own marriage had ceased with my objection to my own death. This was the main change; there were of course many other considerations which we shall probably discuss at some future time. Possibly one of them was that the relation between us had never until then completely lost its inevitable preliminary character of a love affair. . . . The thing being cleared thus of all such illusions as love interest, happiness interest, and all the rest of the vulgarities of marriage, I changed right about face on the subject and hopped down to the Registrar, who married me to her on one leg.

Another thing that changed his mind specifically about Charlotte was that he was becoming affluent. His play *The Devil's Disciple* had enjoyed a long, lucrative run in New York and promised to be the precursor of more such theatrical gold mines. Thus she would not have to support him; he could dig his own gold. Their arrangement about money, in fact, was eminently sensible. They shared basic living expenses, but she was to feel free to spend her own money as she wished, including the maintenance of a lifestyle to which she had become pleasurably accustomed. The only hitch seems to have been her unconquerable itch for traveling, which resulted in his being dragged hither and yon about the world, from Germany to Australia, on the questionable grounds that he repeatedly needed rest and rehabilitation. He generally hated traveling, since it seriously interfered with his writing, although later in life he came to enjoy it almost as much as she did.

Yet she was far more help than hindrance to his writing. She learned to type so that she could make his manuscripts more presentable and handle his growing correspondence. For their first nine years she was his unpaid secretary as well as his nurse and housekeeper. After paid secretaries took over the routine, detailed tasks, she continued as the family accountant. She was a splendid hostess, her parties giving them both opportunities to entertain celebrated artists and writers like Rodin and Mark Twain. She also became adept at warding off unwelcome and time-consuming visitors. Bernard valued her criticism of his writing most highly and accepted suggestions from her, such as those which eventually brought forth *The Doctor's Dilemma* and *Saint Joan*.

Whether they ever consummated their marriage, which was childless, has remained their secret. She feared giving birth after forty, and he, being perhaps undersexed and vociferously disdainful of the purely physical, may have sown enough oats to last a lifetime. Certainly they provided no evidence of an uncontrollable physical passion, and certainly it was a marriage of comfortable convenience. Yet it was also a union of deep, ardent, solicitous affection. Not only did she play constant nurse and helpmeet, but when she suffered flare-ups of her chronic rheumatism, he cared for her most tenderly. And they greatly enjoyed each other's company.

The other women in his life were of no great consequence to Charlotte, with a notable exception. In 1912 came his notorious affair with Mrs. Patrick Campbell, the hypnotic actress who would bring the transformation of the flower girl to life in his *Pygmalion*. The affair was the talk of the town, and this may have been what Shaw had chiefly, if subconsciously, in mind. It also gave him countless opportunities to write about his love without really doing anything about it. One of his letters, written when Mrs. Pat had refused to see him for several days, provides a sample of his feverish prose: "I want my plaything that I am to throw away. I want my Virgin Mother enthroned in heaven. I want my Italian peasant woman. I want my rapscallionly fellow vagabond. I want my dark lady. I want my angel—I want my tempter. I want my Freia with her apples. I want the lighter of my seven lamps of beauty, honor, laughter, music, love, life and immortality. I want my inspiration, my folly, my happiness, my divinity, my madness, my selfishness, my final sanity and sanctification, my transfiguration, my purification, my light across the sea, my palm across the desert, my garden of lovely flowers, my million nameless joys, my day's wage, my night's dream, my darling and my star." Yet, when he did visit her, he always managed to leave in plenty of time to get home for dinner with Charlotte.

Although the affair was almost certainly no more than a display of plumage, and although Bernard pretended to himself and others that Charlotte found it vastly amusing, it hurt her deeply enough to turn her to religion, especially of the mystic guru type. Yet she was resilient, and in September 1913, during a visit to Europe, she had it out with Bernard, who reported to Mrs. Pat: "After two perfectly frightful scenes with me, in which she produced such a case against my career and character as made Bluebeard seem an angel in comparison, she quite suddenly and miraculously—at a moment when murder and suicide seemed the only thing left to her—recovered her intellectual balance, her sanity, and her amiability completely, and became once more (after about two years) the happy consort of an easygoing man. . . . The relief is enormous: I have such infernal powers of endurance that I never realize the weight of a burden until it is lifted from my shoulders." Charlotte had gotten it out of his system as well as hers, and the marriage, although perhaps never quite the same again, at least returned from crowd to company.

Yet it was company, his company, that she enjoyed less and less as he grew busier and busier. He was out a great deal—lectures, debates, meetings of all sorts—and at home, absorption in his work limited their opportunities for conversation. Ironically, during the twenties and thirties it was she who took up with someone else—not romantically, for T. E. Lawrence was young enough to be her son, but nonetheless emotionally. It was largely due to her encouragement that *The Seven Pillars of Wisdom* was completed and published. When he was posted to military bases in India and the Middle East, they corresponded faithfully. It was a sad day for her when, in 1935, he was killed while riding the motorcycle that the Shaws had given him as a present.

By then they were in their late seventies. Charlotte grew increasingly ill with lumbago and was often painfully immobilized as they passed into their eighties. Bernard cared for her lovingly, spending more time with her, helping her to get about, singing and playing the piano for her. When she died in September 1943, at eighty-six, he wrote to Sidney Webb, who had just recently lost his Beatrice: "I also am a widower. Charlotte died this morning. . . . As she lies now she is not a crippled old woman; she is just like the portrait Sartoric made in Italy when she was in her first youth. The change is inexpressibly touching."

Among the Shaws' most interesting and satisfying friendships was a late one, with the gentleman boxer Gene Tunney and his wife, whom they met in 1928. Years later Tunney remembered it fondly. "It was wonderful to be with G.B.S.," he recalled, "but Charlotte was a good half of it."

Eleanor Roosevelt
and
Franklin
Delano Roosevelt

⌣

"**C**ousin Eleanor," an eighteen-year-old Franklin Roosevelt reportedly told his mother, "has a very good mind."

Cousin Eleanor fortunately was not there to overhear that comment. The poor girl already thought of herself as unprepossessing, ungainly, unremarkable, unattractive, and uncommonly undesirable. But she was not so for Franklin, who came to appreciate not only her head but also her heart and the rest of her as well. The pictures of Eleanor as the gadabout personal ambassador of a crippled president, as well as the publicity lately given to Franklin's enduring fondness for Lucy Mercer, have clouded over the solicitous affection, thoughtful attachment, and deep mutual devotion that characterized their love affair. For her, in their courtship days, he was a Greek god with a rollicking sense of humor. And as for him, he was elated (he wrote his mother) at the thought of "gaining anyone like Eleanor to love and be loved by."

It took a strong love indeed to survive his mother's opposition. His father had died when Franklin was a college freshman, and the forty-six-year-old Sara Delano Roosevelt turned the full weight of her emotional dependence onto her only child. He was, after all, she insisted, "a Delano, not a Roosevelt at all." She arranged to be with him as often as possible, to be near him as much as possible, and to indulge his every wish so far as possible, except any wish that he might have for independence. His announcement late in 1903, when he was twenty-one, that he had proposed to Eleanor, who was nineteen, therefore struck Sara as a declaration of independence no less serious than that of 1776.

Eleanor, after all, was only a Roosevelt. Since both her parents had died while she was still a child, she was virtually an orphan. Her father and uncles had suffered from an embarrassing, if genteel, alcoholism. Franklin could do *so* much better. Indeed, what could be better than spending his life at Hyde Park and Campobello with his loving mother? They were so young, she told them when they visited her in New York. Why, her beloved father waited until he was an established, affluent thirty-three before he married. (She did not mention that she, at twenty-six, had married James Roosevelt, then fifty-two, against her father's wishes.) Did they care for each other enough to make such a commitment so soon? To her restrained chagrin, they answered yes. Well then, she countered, would they wait a year, keeping their engagement secret and informal until January 1905? Reluctantly, they agreed. It was a shame, a relative commented later, that Eleanor, after being unhappy for so much of her young life, should wind up with a mother-in-law like *that*!

But Eleanor loved Franklin enough to love his mother, too. She went out of her way, continually, to reassure Sara that she "had not lost a son but gained a daughter," although the gain was so obviously unsolicited. Soon after their little talk, Sara whisked Franklin off on a five-week winter cruise of the Caribbean. After their return, Eleanor asked Franklin to try to keep his mother from feeling that this would be her last trip with him, to let her know that the three of them could take trips together in the future. Meanwhile, Sara was importuning the American ambassador to England, who was in the United States to consult with President Theodore Roosevelt, to take Franklin back with him to London as his secretary. But the ambassador already had a secretary, and this proved to be Sara's final ploy.

She could be gracious in defeat. She turned Hyde Park over to the newlyweds for a preliminary honeymoon while she stayed with a sister. It was, she wrote in a note to them, "a delight to write you together and to think of you happy at Hyde Park, just where my happiness first began." Nor was she necessarily being hypocritical. On their wedding night she confided to her diary, "Franklin is calm and happy. Eleanor the same." Eleanor responded in kind. After Franklin completed his current year at Columbia Law School, the young couple left for a fifteen-week honeymoon in Europe, and during the trip they both wrote her with unrelieved frequency. Eleanor's letters were sometimes too effusively affectionate for any-one else, removed from her relationship with Sara, to read with composure. But she probably felt that, however heavily troweled the effusiveness, Sara would consider it only her due. Her letters could safely err on the side of extravagance.

The trip—through England, France, Italy, and Germany—was a joyous one for the honeymooners, although for Eleanor the sexual component was an unwelcome novelty for which society, still suffering from its Victorian hangover, had left her quite unprepared. To proper young ladies of her upbringing, sex was a duty, an ordeal to be borne for the preservation of the race. This was not a time when "loving" and "making love" were epidemically synonymous. Eleanor's submission to Franklin may not have transported her into erotic ecstasies, but that lack of pleasure need not have kept it from being a genuine act of love. In one sense, perhaps, quite the contrary. Yet her distaste for its physical aspects doubtless had much to do with the most important crisis in their married life.

After their return from their honeymoon trip, they rented a house in New York not far from Sara's and settled into a routine; Franklin continued working toward his law degree while Eleanor took courses from Sara in such subjects as home management and matronly deportment. After their first child, Anna, was born in May 1906, other courses were added to the curriculum, even though Sara had wanted a boy. Franklin countered this achievement of Eleanor's the following May by gaining admission to the bar. The routine included summers at Campobello Island, where Eleanor, overcoming her fear of water, learned to share her husband's love for sailing. In other respects, however, her inhibitions interfered with their companionship. She could not learn to play, or enjoy, tennis or golf well enough to join him, nor could she summon up much enthusiasm for horseback riding. Their joint activities outdoors were largely restricted to picnics and walks. The situation was not helped by her frequent pregnancies, which interfered also with their social engagements.

Nor was it helped by Franklin's embarking on a political career, first as a state senator in Albany and then as Assistant Secretary of the Navy in the Wilson administration. Although Eleanor handled her role as a politician's wife with consummate competence and even came to enjoy it, it tended to relegate her to helpmeet status. And finally there was Franklin's considerable attractiveness and attraction to women; though hardly a philanderer, he was not oblivious to feminine charms other than Eleanor's. He was by no means oblivious to those of Lucy Mercer, the well-bred but impoverished young lady who served as Eleanor's social secretary from 1913 to 1918. During those five years, Eleanor's suspicions and jealousy grew bit by uncertain bit, though never enough to cause her more than a vague uneasiness. She recognized that Lucy was more like the fun-loving Franklin than she, and she could only hope that the fun they loved together stopped short of that mysterious fun that she had never understood—except to know in the abstract that some other women could enjoy it quite avidly. And then one day in September 1918, when Franklin had come home ill from an official trip to Europe and she was handling his mail, she chanced upon some letters from Lucy revealing that the fun had not stopped short. She was devastated.

She offered Franklin a divorce. She would not demand one, chiefly for the children's sake, unless he wished to preserve the triangle. No more Lucy. Under pressure from an angry Sara and an anxious Louis Howe, his new political Svengali—and even in a sense from Lucy, who as a Catholic was not eager to marry a divorced father of five children—Franklin buckled and agreed. How much his love for Eleanor affected his decision was something she could never really know.

But his love was strong enough to change his behavior toward her. He seemed genuinely contrite, trying to please her and to be more thoughtful of her, although failings like his chronic unpunctuality could still nettle her puritan soul. She reciprocated, trying to be gayer for him, more gregarious. She worried about him, sometimes unnecessarily, as when he was in Washington during the racial violence of 1919. And although she was determined to be more independent of him, she seemed to care for him, in both senses of that phrase, as much as ever. Perhaps she could not otherwise have been so ready for the next great crisis in their lives.

This was, of course, the polio attack. In 1921, after a strenuous if unsuccessful campaign as the vice presidential candidate on the Democratic ticket, Franklin was eager for a summer vacation at Campobello. Once there, instead of going horizontal for long rest periods, he flung himself into ceaseless activities—tennis, baseball, swimming, sailing—until he was tired enough to drop. And drop he did, into bed after looking through the mail in his wet bathing suit and catching a proper chill. The next morning, August 11, he had a high fever and had difficulty moving his left leg; by afternoon he could not move his right leg. And by Friday he was paralyzed from the chest down, including his arms and hands. Doctors were called, and the diagnosis was that a blood clot probably was interfering with the lower spinal cord and causing a temporary paralysis.

A trained nurse was requested from New York City, but none was immediately available. For the next two weeks Eleanor nursed Franklin night and day, sleeping whenever she could on a cot in his room, caring for him so tenderly and faithfully that one of the doctors later, in a letter to Franklin, called her "one of my heroines." He was impressed also with Franklin's dauntless courage, although Eleanor knew that one of her hardest tasks was to lighten the frequent dark periods of discouragement. Not only was he in pain, almost continuous and often excruciating, but he had no assurance that he would get any better, especially after his condition was diagnosed as poliomyelitis—a diagnosis which, to add to his troubles, rather embarrassed him, because polio was normally a child's disease. To his doctors and visitors and family he showed a brave and cheerful face. It was only Eleanor who saw him in the depths of his despair.

She understood his occasional visits to those depths, but she could not let him live there. Against Sara's urgent opposition but with the stalwart help of the incredibly loyal Louis Howe, she maintained Franklin's morale by refusing to treat him as a helpless invalid. After the nurse had arrived to take care of his medical and therapeutic needs, she and Howe (who had moved to Campobello for the duration) kept their patient distracted with things to be done and plans to be made. She served as his secretary, managed the large and complicated household around him, encouraged visitors to come but also to leave whenever he began to show the strain, arranged his trips to New York and Boston for treatment, and generally sacrificed herself completely to his recovery, his interests, his morale, his future.

She was tough and resilient, and so was he. Slowly, painfully, his body began its partial recovery. The paralysis left his hands and arms and torso, and before long he could even move his legs, although they never again would be able to bear his weight unaided. His exercises gave his arms and upper body great strength, so that when necessary he could haul himself along a floor with astonishing agility. By April 1922, with leg braces and crutches, he could even walk a little. And that is how he managed, in the summer of 1924, to get up before the Democratic National Convention and nominate Al Smith for President of the United States. And how he managed, four years later, not only to do it again, more successfully, but also to become governor of New York. But through it all, his real support came not so much from braces and crutches as from Eleanor.

Some twenty years later, after Franklin's death, and after learning that Lucy, now Mrs. Rutherford, had been one of the people with the president at Warm Springs when he died, she told friends that she had not been in love with him since her discovery of his affair with Lucy but that she had cared for him as she did because of his ideals and his talent for leadership.

Maybe so. But subsequently she said something else. She was very much in love with Franklin during their courtship, she wrote in her autobiography, but only years later did she understand "what loving really meant."

Clementine Hozier
and
Winston Churchill

~⦿~

During his long career Winston Churchill said many stirring things of worldwide importance. He also had something to say about personal relationships, especially in marriage: Never go to bed mad. Of course, he put it in a more dignified, biblically cadenced way, "Let not the sun go down on your wrath." (Eph. 4:26).

They were very different people. He was gregarious; Clementine was reserved. He was extravagant; she cautious. He was demanding, up to a point, and she acquiescent, up to a point. Beyond those points, both could be irascible. In the 1930s the financial strain of maintaining their Chartwell country home was considerable, especially maintaining it in the comfortably elegant style to which the expansive Winston was eager to become accustomed. His cheery attitude toward expensive "improvements" and overdue bills gnawed at her Scotch insecurity, provoking her on one occasion to throw a plate of spinach at him, forcefully if inaccurately. After that incident

136

they made up quickly, but Clementine resolved to present her arguments in writing as often as possible thereafter. (She was essentially right about Chartwell; in the late thirties Winston, whose rather unreliable income depended mostly on his writing, came close to selling it.)

As late as 1954, during his second stint as prime minister, when he was nearly eighty and she nearly seventy, the spats continued, ever followed by evening reconciliations. Sometimes, it seems, Winston may not have reached the reconciliation stage before Clementine went to bed. In her biography of Clementine, their daughter quotes a note found in their effects, evidently written by Winston after a combative evening and left out for Clementine to find in the morning. "Fondest Love," it began, "I am so sorry I was awkward at dinner." The sun must have gone down, but the note was not received too late.

As in this instance, their love was nourished by the written word throughout their years together. Or, rather, their years apart, for they were often forced apart by the strenuous demands of his remarkable career, to their persistent and mutual dismay. During these times of separation they sustained themselves with streams of letters, flowing both ways, letters filled with words of love and longing. Sometimes even a letter to a third party would give a hint of their affection, as when Winston wrote his mother in September 1908 from their European honeymoon, with a characteristic flourish, "We have only loitered and loved, a good and serious occupation for which the histories furnish respectable precedents."

Two years later Clementine suffered a brief period of jealousy over Violet Asquith, the prime minister's daughter, a young woman of scintillating intelligence and other charms whom Winston occasionally saw at No. 10 Downing Street. The young wife must have revealed her feeling, inadvertently or otherwise, to Winston, for a note survives in which he reassured her in the gentlest terms. He found her suspicions depressing and vexing, he wrote, although he recognized "that they originate in the fond love you have for me. . . . You ought to trust me for I do not love and will never love any woman in the world but you and my chief desire is to link myself with you week by week by bonds which shall ever become more intimate and profound." In their correspondence she was his "Kat" and he her "Pug" (and sometimes, later, her "Pig"), and their letters were often signed with appropriate sketches. In one letter she promised him to be agreeable "especially if you stroke my silky tail," without getting into specifics.

On their eleventh wedding anniversary, in September 1919, with World War I in its closing weeks, he wrote her from France about his "great good fortune on that day" and paid tribute to their ever-growing "bonds of deep affection. I can never express my gratitude to you for all you have done for me and all you have been to me." In her reply she wrote, "I love to feel that I am a comfort in your rather tumultuous life. My Darling, you have been the great event in mine. You took me from the straitened little by-path I was treading and took me with you into the life and colour and jostle of the high-way." But in that life and color and jostle her "sweet love and comrade-ship," as he put it, was the harbor for which he always yearned and to which he always returned. "I miss you very much," he wrote her during the famous conference at Yalta in 1945. "I am lonely amid this throng."

The jostle on the Churchills' highway was exhausting. Clementine, though energetic, was not inexhaustible—she once remarked to one of their children that just keeping up with Winston drained all her energy—yet her wholehearted dedication to her whirlwind spouse and to his career brought her a life of often feverish and usually burdensome activity. (Even Franklin Roosevelt once remarked to her that her husband was a "great fellow, if you can keep up with him.") Winston fought fifteen electoral campaigns in his political career, and she fought by his side in every one of them, even in those after World War II, when she felt strongly that they ought to be enjoying his retirement. She gave countless stump speeches and was often shouted down, even spat upon. In 1912 she accompanied him on a trip to Ireland on the grounds that her being there with him might make it less violently dangerous for him (and the violence was indeed less than expected). Her role as wife of the prime minister was onerous, especially for someone not given naturally to unceasing social activity; among the surviving records is the information that during the first nine months of 1944 the Churchills gave seventy-five luncheon and nineteen dinner parties, averaging more than ten a month, in addition to those that they attended as guests. It is small wonder that she objected strenuously to their returning to No. 10 Downing Street in 1951, after he had been out of office for six years, although she supported him fully once he decided to accept the, for him, irresistible challenge. With a husband like Winston, loving one's man was not always sharply distinguishable from loving one's country.

When he needed defending, she was there to defend. On one occasion, when the rough-and-tumble of British politics became too literal for comfort, she saved his life. As they emerged from a train at Bristol Station one day in November 1909, a young and rather athletic suffragette bore down on Winston and tried to alter his countenance with a riding whip. To thwart her project, he grabbed her wrists and held them tight, but she responded by pushing him through the crowd toward the edge of the platform. By now the train was moving out, and Clementine, some yards away, suddenly recognized that her husband was in imminent danger of being jostled into the space between the moving train and the platform. The considerable luggage between them proved but a minor obstacle course: She was next to him in a moment, fiercely grabbing at his coat and pulling him away from the danger. It was true that she had never been able to persuade him to share her feminist ideas, but she considered the young woman's debating technique well beyond the pale. And so, needless to add, did the bobbies on the scene, who carted the bellicose maiden off to a less permissive environment.

In 1915, after the disaster at Gallipoli for which Winston was unfairly blamed and which cost him his job as First Lord of the Admiralty, Clementine (as she said later to one of his biographers) "thought he would die of grief." She was his support and comfort during these dark days of shabby treatment by the government, the press, and even much of the public. At the time, she wrote a very sharp, if futile, letter of protest to the prime minister, and some months later, in March 1916, she let herself go in an indignant outburst. It was at a luncheon attended by Lord Fisher, who had undercut Winston at the Admiralty and then tried to take over his job and who was now badgering Lieutenant Colonel Churchill, on leave from the front, to attack the Admiralty's conduct of the war at sea. "Keep your hands off my husband," Clementine cried out. "You have all but ruined him once. Leave him alone now!" (She was no great respecter of rank. She once described a British officer as "one of the few unblighted generals in the general mildew.")

Again, during World War II, she lost her temper while keeping her poise. It was July 1940, shortly after Winston had become prime

minister. She had watched him agonize over a decision made necessary by the fall of France, resulting in the destruction of a goodly
portion of the French fleet by the Royal Navy, to keep the French
ships out of German hands. At a luncheon at Downing Street she
remarked to General de Gaulle that she hoped the remaining French
warships would join in battling the common enemy. He replied
rather harshly that the French naval forces would like best to turn
their guns "on you," the British. This provoked a response, in her
fluent French, to the effect that it ill behooved an ally, and a guest, to
make such an ungracious remark. Winston, on the other side of the
table, gathered that things were not going well and, in an effort at
conciliatory humor, suggested that perhaps sometimes his wife's
French was too fluent. But Clementine interrupted him, protesting
that there were some things that only a woman could say to a man,
"and I am saying them to you, General de Gaulle!" The formidable
de Gaulle, quite unused to this kind of confrontation, offered his
apology in some confusion, and the next day reinforced it with an
enormous basket of flowers.

And again, in 1963. In 1959 the aging couple (he was eighty-five,
she seventy-four) had conducted their fifteenth and last electoral
campaign. Now, in 1963, Winston was about to retire from the
House of Commons after serving in it for fifty years, most memora-
bly. The House drafted a resolution of thanks for this service and
submitted it to Clementine for her comments, which proved to be
quite acid. In her reply she compared the routinely worded statement
with the generous expression of thanks offered to the Duke of
Wellington and suggested that the latter was in sharp contrast to this
"mangy resolution." When Winston retired formally in July 1964, the
recast resolution was a glowing tribute to his inspiring leadership.

He died in January 1965. About two years earlier Clementine had
received perhaps the definitive tribute to their marriage from her
suspected rival of years before, Violet Asquith, now Violet Bonham-
Carter:

My Darling Clemmie,
    I must write you a line (*not* to be answered) to say how moved
I am, whenever I see you, by your amazing courage under this
long strain [Winston's long illness and decline], and by your
gaiety and tenderness to beloved W. It is as though you alone

could reach him with comfort and amusement. Your "private line" with him has remained intact. . . . I am filled with admiration and emotion when I see you together.

In a way Winston may have had the last word. After his death his paintings—his "little daubs," as he described them—brought some very respectable prices, helping his darling Clementine to live out her days in comfortable dignity.

Alice B. Toklas
and
Gertrude Stein

~~~

After reading Gertrude Stein's *Things as They Are*, the critic Edmund Wilson conjectured that the obscurity of her writing may have been due to "a need imposed by the problem of writing about relationships between women of a kind that the standards of that era would not have allowed her to describe more explicitly." As for Gertrude, she had something to say in *The Making of Americans* about the variety of ways of expressing love. "Some say alright all but one way of loving, another says alright all but another way of loving," she wrote. "I like loving. I like mostly all the ways any one can have of loving feeling in them. Slowly it has come to be in me that any way of being a loving one is interesting and not unpleasant to me."

In the fall of 1907, when Alice B. Toklas arrived in Paris from her native San Francisco, Gertrude had been living there with her brother Leo, at 27 Rue de Fleurus, for about four years. She already knew a good deal about Alice, for a mutual friend had been showing her the

San Franciscan's letters. She knew, for instance, that they were about the same age (she was thirty-three, Alice thirty), enjoyed modest but reliable independent incomes, and shared many cultural tastes. When Alice visited her on her second day in Paris, Gertrude saw a pneumatic young woman with hair of glistening ebony, deep pools for eyes, sensual lips, and a pleasing figure colorfully attired—altogether a much more attractive picture than the spinsterish photos taken of her years later. Alice saw a stolidly handsome woman with a head and face reminiscent of Greek statuary ("a golden brown presence," she wrote later, "burned by the Tuscan sun and with a golden glint in her warm brown hair"), and she heard a voice "unlike anyone else's voice—deep, full, velvety like a great contralto's, like two voices"— especially when Gertrude laughed, as she did a great deal.

Alice was late for her appointment, and Gertrude made a bit of a fuss over such disregard for court regulations: "She came late I state that she came late and I said what was it that I said I said I am not accustomed to wait." She quickly got over her pet, however, and the two women went out for the first of their countless long walks. Their affectionate friendship and constant companionship would last for almost forty years.

Alice's timing was quite remarkable. She was looking for someone to take care of, being that kind of person, and Gertrude needed someone to take care of her, being that kind of person. Brother Leo had been filling the caretaker role to a great extent, but he and Gertrude were growing apart. She was becoming ever more restive under the burden of his aesthetic dogmas, and he was as appalled by her nonrepresentational writing as he was by her friend Picasso's nonrepresentational painting. The two of them, in his opinion, were "using their intellects, which they ain't got, to do what would need the finest critical tact, which they ain't got neither, and they are in my belief turning out the most Godalmighty rubbish that is to be found." Very gradually, *very* gradually, Alice began to take his place. She learned to type in order to make Gertrude's manuscripts legible, if not intelligible, working on them with their author through long hours, often coming home so late at night as to worry Harriet Levy, the friend with whom she had come to Paris and with whom she was staying in a flat some distance away. Any tension that her preoccupation may have caused evaporated in 1909 when Harriet returned to the States and Alice accepted Gertrude's invitation to move in with her and Leo. Four years later this increasingly uneasy symbiosis came to an end: Leo moved out, almost never to be seen again, at least by Gertrude.

By then Alice had settled in as Gertrude's housekeeper, cook (exotic), auditor (prosaic), protector, laundress, grocery shopper, ticket buyer, travel agent, typist, diffident but valued literary consultant, and tireless factotum, among other things. Even barber—it was she who gave Gertrude, somewhat inadvertently, the celebrated crew-cut appearance. Her easygoing nature, filigreed with a wry sense of humor but resting on a bedrock of adamant, enabled her to put up with Gertrude's more mercurial character, with her willful taste for disorder, and with her often intense but dependably brief tantrums ("I am often angry. Sometimes I cry. Not from anger. I only cry from heat and other things. I love to be right. It is so necessary"). The difficulties of daily life during World War I aggravated minor frictions ("Don't turn the leaves / Because they make a noise"), but their differences barely scratched the surface of their abiding, taken-for-granted unity of mind and heart. Gertrude was boss ("I am very fond of yes sir"), and Alice felt that this was only to be expected ("Y is for you and us is for me and we are as happy as happy can be").

In this sense the relationship was emotionally heterosexual— "Pussy how pretty you are," "Alice B. is the wife for me," "She is my sweetheart," and so on. Alice was the retiring female, aggressive only in protecting Gertrude from unsolicited attention, a second but ever indispensable fiddle. For the famous salon gatherings and other social affairs—for Ernest Hemingway, Zelda and Scott Fitzgerald, the Paul Robesons, Pablo Picasso, Thornton Wilder, Eric Sevareid, countless doughboys and GIs during two world wars—Gertrude played host and Alice played hostess. At bullfights in Spain "Gertrude would say, Do not look, when a horse was being gored." During the first of the world wars, in distributing supplies to hospitals, Gertrude drove her converted Ford truck and Alice prepared the supplies. (In the second war, it behooved two American Jewesses to keep a low profile, and they did.)

How much of Alice's literary talent went into the whimsically titled *The Autobiography of Alice B. Toklas*, Gertrude's reasonably straightforward and uniquely profitable book, is anyone's guess. Most guesses answer "a lot." The style is much like that of Alice's own *What Is Remembered*, published thirty years later. Virgil Thomson felt that the *Autobiography* was "Alice Toklas' book," at least "in every way except actual authorship." A close friend of the odd couple wrote, "One way to rile Miss Toklas, and one out of many, is to tell her that you suspect her touch in the Stein genius, though it is of course quite a natural suspicion for which Miss Toklas should blame, not her admirers, but Miss Stein herself, author of the Toklas *Autobiography*; and for that matter, the better you knew them, the more you wondered whose light was being hidden under whose bushel." But neither woman was a "bushel" in that sense. They were both lights, and one doubtless was used to brighten the other.

Two short passages may illustrate the two books' similarities, at least in the flavor of the wit. In *What Is Remembered*, Alice wrote of some friends who met her after one of Gertrude's lectures. "One of them said to me, You know we were tremendously fond of your father, your mother was an angel, and you are very dear to us. I noted the descending order." In the *Autobiography* the author gives an account of a luncheon party. "Later I was near Picasso, he was standing meditatively. Do you think, he said, that I really do look like your president Lincoln? I had thought a good many things that evening but I had not thought that." Perhaps the last two paragraphs of the *Autobiography* reveal a good deal about the relationship between the two women, not only in relation to the book, but in general:

> I am a pretty good housekeeper and a pretty good gardener and a pretty good needlewoman and a pretty good secretary and a pretty good editor and a pretty good vet for dogs and I have to do them all at once and I found it difficult to add being a pretty good author.
>
> About six weeks ago Gertrude Stein said, it does not look to me as if you are ever going to write that autobiography. You know what I am going to do. I am going to write it for you. I am going to write it as simply as Defoe did the autobiography of Robinson Crusoe. And she has and this is it.

There was very much of Neil Simon's odd couple in this pair, and something of the sisters in *Arsenic and Old Lace*, without the homicidal avocation. Spinsters in tandem were a common phenomenon in the first half of the twentieth century, on both sides of the Atlantic, and doubtless the relationships involved ran through a spectrum of spectra. The extraordinary pair at the Rue de Fleurus and later the Rue Christine screened the details of their relationship, Gertrude more or less effectively behind her third-person device and her natural talent for obfuscation, Alice quite effectively behind her natural talent for reticence. Yet even Alice could let drop a telling phrase now and then about the affection that united them. When she was evicted from the apartment at the Rue Christine after Gertrude's death (the landlord wanted it for some friend or relative), she wound up in a more modern, brighter apartment that simply depressed her: "Gertrude is not *here*."

Gertrude was taken to a Paris hospital late in July 1946. Alice's account of her last moments with her lifelong friend is typically terse. Gertrude, before the surgery from which she would not emerge, groggily asked Alice, sitting beside her, "What is the answer?" Alice, thinking her barely awake, did not reply. Gertrude then asked, "What is the question?" Again Alice was silent, this time trying to formulate some response. "If there is no question," Gertrude wearily concluded, "then there is no answer." Those were her last words. Then "later in the afternoon they took her away on a wheeled stretcher to the operating room and I never saw her again."

She expected to see her again, however. She was sure that there must be a heaven, where she knew they would be reunited.

Frieda von Richthofen
and
D. H. Lawrence

~⌐

In the spring of 1912 Frieda von Richthofen was a thirty-two-year-old housewife and mother of three children, and she was bored. Her husband, Ernest Weekley, a professor of languages at the university in Nottingham, was a good provider, a vigorously competent scholar, and a conventionally solicitous husband. As a lover, however, she found him quite inadequate, especially after a visit to her native Germany during which she bedfellowed with a passionately adequate practitioner of free love. As a result, after her return home to staid old Nottingham she pursued a program of extramarital adventures discreetly enough to avoid scandal but energetically enough to provide some distraction. Thus she was sufficiently acquainted with such distractions to be reasonably prepared for the one that would change her life.

It arrived that spring in the person of David Herbert Lawrence, a twenty-six-year-old former student of Professor Weekley's who

147

wanted advice on finding a job as a lecturer in a German university. At the professor's invitation, he showed up for lunch late one morning, but his mentor had not yet arrived home. So he and Frieda talked for half an hour while her children played outside. She was attracted by his "long thin figure, quick straight legs, light, sure movements," as she later recalled her first impressions, and he was struck by her blond, statuesque Teutonic comeliness. For him it was, he said afterward in an unusual reliance on cliché, love at first sight. Evidently they became at least conversational soul mates at first breath, for Ernest arrived, had lunch with them, and departed without discussing Germany and indeed without seriously interrupting the tête-à-tête, which continued until dusk callously ended it. Lawrence was entranced. Frieda had been an attentive listener, sympathetically hearing him out as he described his current problems, for instance, with his revision of *Sons and Lovers*. Yet he had had listeners before, notably a young model for the girl Miriam in that novel. He found Frieda stronger, more self-assertive, more challenging than the women he had loved and left; in addition, there was his oedipal fixation on his late mother, readily transferable to this attractive matron. When he got home from his visit, he sent her a note: "You are the most wonderful woman in all England."

On his next visit Professor Weekley was away, and Frieda suggested that he spend the night with her. It was an invitation which she naively expected him to welcome but which he angrily refused. He would not, he protested, take such advantage of the professor's hospitality. Further, she discovered, it was not that he did not want to play, but rather that he wanted to play for keeps. He issued an ultimatum: Tell Ernest we are hopelessly in love and intend to go away together, or you will never see me again. Frieda's terror at the thought of losing this poetic, articulate young genius proved greater than her fear of leaving her husband and children. She agreed and even recommended a plan: She had to be in Metz, Germany, by May 4 for the golden anniversary of her father's enlistment in the army, and they could go together. After her painful meeting with her astonished husband, and after leaving her two young daughters with her puzzled in-laws, presumably for some sort of safekeeping, she joined her new lover for a week's honeymoon in Metz.

The rapture evaporated quickly. The mercurial Lawrence, an irredeemable snob of humble origins, had been mightily impressed by the fact that Frieda's father was Baron von Richthofen, and may have been severely disappointed to discover that she belonged to a minor twig on that ubiquitous family tree. More important, she left him at the hotel while she visited the family, keeping him at a long arm's length except for a brief visit with her two freethinking and sympathetic sisters. Unable to speak German, he felt quite abandoned. She did find time to take him on a tour of the local fort, where they were heard speaking English and he was arrested on a charge of being a British spy. To invoke the baron's intercession, she had to go home and tell all during an acutely uncomfortable confrontation, but the baron did manage to straighten things out with the overzealous authorities. Once released, and after an introduction to the von Richthofens at a rather frosty tea party, Lawrence left Metz hurriedly for nearby Trier, where Frieda joined him soon afterward. The less than happy couple quarreled, however, and Lawrence left for the Rhineland to visit some distant relatives. For a while the two of them exchanged some rather snappish letters, but by the end of May they were together again in a small town just south of Munich, where they finally had the happy honeymoon that they had planned for Metz. The doubts they had entertained about their being meant for each other now seemed utterly dispelled.

The doubts were more his than hers, as had been the case in his earlier love matches. She remained eager for her divorce and their marriage, while he coolly advised patience. Even after the honeymoon, after they moved to Italy and more or less settled down, relations were strained by her wistful hankering for a visit to or from her children, to which Lawrence was indifferent and Ernest Weekley was implacably opposed. They took to quarreling, establishing a habit that would last their lifetime together—and to making up, another enduring habit that could close wounds and even heal them, at least till the next round.

When they returned to London in the summer of 1913, *Sons and Lovers* (which Frieda rather disliked) had just been published and generally well received by critics, although it would not sell well for a while. Frieda managed sneak visits with her thirteen-year-old son and two younger daughters, who were living with their father's family, but the brief and not very affectionate meetings simply whetted her appetite for more. More being impossible, the couple took off for Germany and then Italy with their baggage of invigorating quarrels and reconciliations. In Italy, in May 1914, they received the surprising news that Frieda had finally been divorced, and that summer they were married in England, shortly before the outbreak of World War I.

The war brought them some discomfort amid the sufferings of millions, partly because of prejudice against the very Germanic Frieda and partly because the military gave Lawrence what he considered a bad time during physical examinations after conscription was introduced (his tubercular condition exempted him from service), but mostly because of the suppression of Lawrence's novel *The Rainbow* on grounds of indecency. They became determined to leave England for Florida, where they would establish "Rananim," an ideal community of like-minded refugees from a world of nations bent on common destruction. But they found this far easier determined than done in wartime, and so they resigned themselves to a rather nomadic way of life, moving from friends' house to friends' house, brawling and cherishing, always unconventional, disaffected, impoverished, fascinating nuisances.

In October 1919 they made their escape from England, never to live there again. To Lawrence's simmering chagrin, they were separated for a month while Frieda visited her widowed mother and other relatives in war-spent Germany and he went on to Florence. There, after her family visit, he met her train at four in the morning and immediately hired a carriage to take her on a tour of such sights as were on display at that benighted hour. Again they embarked on a period of restless touring—Florence, the Abruzzi Mountains, Capri, Sicily, Sardinia, then back to Germany and Austria. Meanwhile his finances began improving, for his books had begun selling in America and to some extent in Britain—*Sons and Lovers*, *The Rainbow*, *Women in Love*, and such new ones as *Sea and Sardinia* and *The Lost Girl*, since he never stopped writing.

One autumn day in 1921 a letter came from a Mabel Dodge Sterne, a resident of Taos, New Mexico, who had recently read *Sea and Sardinia* and admired it so extravagantly that she wanted Lawrence and Frieda to come to Taos and live in an adobe house which she would provide and furnish for them. (She was a millionaire refugee from Buffalo, New York.) Thoroughly intrigued, Lawrence jumped at this chance to live among Native Americans in an isolated village seven thousand feet up on the side of a mountain, but soon he began harboring doubts about putting their lives in the hands of a woman he did not know in a distant land he did not know. He decided, instead, first to accept some friends' invitation to join them in Ceylon for mystic Buddhism, thus making the remarkable choice of going from Europe to New Mexico by way of the Far East.

He was utterly taken by Ceylon (Frieda less so, but her reactions were almost always of secondary importance). Immediately he decided, "I shall never leave it," and six weeks later he was writing to a friend about the East's "boneless suavity, and the thick, choky feel of tropical forest, and the metallic sense of palms and the horrid noises of the birds and creatures, who hammer and clang and rattle and cackle and explode all the livelong day, and run little machines all the livelong night; and the scents that make me feel sick, the perpetual nauseous overtone of cocoanut and cocoanut fibre and oil. . . . I am going away. Moving on." Furthermore, he explained in another letter, "I detest Buddha."

They left for Australia to visit a friend whom they had met on the voyage to Ceylon while she happened to be reading *Sons and Lovers*. After spending a month with her in Perth, on Australia's west coast, they crossed the continent to Sydney, where they rented a cottage near a primitive mining village some thirty-five miles south of town. Frieda loved the house, which she described as being "right on the sea . . . and a stretch of grass going right down to the Pacific, melting away into a pale-blue and lucid, delicately tinted sky." She also loved the solitude (for no one knew who they were, or cared). "I was happy: only Lawrence and I in this world." She wanted to stay there for the rest of their lives, but Mabel had continued writing them and Lawrence had decided on Taos. And since Frieda "had always regarded Lawrence's genius as given to me," presumably in trust, she decided on Taos too. They arrived in San Francisco in late August 1922.

At the hotel they found a note of welcome from Mabel together with train tickets to Taos. They were, the note insisted, to be her guests while in the States. On September 10 they were welcomed to New Mexico by Mabel and her Pueblo Indian lover, Tony Lujan, who had recently replaced her third husband, Maurice Sterne. Mabel immediately felt that Lawrence needed another sort of woman than Frieda, and "the womb in me roused to reach out and take him," although she managed to restrain it at the railroad station. When she did get a chance to release it, she discovered, to her surprise and doubtless to Frieda's, that his wife's hold on him was too strong for her, that he was not for the taking. This situation created so much tension that the Lawrences retreated to a cabin of Mabel's perched in the mountains north of Taos. There they spent a bracing winter, with little more than their intense love–hate relationship to keep them warm.

In March 1923 they took off for Mexico, where they maintained that relationship even where it was not needed to keep them warm. An American who knew them there commented on their passionately "bad manners" in a letter to a friend. "Never before or since have I heard a human being, in educated society, repeatedly release such flow of obscene vile abuse on his wife (or on anyone) in the presence of comparative strangers as Lawrence did on Frieda; nor, I must admit, have I heard such apparently uninhibited response. . . . Lawrence was far more eloquent, more varied in his vituperation, but Frieda hardly less emphatic." Yet they seem never to have wanted for friends, or at least acquaintances. The surprising thing is that Lawrence had time to write *The Plumed Serpent* during his brief stays in Mexico, just as he was able to write *Kangaroo* during his brief visit to Australia. He apparently socialized and fought with Frieda much less efficiently than he wrote.

In August they separated. Frieda could not bear another day without seeing her children, and Lawrence could not bear the thought of returning to England. They arranged very tentatively that he would go to California, where she would join him sometime in October. But she found herself very comfortable in England, despite her children's adult independence and despite her sense of sacred trust concerning Lawrence. The nation at peace proved far more hospitable than it had been at war, and she began urging him to join her. October came and went without her appearance in California. He returned to Mexico for a while, but finally his longing for Frieda's company overcame his distaste for England, and in December he sailed for London. She met him at the boat train. And again his sojourn lasted about three months.

Although his work was selling better and receiving better reactions from critics and other literary scrutinizers, England did not give him the degree of obeisance that he felt he deserved. Again he returned to his recurrent obsession with the chimerical Rananim community, this time proposing to a group of friends that they establish it in New Mexico, with him of course as head guru. When he and Frieda sailed for America in March 1924, they did so with one recruit, Dorothy Brett, an aristocratic, deaf painter equipped with a formidable ear trumpet named Toby. In America they headed for Taos, where Lawrence could bask amid the competitive attention of three variously solicitous women. Five weeks later he grew restless again, and Mabel on impulse gave the couple the ranch property north of Taos, where the adoring Brett had plenty of opportunities to side with her idol during the obligatory fracases, as well as to deal with Frieda's intermittent jealousy. But both women had plenty of something to share—anxiety—when Lawrence, for the first time in his life, spat blood.

Although a few days' rest seemed to restore him to his normal ill health, the doctor's prognosis made it imperative to go south for the winter. In October the motley threesome fled to Oaxaca, Mexico, where they rented some rooms from an Englishman after Frieda had arranged for Brett to live at a hotel some distance away. The distance proved inadequate, however, and in January, the coldest month of the year, a crestfallen Brett went back to New Mexico—only to be rejoined there in late March by Frieda and Lawrence after the latter became desperately ill with what was finally diagnosed, by a doctor in Mexico City, as tuberculosis.

They stayed there through the summer while he regained some strength. In September they were on the move again. Brett reluctantly went off to Capri, alone. Frieda and Lawrence, after a winter in England, traveled to Italy, where they had a brawl vicious enough for him to leave her and join Brett in Capri, to Brett's immeasurable joy. Naturally, they soon moved, and Lawrence tried vainly on two successive nights to have sex with this woman whose eagerness was matched only by her inexperience. After the second failure he gave up in disgust, explaining that her "boobs were all wrong" and turning her joy to ashes. She left for the States, where she had taken out citizenship papers, and he returned to Frieda.

Brett suspected that the failures may not have been entirely her fault. She wrote later that she thought that he "was struggling to be successfully male." Doubtless she felt somewhat vindicated when she learned, presumably indirectly from Frieda's widely broadcast complaints, that the increasingly tubercular lover was rendered completely impotent later in 1926. He had only three years more to live. Frieda stayed with him as he continued to move restively about Europe. He resumed his painting, such as it was, and of course continued to write—some poetry, but mostly *Lady Chatterley's Lover*. His health worsened steadily. One evening in March 1930, at Vence in southeast France, with Frieda and the Aldous Huxleys at his bedside, he died. Frieda soon thereafter returned to an Italian army officer with whom she had earlier sought refuge from Lawrence's impotence. He left his wife and family to live happily ever after with her in New Mexico. They were married there twenty years later, when he was fifty-eight and she was seventy-one. She died in 1956, leaving half of her estate—respectably swollen now by receipts from the sale of books and movie rights—to her children and the other half to her Italian, who promptly rejoined his former wife.

The Lawrences' was a roller-coaster affair both in its bright peaks and gloomy canyons and in the fast pace and excitement that it provided for them in their eighteen years together. To some they were an almost repellent couple, self-centered and demanding, while to others they were a colorful, welcome distraction from drab routine. Frieda won men's admiration, often their respectful admiration; one male friend described her as a "solid, hearty, wise, and delightful woman" whose "love for Lawrence, probably her worst fault, is genuine and forgivable." Lawrence could enthrall some women (he preferred them as thralls), though by no means all. Much of his appeal surely had its source in his mother's-boy appearance and behavior as well as his frequent flights of romantic eloquence. Emily Hahn, in preparing her biography of Lawrence, asked Dorothy Brett how she could allow the man to interfere with her painting, as he often did in his aggressive, high-handed way.

"She laughed a little sheepishly. 'He was such a dear,' she said."

Bess Wallace
and
Harry Truman

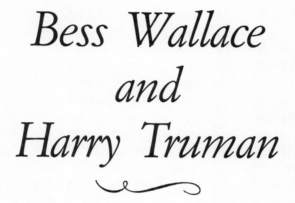

Often President Harry S. Truman, after hearing a good story, would follow his laughter with "Wait till I tell the missus!" A fairly ordinary reaction, but one that pretty well sums up the love of sharing, and the sharing of love, that characterized the lifelong romance of Bess Wallace and Harry Truman.

One can hardly make a case for love at first sight, since they first met, in 1890, when she was five and he was six. Yet despite their differences—in social status, with Bess on the brighter side of the tracks between them; in athletic ability, with tomboy Bess a versatile sportswoman and myopic Harry an insatiable bookworm; and in education, with Bess enrolled in a finishing school and Harry forced by bitter economics to forsake college for work on his grandfather's farm—despite such differences, they came together in the kind of gentle romance typical of turn-of-the-century small-town America. (Independence, Missouri, was small-town without being a very small town.) As they grew up, Harry became increasingly attentive, and Bess welcomed his attentions. Her mother, though recognizing that her daughter's book-reading, piano-playing suitor was no ordinary farm boy, was nonetheless disdainful—a feature of her character that some people said had driven her husband to suicide when Bess was only sixteen. But Harry was not one, never would be one, to be put off by disdain. Every Saturday he would visit Bess armed with a bouquet, and they usually would take long walks in the nearby woods or go fishing—Bess did the fishing while Harry read to her. After spending the night with relatives, Baptist Harry would escort Bess to Sunday services at the Trinity Episcopal church.

They had fun together at parties, although one thing that he never learned to share was her love of, and skill in, dancing. He made up for this lack, however, with his versatile, entertaining piano playing. Their times together were pleasant times, but the prospects for marriage seemed to dim as the years slipped by and Harry lost his savings in ill-starred business ventures. When World War I came to the United States in 1917, they were in their early thirties and still unmarried. His National Guard unit was activated, and he became a first lieutenant with a ticket to France. Bess wanted to get married before he left, but he argued that they ought to wait until he came back in one piece. Then, if she hadn't changed her mind. . . .

Harry would not allow a mere four thousand miles to interfere with his courtship. Although he had been made captain of a notoriously unruly artillery battery and was involved in much heavy fighting against the enemy as well, he wrote Bess every day, and she replied in kind. (Years later, in the White House, he discovered her burning his letters and protested that she ought to think of history; she retorted that she was.) He returned in the spring of 1919, still in one piece and with his savings from his captain's pay. When they were married in June, they had been "going together" for something like twenty years.

After a brief honeymoon they "moved in with her folks"—a fate more customary for newlyweds in those days than in these, though no more comfortable. Although Harry had given up working on the farm, Mrs. Wallace had not given up her disdain. The family home contained fourteen rooms, and the only residents besides Bess and Harry were her mother and grandmother, both widows; yet the living was really too close for comfort, especially when the two older women made Harry feel, as he confided to a friend, like "a small boy with dirty knees." He reacted to their barbs with iron-willed equanimity, however, while Bess took on the uneasy role of resident diplomat.

The couple's predicament was not eased by the failure of the haberdashery in which Harry and a friend had invested their savings and untold hours of hard work. Bess helped out as bookkeeper, advertising manager, and general factotum, and for a year or so after opening in November 1919, the store did splendidly. But the recession of 1920–21, which hit the farm belt especially hard, impoverished most of the store's customers. When the store folded, Harry, in debt but reluctant to declare bankruptcy, instead returned the leftover inventory and promised to pay off the debt in installments. As a result the Trumans, never profligate, lived with self-imposed frugality until, in the mid-1930s, the debt was finally paid.

He had been studying law on the side, at Bess's urging, and this may have been partly responsible for his being offered a county judgeship in 1922. At least as responsible was his wartime friendship with the son of Mike Pendergast, whose political family in Jackson County was often compared with that of Boss Tweed in New York. The judgeship was an elective office, but that was a mere formality under the circumstances. Over the next dozen years, except for a brief two years out of office, Judge Truman grew into a public figure. In Missouri such "judgeships" were not judicial but administrative jobs, somewhat like those of county supervisors elsewhere. Harry supervised county projects supported by more than sixty million dollars in public money, earning himself a reputation for efficiency and honesty, whatever his political connections. To earn extra money to support his wife and child (Margaret was born in 1924), he turned not to graft but to moonlighting. In his campaigns for election and then reelection, he discovered that his impromptu speeches were more forceful, more appealing to audiences, than the speeches he read. Bess quickly recognized this, too, and it made her nervous over the possibility that he might say "something embarrassing." She never fully eliminated that tendency of his, but she did overcome the embarrassment. To some extent, at least.

A famous story in this connection, illustrative if apocryphal, concerns a visit paid by President and Mrs. Truman to a garden show in Washington. At one point Harry, impressed by a particularly luxuriant plant, exclaimed that it must have required a lot of manure. Later one of the primmer ladies suggested to Bess that perhaps she could persuade the president to use a more, er, dignified word, like "fertilizer." Bess promised to try, but warned the lady that it had taken her twenty years to bring him up to "manure."

In the 1934 congressional elections, the support of the Pendergast machine helped Harry to win a seat in the U.S. Senate, but that support also burdened him with the image of a puppet controlled by strings reaching all the way back to Missouri. Both he and Bess had to look up the noses of some Washington old-timers who considered themselves holier than they. Neither of them was much given to taking up such a position. Turning to each other as usual for moral support, they managed to survive that trivial aspect of the puritan heritage while Harry built himself a reputation as a conscientious senator. Bess helped in this project by working as a staff aide in his office, with special responsibility for keeping in touch with his constituents. Although her working in this paid job caused a bit of a flap, the commotion generally subsided when it was realized that she worked much harder, longer hours than could be covered by her standard salary of $4,500 a year.

By reelection time in 1940 Harry had earned acceptance into the senatorial "club," and he and Bess were receiving more social invitations than they really wanted. President Franklin Roosevelt, however, felt that the decline of the Pendergast organization in Missouri (Boss Tom Pendergast was now in prison for tax evasion) meant that Harry could not win reelection. He offered him an appointment to the Interstate Commerce Commission, but Harry, backed up by Bess, stoutly insisted on making the race. He did—they did—and won, narrowly but unmistakably. No puppet strings this time.

They went back to working together. Bess was busier than ever, especially after Harry was made chairman of the Special Committee to Investigate the National Defense Program, which he had proposed as an antidote to the kind of graft and other corruption that had infected the arms buildup in World War I—and which, under his leadership, not only stepped up war-production efficiency but also saved the country an estimated billion dollars in times when a billion dollars meant something. Although his efforts involved a great deal of traveling, they brought him also a great deal of flattering attention.

Reader's Digest called him the "Billion-Dollar Watchdog," and he turned up on the cover of *Time*.

Franklin Roosevelt was impressed. He had been impressed also by Harry's gutsy reelection fight in 1940. He insisted that the Missouri senator's name be placed in nomination for vice president at the 1944 Democratic convention. Harry and Bess both had mixed feelings about his leaving the Senate for the country's most notorious sinecure, but the matter was very much out of their hands. He won the nomination. Beth's invaluable contribution to the convention was to persuade her husband to make one of the shortest acceptance speeches on record, just ninety-one words. It was barely more than a short thank-you note, but it stood out amid all the general logorrhea.

Their concern about enforced idleness in the new job was tinged with quite different misgivings. In view of the spreading rumors about Roosevelt's poor health, Harry just might wind up as president of the United States. Their premonitions were reinforced at Harry's first meeting with FDR to discuss campaign strategy. Roosevelt's hands shook so uncontrollably that he could not pour cream into his coffee, and he had trouble speaking clearly. The implications were unnerving, but the die was cast.

During the campaign Bess stayed home with Margaret while Harry jaunted about the country, engaging in the usual campaign hijinks, including joining in Indian war dances and cow-milking contests. When he phoned her, as he regularly did of course, she told him to behave himself.

Some six months later, when Roosevelt died in April 1945, Harry became president—and learned that the United States was building an atomic bomb. That summer, informed that it was ready to go, Harry decided to use it. Bess supported his decision, convinced that invading Japan would cost not only American but also Japanese casualties far greater than the toll from the bomb. This choice between two horrifying alternatives was another presidential burden as unwelcome as it was unavoidable. Five decades later that decision still evokes hot controversy, much of it based on sober second hindsight.

Hot controversy also was detectable in the 1948 presidential campaign. It split the Democratic party, with former vice president Henry Wallace heading a Progressive ticket and Governor Strom

Thurmond heading a States' Rights, a.k.a. segregationist, ticket. For a number of reasons—the United Nations action in Korea, economic conditions, the contrast with Franklin Roosevelt—Harry's political support was eroding at an alarming rate. Some Democratic leaders were openly suggesting that the party should get rid of Truman and call on General Dwight Eisenhower to make the race.

Neither Bess nor Harry was disposed to take this treatment and obsequiously retire. Although she had been looking forward to private life in Independence, she urged Harry to run. Perhaps the smug confidence of Republican candidate Tom Dewey, who looked as though he had canary for breakfast every morning, helped them to make this decision, especially since Dewey represented the kind of business interests that had always given Harry indigestion. After Harry had been nominated by a Democratic party shrunken by defections, and after columnist Drew Pearson had joined the national consensus by giving him one chance in a thousand to win reelection, the Truman family got to work. For seven weeks Harry, Bess, and Margaret lived in the presidential campaign railroad car, covering thirty thousand miles and countless whistle-stops. The famous uphill campaign ended with a famous picture of the indomitable Harry, with a triumphant grin, displaying a copy of the *Chicago Tribune*'s prematurely gleeful headline, DEWEY DEFEATS TRUMAN.

But in 1952 the couple felt much differently about the prospects of another campaign. After a term that included such delights as four more years of the Korean War, an assassination attempt, the insubordination of Douglas MacArthur, the forked tongue of Senator Joe McCarthy, and the pitiless glare of publicity, they decided that enough was enough. Harry might have been gulled into running against Dwight Eisenhower, but Bess insisted on going home. Which they did, in January 1953.

In all their years in Washington they had rarely been apart. He was her admirable, irrepressible Harry, and she was his devoted, solicitous, wise-counseling Bess—as one friend put it, "his cold towel, brandy, and chicken soup all rolled into one." Their love was exclusive and impregnable. In 1946 Richard Nixon, running against Helen Gahagan Douglas for a California seat in Congress, implied that President Truman might be supporting his opponent because there was some hanky-panky between them. Bess found the suggestion hilarious. On an earlier occasion Senator Truman was part of a congressional delegation making a tour of Central America during which groups of call girls were furnished for the legislators' comfort and convenience; Harry invariably retreated to his hotel room, alone.

Shortly before they left for Washington in 1935, Bess was asked, more or less wittily, by some friends during a bridge game whether she would be anxious about Harry's working with all those devastatingly attractive government secretaries. "No," she answered. "Three no trump."

Mamie Doud
and
Dwight Eisenhower

Dwight Eisenhower was a strategist, military and otherwise. In the otherwise department he demonstrated his talent when, as a shavetail fresh out of West Point and stationed in San Antonio, Texas, he was courting Mamie Doud. His problem was that, although he had been squiring her about for some time and was on very friendly terms with her parents, she was entirely too popular. The competition was exasperating. To reduce it, Ike Eisenhower made a practice of dropping in on the Douds on evenings when Mamie was out on a date. Mrs. Doud enjoyed talking with him (and may well have been a coconspirator), and he usually could stay late enough to greet Mamie when she came home. Eventually the competition began disappearing out of discouragement, and Ike had Mamie all to himself. Fortunately, by then that was more than all right with her. They were married in July 1916, in Mamie's home town of Denver, when he was twenty-five and she was nineteen.

She was the spoiled child of affluent parents; he was a poor farm boy whose prospects for affluence as an army officer were about as good as Mr. Micawber's. Many friends and relatives thought her too young to commit herself to the limited means and nomadic style of army life. She probably was, but she was also strong willed, and she wanted Ike more than anyone else in the world.

Because they were both strong willed, only a few days later they had a violent quarrel—not physically violent, but long and loud and heated. They had gone to *his* hometown of Abilene, Texas, for her to meet his family. That afternoon Ike left the house to go downtown and visit some old friends, after casually promising to be back in time for supper. Suppertime came and went, with no Ike. Mamie began working up a full head of steam. When he was finally found, by telephone, he explained that he had fallen into a poker game, was losing, and could not leave until his luck turned. Mamie exploded, demanding that he—come—home—*this*—*minute!* But he declined this pressing invitation and in the event came home unmistakably after midnight. He was met by a simmering wife, and they shook the rafters with their confrontation until, at sunup, exhaustion closed eyes as well as mouths and doubtless relieved many ears. This first quarrel, though by no means their only one, was remembered by Mamie as their worst.

The incident may have been helpful, for Mamie had some adjusting to do. *She* may not have been able to get Ike to do something "this minute," but the army could. They were destined to move, for example, three dozen times in about the next three dozen years, living in everything from tents to mansions, eventually including the White House. She had to accept the fact that, in matters of duty, Ike was a soldier first and a husband second. But by sticking it out, she also learned that he was wholeheartedly in love with her, deeply concerned for her, and very dependent on the love she felt for him.

They were separated a great deal during World War I, in which Ike was busy on a number of training assignments. (He was ordered to report for an overseas assignment on November 19, 1918, about a week after the Armistice was signed, and thus never left the country, to his distress and Mamie's delight.) After the war they were together much more, but in January 1921 their happiness received a crushing blow in the death, from scarlet fever, of their first son at the age of three. They had been so overjoyed with the little boy, so emotionally dependent on him as a precious distraction from the drab routine of peacetime army life, that they never fully recovered from the experience. It was especially hard on Ike, not only because the father-son relationship was important to him but also because the tragedy came at a time when he was in the professional doldrums. The popular disillusion following the war, accompanied by a popular determination never to get into another, promised to make a military career a dead-end exercise in futility. Having just been rejected for officers' infantry training school, he was seriously considering quitting the army for civilian work. Mamie, as was usual in important matters, left the final decision up to him. (The notable exception was her insistence, earlier, that he not join the budding Army Air Corps. She could not face the risk of losing him. But he did learn to fly some years later.)

He put off the decision, and over the next year or so three things happened to brighten their lives and their prospects. One was a new friendship with an older couple, Fox and Virginia Connor. General Fox Connor was commander of U.S. troops in Panama, where Major Eisenhower was assigned as his executive officer in January 1922. Panama was a steam bath with bugs, an environment hardly designed to make the still grieving young couple any happier. But the Connors took quite a parental shine to them. The general proved very helpful to Ike, both in Panama and in later years when he became deputy chief of staff. Another, related thing was that his wife, recognizing that the youngster's death was threatening to take the life out of the Eisenhowers' marriage, and sharing Mamie's fear that Ike was growing rather cold and distant, urged the young wife to embark on a program of "vamping" her husband. Mamie had quite enough of the flirt left in her to take this advice. Her tactics, which included considerable personal refurbishing—Ike found her new hairstyle so fetching that the famous bangs became a permanent trademark— reinvigorated the marriage. The third thing, the birth of son John in August 1922, brought back the sense of secure togetherness that they had almost lost.

General Connor had given Ike some hope for his career by persuading him that World War I had been inconclusive and that the United States would need good soldiers sooner than anyone dared anticipate. On the general's recommendation Ike was selected for the Command and General Staff School. Although he and Mamie were together during his stint there, he forced himself into such a time-consuming, arduous study program that he might as well have been on the moon. She supported him as best she could, however, and their sacrifice paid off when, in 1926, he completed the notoriously tough curriculum and was graduated with first honors in a class of 175. This brought him to the Army War College and to another graduation two years later.

After some piddling assignments—the army in its notorious wisdom, for instance, made the first-honors graduate a football coach at Fort Benning for a spell—he took on the writing of a guidebook, *The American Battlefields in France*, for none other than the towering hero of World War I, General Pershing, to whom Connor had recommended him. Pershing, impressed with the finished product, wrote a warm letter of tribute that spoke of his "splendid service," his "unusual intelligence," and his "constant devotion to duty." The letter, which went into Ike's personal file, did him no harm whatsoever. Mamie, who had urged him to do the job for Pershing despite his own reluctance and misgivings, was proudly delighted.

He similarly impressed Chief of Staff Douglas MacArthur, to whom he was assigned as an aide in 1933. When MacArthur was appointed military adviser to the new Philippine Commonwealth in 1935, he asked Ike to come with him as his assistant. Mamie urged her doubtful husband to accept the invitation for his career's sake, although it meant that she would have to stay in Washington to see son John through his last year of grade school, where he was doing too splendidly to leave in midstream. But a year later they were together again, in the Philippines, where the climate was downright Panamanian but the housing was downright palatial.

After four years of "studying dramatics under Douglas Mac-Arthur," as Ike put it privately many years later, they found themselves back in the States. After a year of being shunted from post to post, they wound up in San Antonio again in the summer of 1941. But this time he was a full colonel, chief of staff for the Third Army. He spent most of the summer planning maneuvers, a job so well done that he was made a brigadier general that September. On December 7 the news that he had long expected finally came from Pearl Harbor, vindicating the viewpoint that had earned him the title, among some of his fellow officers, of "Alarmist Ike." He was soon transferred to the War Plans Division in Washington at the request of the army chief of staff, General George C. Marshall. In March 1942, Major General Eisenhower, now head of the War Department's Operations Division, was made responsible for drawing up plans for the unification of all American forces in Europe under one commander. He completed and submitted his plans in June, and was appointed that commander. A week or so later he was in his new London headquarters. He would not be able to return to Mamie until October 1945, except for a hurried and secret official visit in January 1944.

And so he took pen in hand—pen, because Mamie could not abide receiving letters from him typed by a stenographer. He wrote 319 letters in about half as many weeks—or more, since not all may have survived. They were love letters not only because of their continual expressions of his love for her but also because of the time and effort they required from one of the busiest men in the world. He was neither poetic nor especially eloquent, but surely no woman reading these letters could doubt where his heart was.

The letters were especially important to Mamie after the summer of 1942, when the titillating rumors about Ike's alleged affair with Kay Summersby began ricocheting about in Washington. They seemed so plausible—a glamorous man in his vigorous early fifties and a glamorous divorcée some twenty years his junior, both lonely, impelled into each other's arms by wartime circumstances—so plausible from thousands of miles away that Mamie, for all her trust in Ike, could not help feeling some anxiety, even some rejection. In her loneliness she began drinking more heavily than usual, but stopped when a concerned close relative pointed out to her what she was doing. She might not have been able to stop so decisively if it had not been for her husband's continual reassurances. Today those reassurances seem quite truthful; the affair seemed plausible only at a distance. Ike was kind to Summersby, even solicitous, especially after the battlefield death of her fiancé, but the romantic and erotic aspects of their relationship while she was on his staff seem to have been a triumph of imagination over memory in an otherwise gallant woman who in her final years was desperately ill and desperately short of money.

The gossip would not die, of course. It surfaced again for the Eisenhowers in February 1951 in a hotel room in Paris. Ike, after a brief, unmemorable stopover in the presidency of Columbia University, had been asked by President Truman to take command of North

Atlantic Treaty Organization forces in Europe. On the evening of the day that Ike and Mamie arrived in Paris, an exhausting day choked with meetings and receptions, they wound up having dinner alone in their hotel room. Over the radio they heard a play, sponsored by the French Communist party, depicting Ike in crapulous revelry with a very private secretary, and their French was good enough for them to get the drift. Ike took some of the sting out of it with a quiet, gentle embrace.

Their eighteen months in France meant that they were together, yet they were separated from John and his wife and their three grandchildren, who had often come down from West Point (where John was teaching English) to visit them at Columbia. But those months also gave Mamie good training in hobnobbing with kings, queens, princes, prime ministers, and other such dignitaries, training that would serve her well later. Soon, in fact—for in June 1952 they returned to the United States. Ike retired from the military and, after much urging from friends and opportunists, ran for the presidency. In June 1953 he and Mamie found themselves ensconced in the White House. During the campaign, through which the couple followed the example of the whistle-stopping Trumans, James Reston estimated in the *New York Times* that Mamie was "worth at least 50 electoral votes."

Unlike Bess Truman, Mamie rather enjoyed being First Lady. She liked the perks, and she found the second-floor living quarters of the White House, after some minor alterations, much more comfortable and homelike than she had expected. Indeed, she and Ike liked them so well that they disappointed many in the butterfly set by spending most of their evenings there alone. Nevertheless, within a few months she began planning a home for Ike's retirement. They had recently bought a farm near Gettysburg with this in mind. Remodeling the old farmhouse became an absorbing preoccupation over the next couple of years, as well as a project costly enough to create some marital friction ("Mamie, the kitchen is *big enough!*"). But the absorption and even the friction were vindicated, for the Gettysburg farm became a weekend refuge for the couple as well as a pleasant place to bring such official visitors as Nikita Khrushchev—and such more welcome guests as the grandchildren.

Despite her adjustment to the publicity and other inconveniences of presidential life, Mamie was eager to enjoy the farm more privately. She was therefore far from eager for Ike to run for a second term. When he suffered a major heart attack during a visit to Denver in September 1955, she made it clear that they would retire to Gettysburg in January 1957 and "lead our own lives in our own way from here on out." In the Fitzsimons Army Hospital near Denver she spent nineteen days at Ike's bedside or in an adjacent room. She took care of the flood of solicitous mail, read to him, waited on him, sometimes simply sat and held his hand. When they got back to Washington in November he bought her an official-looking medallion commemorating her love and devotion beyond the call of duty.

Yet he also informed her, about three months later, that he felt he should run again. She had been told by his doctors that a man of his restless vigor might decline faster in retirement at Gettysburg than at work in the White House. She accepted this opinion, his decision, and four more years in Washington. But in January 1961 they finally did retire to the farm, if not quite to the privacy which she had been looking forward to so eagerly.

Ike's health had never been the same after the heart attack. In 1965 he suffered two more attacks, and over the next four years experienced several other related illnesses. By the spring of 1968 his health had deteriorated so badly that he was assigned to a suite in Walter Reed Hospital for continuous care. There he and Mamie lived for almost a year. Some days he was better, some days worse, but the long-term trend was unmistakable. When he finally died in March 1969, Mamie was at his bedside, and they were holding hands.

Marion Davies
and
William
Randolph Hearst

∽

When Marion Davies (then Marion Douras) was born in January 1897, William Randolph Hearst was already, at thirty-three, the owner and publisher of three newspapers which he had nursed from feeble destitution into flamboyant prosperity. He was about to launch his famous, or infamous, campaign to goad the United States into war with Spain over Cuba and thereby to demonstrate that he could be as influential as he was colorful.

When he first came across Marion eighteen years later, she was a Broadway chorine and he was the owner and publisher of ten newspapers and seven magazines, a multimillionaire landholder, a husband, and a father of five sons. In 1903 he had married a professional dancer and had established a household and family environment befitting their affluence and rather exalted social status. He was not utterly dedicated to the life monogamous, however, and showgirls could provide a welcome distraction. But Marion proved to be more than a fleeting distraction. He was thoroughly captivated. She had a lovely face, a trim figure, and the shapeliest legs in the line. She also, he found, had an agile if untrained mind, a pointed wit, and a love of fun rivaling his own. What he felt for her may not have been love at first sight, but it was something very powerful at first sight. It was the beginning of a love affair destined to last, through better and worse, till death did them part.

Only Millicent's adamant refusal to agree to a divorce prevented the marriage. Husband Bill even employed detectives in the hope of establishing grounds for divorce, to no avail. Eventually he and Marion simply lived together for the rest of his life, more and more openly as time went by. They wound up living in southern California while Millicent lived in New York, where she maintained a decorous home to which he occasionally repaired for important social functions. Since he and Marion felt no urge to tweak blue noses in the East Coast's relatively structured and judgmental society, after 1924 they stayed in the more relaxed and tolerant atmosphere of California. At San Simeon, his fabulous estate some two hundred miles north of Los Angeles—with its 240,000 sunny acres, fifty miles of ocean shore, four castles and unbelievable art treasures—she was accepted virtually without reservation for a quarter of a century.

But it was not blue-nosed disapproval that kept her in the West. It was her movie career that eventually moved her from New York to California. By 1917 her reputation as a Broadway showgirl had stirred some interest in the growing film industry. She began receiving movie offers. Although she was doing well in the Ziegfeld Follies and other revues, her prospects as an actress in speaking roles were dimmed by a lifelong stammer. This minor handicap was not serious in ordinary conversation. It was if anything rather appealing—Hearst certainly found it so—and at times may have provided an element of timing that enhanced her reputation for ready wit. She managed, with sharply focused effort, to get through the few lines assigned to her in occasional comedy skits, and of course, as with most if not all stammerers, her singing was not affected, but no theatrical producer or director was likely to take a chance on her in a major speaking role.

Silent movies thus offered her an opportunity denied her in "the legitimate theater." Her interest in film acting was further stimulated by a family connection. Sister Reine had starred in a few films, one of them produced by her ex-husband George Lederer, and was under contract to Lewis Selznick's World Film Corporation. Reine's enthusiasm over the new medium was infectious, and soon Marion became determined to have a go at becoming a movie star. She may have been motivated partly by a hope that such celebrated status might make it easier for W.R. to divorce Millicent and marry the woman to whom he was now, in 1917, obviously and delightedly in thrall.

Although he could have helped her, he did not. He temporized. Since 1913 he had been active in filmmaking, at least financially, chiefly in newsreels, serials, and short subjects. His hesitancy may have been due to a genuine, if fading, hope that Marion would eventually be the second Mrs. William Randolph Hearst, thereby incurring family and social responsibilities that would preclude a serious movie career. As it turned out, Marion did not need his help to get started. Lederer offered to star her in a picture which another friend offered to finance. *Runaway, Romany* was the story of a rich young girl who leaves home and joins a band of gypsies, and of her father's frantic efforts to find her until they are 'at last happily reunited, together of course with the girl's handsome and sturdily reliable young swain. Though the corn was higher than any mere elephant's eye, it was fairly typical of the movie fare of the time. The story, indeed, may have been all too typical, for the picture, released in December 1917, made no memorable waves. Marion's performance was static by direction, displaying a great deal of her beauty but none of her inborn talent for comedy. Yet Hearst, to her surprise, found it breathtaking. She was a natural for movies, he told her, and he was determined to make her a star. He probably had begun to despair of ever getting a divorce, and perhaps to think in terms of compensation.

The movie industry in 1918, such as it was, was still concentrated in New York. Hearst rented a capacious building that had housed a nightclub and transformed it into one of the city's best equipped and most competently staffed studios. His first effort, a maiden-in-distressful-danger serial, proved severely disappointing: Marion's perils failed to match Pauline's in audience appeal. So he turned to publicity, using the power of his enormous journalistic empire to persuade millions of moviegoing readers that Marion Davies was already a firmly established movie star. To provide her with a lifestyle that such readers would expect, he ensconced her whole family (except her estranged father, who later moved in next door) in a palace of white marble on Riverside Drive, lavishly refurbished. He also generously enlarged her personal bank account. His devoted support was to be the making of her as a movie star and her undoing as the memorable comedienne she might have been.

He launched her career with *Cecilia of the Pink Roses*. For its opening in New York in 1919 he had the screen flanked with masses of roses whose perfume was wafted to the audience during the showing through the theater's ventilating system. Whatever the hypnotic effect of this on the audience, it (among other influences) inspired the Hearst papers into a frenzied welcome of the picture and its star. Their joyous excitement rivaled that with which they had greeted the Armistice the year before. Marion was on her way in earnest now. Significantly, Hearst now allowed himself to be seen regularly escorting her, permitted news photos to be taken of them together, and generally went along publicly with the view of their relationship prevailing among all but the deaf, dumb, and blind.

Although he was quite serious about his movie studio and was accepted by his fellow moguls as a major competitor, he never really managed its activities, never gave it the attention that he gave his newspapers. He even made Marion titular head of the enterprise. Instead of managing, he interfered irregularly but frequently as a kind of ad hoc perfectionist, always in what he considered Marion's best interest and usually in some trivial matter like the authenticity of a piece of eighteenth-century furniture. Much shooting time was wasted in favor of combing through his already vast but still burgeoning collection of art objects to lend an imaginary reality to movie sets for audiences who could not have known or cared less. If he had limited his interference to trivia, the damage might have been correspondingly trivial. But he also controlled the selection of scripts. Although he hugely enjoyed Marion's puckish, pomposity-pricking, self-deprecating, clownish sense of humor—Chaplin reveled in putting on impromptu skits with her at parties—he could not bring himself to display her comic talent on the screen, apparently because of a gut feeling that a beautiful woman is somehow demeaned by any behavior other than a kind of decorous posing. As a result, Marion became so widely associated with movies fraught with stately sentimentality that late in 1922 Hearst's own movie columnist Louella Parsons complained in print, "Why don't you give Marion Davies a chance?" and described her as "a good actress, a beauty, and a comedy starring bet." But Hearst continued to play wet blanket despite the criticism, so that Marion's comedy starring remained largely limited to entertaining guests in tandem with Chaplin and others, and to indulging in jokes and horseplay between takes on the set.

Their relationship in 1919 was strained by separation. She was working in New York while he spent most of his time in California, feverishly busy at his imperial business headquarters or at his imperial estate at San Simeon, where Xanadu was under construction. Acutely jealous man that he was, by early 1920 he could no longer tolerate the arrangement. Fortuitously concluding that the future of the movies lay in the West, he persuaded Marion to move to California, although he had just spent a million dollars renovating the Riverside Drive mansion. Her stay there lasted only several weeks, despite a brief "honeymoon" at an inn in Santa Maria from which they emerged more deeply in love than ever. She was not working, despite his hopes, and her interest in San Simeon and its "things" was never as fervid as his. She soon grew restless and returned to her studio and her family in New York.

He followed soon thereafter, ostensibly because of his interest in the presidential campaign. (He was a frustrated politician all his life.) Once in New York, he took Marion and some friends on a yacht trip to Mexico. On his return he was accosted by an angry Millicent, who demanded a trip to Europe as compensation. He and the family left for London, but he arranged to have Marion sail in their wake and take up residence, luxuriously, at a hotel across town from theirs. When this uneasy arrangement proved inconvenient, he booked passage for New York, leaving the family in London but reserving a separate suite for Marion on the same ship. Marion was delighted to get back to New York. She had gone to England reluctantly, at Hearst's urging, and the visit had proved quite as uncomfortable as she had expected.

In the States they again were separated more often than not by the three thousand miles from sea to shining sea, linked through Hearst's incessant letters, telephone calls, and multiple-page telegrams. Marion starred in two or three forgettable films, but late 1922 saw the release of *When Knighthood Was in Flower*, a casually historical romance in which she starred as an irrepressible Mary Tudor. The role was more demanding than she was used to, and it even gave her some moments of energetic comedy. She met the challenge, receiving good notices in even the non-Hearst press. And the picture, although an outrageously expensive production, actually made money. Marion could now be mentioned in the same breath with Mary Pickford.

Knighthood was only one of five Marion Davies movies released in 1922–23. The four others were received less enthusiastically, although *Little Old New York* was described as "exquisite" by the *New York Times* and *Adam and Eve* elicited praise from *Photoplay* on Marion's "graceful performance," which "makes us think that her forte is light comedy." In 1924 Hearst moved their cosmopolitan production facilities to Hollywood. Marion joined him in California, where she starred in eleven more silent movies before the advent—indeed, the onslaught—of sound. Her last, *Show People*, a satire on Hollywood life directed by King Vidor, was her best, earning a tribute from the *New York Times* for her "unusually clever acting."

Like many another star of the silents, Marion was terrified by the inevitable coming of talking pictures. Although her voice was pleasant enough, she assumed that her stammer meant the end of her career. Hearst, sharing her anxiety, had her take training in voice control and diction from the best coaches available. This brought some improvement, but she had to grit her teeth to get to her first sound screen test, for Irving Thalberg. On the set she was handed a test script containing what she considered "stupid dialogue" (it was an artificial test for enunciation). In response she persuaded the actor playing opposite her to let her ad lib, and the result was so funny that Thalberg not only gave her a contract but also offered to raise the salary of whoever had written the script. Between 1929 and 1937 she starred in sixteen talking pictures with never a complaint about a stammer.

The opening of the 1930s, however, marked the beginning of a gradual decline in her fortunes, and in Hearst's as well. Despite her starring in pictures with male leads like Leslie Howard, Clark Gable, Gary Cooper, and Bing Crosby, she was hampered by mediocre scripts. This may have been due partly to Hearst's meddling; among other things, he could be very puritanical in vetoing the way she might appear on the screen and the lines she was given to say. It may also have been due to the rise of a competitor, Norma Shearer, an attractive star whose new husband, Irving Thalberg, was naturally inclined to show her some preference. (For years, Shearer's name never appeared in Hearst newspapers.) As for Hearst, his years of uninhibited profligacy were beginning to catch up with him. He had exhausted his inheritance and was juggling bank loans with a wonderful but perilous dexterity. But the elaborate parties continued unabated at San Simeon and at Marion's less palatial beach house at Santa Monica, which merely resembled a resort hotel. In 1934 he took Marion and a caravan of guests on an extended tour of Europe. His fortunes were declining, but they were falling from a height of about a quarter of a billion dollars.

In 1937 Marion retired. She had made forty-six feature films and was the wealthiest woman in the film colony. It was time, she explained, to enjoy the companionship of the man she loved. It was a companionship he needed, for now, at seventy-four, he had finally spent himself to the edge of bankruptcy. He was possession-poor. Executives of his empire formed a committee to slow its rate of collapse and, if possible, save it. Much of his collection of art objects was taken from his many warehouses and put on sale in department stores throughout the country. Marion lent him a million dollars, over his protests, and, when that proved insufficient, sold jewelry and mortgaged real estate and pleaded with friends until she came up with another two million, which satisfied the importunate banks enough to end the crisis.

To end *that* crisis, but not the fall of the crumbling empire. Not all her goods and chattels were enough for that. Hearst was deeply moved by her efforts to save him, and their mutual travail (her movie career having ended more in whimper than bang) united them in a mutual sympathy. They were both freer now to spend time together, making up for all that lost time spent apart. As the empire continued to crumble and shrink, they continued their fabulous and celebrated social activities in an atmosphere tinged with desperation, like revelers on the eve of Armageddon. They also continued their less publicized but extensive charitable activities. In the spring of 1941 they suffered a personal blow with the release of Orson Welles and Herman Mankiewicz's *Citizen Kane*, in which sugar-daddy Kane and baby-doll Susan Alexander quickly became identified with Hearst and Marion Davies. Although Hearst was not much disturbed by the implication of casual ruthlessness in his business dealings, he was sharply troubled by what some of the picture's other implications seemed to be doing, and indeed did, to Marion's professional reputation. Even more distressing was the depiction of Susan's alcoholism, since Marion's borderline drinking problem had always worried him. But within a few months their personal problems were engulfed by World War II.

Because of the war they left San Simeon, which was considered an inviting target for offshore shelling by a Japanese submarine. He was seventy-eight now, and his health was failing. After the war, which they spent at his estate in northern California, they returned to San Simeon only to be told that its altitude was risky for him. Marion bought him a house on an eight-acre estate in Beverly Hills, using her own money and deeding the property over to him. Moving there was enormously difficult for Hearst, whose heart was wrapped up in San Simeon (Marion always considered it her greatest rival) and who clearly recognized that he could never live there again.

He never did. Gradually their social life dwindled to an almost reclusive withdrawal amid the comings and goings, and stayings, of doctors and nurses. One extraordinary feature of his treatment was his bed, which was rocked incessantly by a motor; both Hearst and the doctors considered this an aid to circulation. One evening in August 1951, as Marion sat beside him, he said three words that stabbed at her heart: "Stop the bed." She knew that he had finally given up.

Within three months she was married. Her new husband was Horace Brown, who strongly resembled Hearst in both physique and personality. Despite some ups and downs, she remained married to him until her death in 1961.

It seems a tragedy that she did so little comedy. In 1937 she was offered the starring role in the comedy *Boy Meets Girl*, but the ironically puritanical Hearst vetoed her taking it on the grounds that the script was "too outspoken," and she never made another movie. She described her career as consisting of "5 percent talent and 95 percent publicity," but George Bernard Shaw thought enough of her talent to want her for the movie production of his *Pygmalion*. She was, Orson Welles said of her many years later, "a delightful and very considerable person."

Wallis Warfield
and
Edward VIII

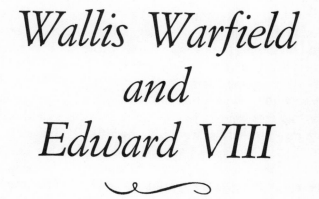

The eyewitness testimony is unanimous. His Royal Highness Edward Albert Christian George Andrew Patrick David was utterly infatuated, spellbound, entranced by Bessie Wallis Warfield Spencer Simpson ("besotted" was the Duke of Kent's word for his condition). The testimony is not so undiluted concerning her feelings for him. Or his early reaction to her.

Their first meeting could hardly have been more casual or, at least for him, less memorable. It was in April 1920, on the American battleship *New Mexico* anchored in the harbor of San Diego, that Wallis and her husband, navy Lieutenant Winfield Spencer, were among those presented to the visiting Prince of Wales and Lord Mountbatten. Some years later she was piqued to learn that, although she had been "dressed to kill," neither visitor could remember her.

A decade passed before they met again. Late in 1930 or early in 1931 (memories differ), after a divorce from Spencer, an entertaining interlude with an Argentine diplomat, and a second marriage to an English-American New Yorker named Ernest Simpson, she and Ernest were visiting London and were invited to a cocktail party by friends of the hostess. The hostess was a viscountess who was at that time the prime object of the prince's unceasing interest in married women. When he dropped in briefly, Wallis and her husband were introduced along with the other guests in a meeting that proved as forgettable as the one ten years earlier. For one thing, she had a miserable cold.

Even after luncheon the next day, when Wallis sat next to the prince and they engaged in some desultory conversation, he remained quite unimpressed. It was he who impressed her as "truly one of the most attractive personalities I had ever met." Still more impressed was Ernest, who took new pride in his English blood. He would live to regret this enthusiasm. Just as Lady Furness would become an unwitting matchmaker, so would he, hoist by the petard of his own ambition. When Wallis had at first decided that her cold was too severe for her to attend the fateful cocktail party, he persuaded her that they should not pass up so golden a chance to meet the Prince of Wales.

The viscountess clearly did not consider Wallis a threat to her preeminent position in the prince's pecking order. She thought her neither chic nor beautiful in face or figure, nor graceful in movement, although acknowledging that she had "alert and eloquent" eyes and "a distinct charm and a sharp sense of humor." After sixteen years with the prince, and being familiar with his appreciation of her own and others' physical charms, she probably considered him impervious to Wallis's less obvious attractions. What she may have forgotten in the press of business was that David, now in his mid-thirties, was maturing in taste and judgment. Whatever she thought, he did eventually find Wallis a stimulating person to talk to, one who showed great interest in the social and political problems that interested him, a degree of interest difficult to feign.

Soon after the cocktail party he left for an imperial goodwill tour of South America, returning to London in time for a court presentation that included the Simpsons, held in June 1931. Once again Lady Furness invited the Simpsons to a cocktail party. This time David, who wrote later that at the court he had been "struck by the grace of her carriage and the natural dignity of her movements," despite the

Furness assessment, was somewhat more attentive to Wallis, complimenting her on the gown she had worn for the presentation. Soon after he left the party, she and Ernest also left, only to find David waiting for them by his car to offer them a ride home. When he dropped them off, he declined an invitation to come in for a drink because of an early appointment in the morning, but he did ask for a rain check. "I'd like to see your flat one day. I'm told it's charming." Although Wallis could hardly have felt swept off her feet in this encounter, and although she was not to see him again for the rest of the year, she later came to believe that "that was how it all began."

David had converted the two-hundred-year-old Fort Belvedere, twenty-five miles from London, into a kind of suburban home. It was here that he invited the Simpsons to spend the last weekend of January 1932 along with several other guests, including the ever companionable Thelma Furness. Over the next couple of years they became habitual guests, and they were often at the Fort when, in the fall of 1933, Thelma, off on a tour of Africa, was absent. They were also there while Thelma the unobservant visited America that winter, having asked Wallis to look after David for her. That January, 1934, he really discovered her lively conversational charms. He began visiting the Simpsons as well as inviting them to visit him. By the end of March, when Thelma returned, he had patently transferred his affections.

She did not guess where at first. In New York and on the voyage home, she had seen a good deal of the notorious Prince Ali Khan, and she thought David's new indifference toward her might be due to jealous pique. But a few days after coming home, she watched Wallis with David at a weekend dinner at the Fort. They were seated together, engaged in what often seemed a very private conversation. Then, during the salad course, David, whose table manners occasionally had a tinge of Henry VIII's, used his fingers to pick up a bit of lettuce only to have his hand slapped by Wallis, gently but reproachfully. Thelma was stunned. Nobody, but nobody, ever took such a liberty with the Prince of Wales, especially this rather touchy Prince of Wales. When Wallis glanced toward her, Thelma threw her a cautionary, beware-of-overfamiliarity look. The challenging look she received in reply stunned her further. She suddenly understood that Wallis had taken her request to look after David very seriously, and would probably do so for some time to come.

David needed, and wanted, looking after, especially from a woman strong enough to help him live through the stifling burdens of monarchy. He hated pomp and circumstance, yet his official life as heir apparent consisted almost wholly of pomp and circumstance. As early as 1927, and intermittently thereafter, he came close to renouncing his right to the throne in order to become a private citizen, or at least as private a citizen as a Windsor could be. He apparently resisted these impulses chiefly out of fear of his bully of a father, who ruled his wife and sons with an iron, if often ineffectual, hand—and whose stiff personality was the reason that David could never bring himself to tell the king that he intended to marry Wallis, no matter what. When the king died in January 1936, David still had not done so.

For not only was she a commoner, she would be a twice-divorced woman, and to marry her, the new king would need the approval of Parliament, the prime minister, the Archbishop of Canterbury, and the dominion governments, all of whom took a dim view of easy divorce and all of whom expected the Defender of the Faith to set an irreproachable example of marital probity. He evidently was counting on his popularity with the people and their representatives in the House of Commons, but he seriously underestimated the animosity in the government establishment, headed by a disdainful prime minister and Archbishop of Canterbury. This hostility was directed not only against his feckless past but even more against the influence of That Woman, who now was running Fort Belvedere and accumulating loads of resentment by flaunting the priceless jewelry that he was lavishing on her while cutting by 10 percent the paltry salaries of the palace staff.

Meanwhile, Ernest Simpson had taken up with another woman, in patriotic cooperation or bitter retaliation or both, and this cleared the way for a quiet little divorce with Wallis technically as the injured party, a status that kept her socially tolerable amid wrinkled patrician noses. After the official mourning period ended in July, the new king, instead of discreetly staying apart from Wallis until after the divorce, continued to see her regularly and to respond eagerly to her incessant telephone calls. Early in August he rented a new, 250-foot yacht to take her, and some more or less appropriate guests, on a tour of the Mediterranean, giving her a taste of the luxury and kowtowing which so delighted her and which would be hers as queen. The tour may be one of history's most spectacular instances of failure to defer gratification resulting in failure to achieve gratification.

Certainly it was a spectacle, a leisurely month of affectionate companionship, sightseeing, and hobnobbing with the very best people of southern Europe, avidly observed and titillatingly reported by the press of the Continent, North America, and elsewhere. Only the British press ignored their shenanigans, out of a traditional, stiff-upper-lipped respect for the king's privacy. Since the lovebirds probably read only British newspapers, they apparently were rather surprised on their return in September to find that their little jaunt, and their relationship, had become an international scandal. A visceral indignation was building up along the church-state axis and spreading throughout the rest of the establishment, casting a dark shadow on any prospect for a Queen Wallis.

Yet the couple both wanted that royal prize so desperately that they could not give up hope. The divorce from Ernest was arranged for late October—a rather close thing, since it would not become final until only a couple of weeks before the coronation in May 1937, leaving enough time for little better than unseemly haste. When the king learned that a ferret for the newspaper tycoon Lord Beaverbrook had discovered the divorce petition listed in the court calendar, he called the Beaver in for a confidential little talk. He had been hoping, he explained, to spare Mrs. Simpson any further embarrassment and would appreciate it if the news of the impending divorce could be suppressed as long as possible; the possibility of his marrying the lady did not come up in the conversation. Beaverbrook made a loyally strenuous and quite successful effort to keep the news from the public: Even the *Daily Worker* and the scandal sheet *Paris Soir* cooperated.

But the rumors could not be kept from the alarmed establishment. Prime Minister Baldwin was besieged by many of its most prominent representatives, including the Queen Mother, to urge the king to get the divorce action dropped and to exercise a little more discretion, or preferably a great deal more. When Baldwin finally did so, he might as well have addressed his plea to the nearest suit of armor. The king avoided direct answers to any questions about his intentions concerning Wallis—indeed, his position initially was that he could hardly be expected to interfere with Mrs. Simpson's personal decisions just because they were friends! Eventually, however, he made his position clear enough for the prime minister to tell Mrs. Baldwin at home that evening that the king had informed him that Mrs. Simpson was the only woman in the world for him and that he could not live without her.

The divorce hearing on October 27 consumed all of nineteen minutes. It was reported in American and French newspapers, with relish, but the British press maintained its incredible silence. That evening David and Wallis dined alone. During the next week or two they saw little of each other while he was held to a packed schedule of public appearances and ceremonies. On November 13, back at Fort Belvedere for some relaxation with Wallis, he received an "urgent and confidential" message from his ministers revealing that the unnatural silence of the British press was about to end, that the publicity would almost certainly bring on the resignation of the government, and that the subsequent election would be conducted chiefly on issues involving "Your Majesty's personal affairs." This statement of informed conjecture was accompanied by a bit of less official advice: that Mrs. Simpson be sent abroad *immediately*.

David, stubbornly and perhaps chivalrously, refused to pack off his "perfect woman" like a discarded royal whore. Although the suggestion enraged him, it seems also to have convinced him finally that he could not marry Wallis and wear the crown. It would have to be one or the other, and in the choice he had not a moment's doubt. A few days later he met again with Baldwin and announced his intention to renounce the throne in order to marry Mrs. Simpson. Baldwin accepted the announcement as "grievous news" but inevitable. The prime minister doubtless was relieved not only by the avoidance of a crisis but also by the imminent departure of a man whom he considered a willful, irresponsible playboy and a potentially dreadful king. Yet, despite his low opinion, he later described the king's demeanor in stunningly romantic terms: "I never saw such a look of beauty on anyone's face. He was like some young knight who had been given a glimpse of the Holy Grail. No reasoning or pleading by family or friend could penetrate that rapturous mist. He was alone with his vision."

Yet the bemused king emerged from that mist with a renewed hope that his popularity with the people would support him against the establishment and that perhaps he could have both Wallis and the crown after all. A few advisers, including Winston Churchill, suggested that he give up Mrs. Simpson, ascend the throne formally in May, and then, after Mrs. Simpson had made herself more acceptable by conspicuously good behavior, gingerly resume his marital pursuit. But this, David decided, would mean "being crowned with a lie on my lips," and he rejected the idea forthwith. Another proposal, for a morganatic marriage making Wallis consort but not queen, was rejected by the Baldwin government, largely on suspicion that consort could soon become queen. Wallis herself recommended a public relations ploy, a Christmas speech in which he could appeal directly to the people over the heads of the establishment, but Baldwin blocked this idea as being quite unconstitutional. Wallis chronically overestimated David's power as king, just as he overestimated his popularity, on this issue, with the people.

On December 3, 1936, the British press dikes burst. Suddenly everyone knew that the king wanted a woman with two living husbands as queen. Page after newspaper page reeked with an accumulation of spicy details of the romance that had gone so long unreported. News photos—of the Mediterranean cruise, for example—from which her image had been brushed out were now reprinted with her on full display. At the king's urging, as though she needed any, she fled to friends in France. David fled to Fort Belvedere, where he stayed for about a week virtually in hiding.

That was his last week in England until the outbreak of war. Despite a last-minute parliamentary effort by Churchill to give him more time, he signed the instrument of abdication on December 11. Thereby, in effect, his younger brother Bertie formally became His Majesty George VI, and David became His Royal Highness Prince Edward, Duke of Windsor. The new king created this resounding title for him, but David later discovered with dismay that it did not extend to Wallis, at least officially. Oversight or otherwise, the omission alienated the brothers and embittered the nonroyal duchess. After saying goodbye to his former subjects in his famous radio broadcast, explaining that his royal burdens would have been too much for him "without the help and support of the woman I love," he was soon ashore on the northern coast of France and on the telephone to Wallis in Cannes. (Churchill, who helped draft the speech and may have originated that famous phrase, later grew weary of it. Even plumbers, he complained to his son Randolph, had taken to saying that they were late "because of the woman I love.")

The static-plagued telephone would be their only connection until April 27, when the divorce became final. The long separation was painful, but he was still a multimillionaire and able to provide for her, from his temporary digs in a Rothschild manor near Vienna, in a style approaching her needs if not her preferences. What he could not protect her from was the predatory attention of reporters and vicious letters in the mail, both of which went far toward making her life miserable. Finally, in June 1937, soon after George VI's coronation, they were married at a chateau near Tours.

For their honeymoon they traveled to Austria with some 250 pieces of luggage and settled into a cozy lovers' nest consisting of a Tyrolean thirteenth-century, forty-room castle provided by an accommodating count. With its swimming pool, tennis courts, stables, hunting grounds, and nearby golf course, and situated as it was in an area frequented by vacationing friends, it seemed ideal. But they soon became bored and, yielding to their shared feelings of defeat and isolation, began quarreling about what should have been. Late that summer they moved to Paris to plan for a visit to Germany and then the United States. The German visit, in October, and especially their gracious hobnobbing with Nazi thugs, proved such a political debacle that they had to cancel their November visit to the States. This disaster seems to have staggered Wallis, who thereafter sought solace in extravagance, lavishly furnishing and decorating their five successive homes over the ensuing years, playing renowned hostess at exalted social affairs, and achieving enduring status as One of the Ten Best-Dressed Women in the World.

World War II brought them back to England in September 1939, but only for a fortnight, during which Wallis was treated by his family as if she did not exist. He was attached, with the rank of major general, to the staff of the British military mission in Paris, and they rented an apartment not far from that headquarters. When the Germans began their march on Paris in May 1940, they fled south, eventually reaching Lisbon, where the duke received a request from Churchill to come to England. He agreed to do so on the irrevocable condition that his wife be recognized as a royal highness. And that is why, instead of returning home, he became governor and commander-in-chief of the Bahama Islands for the duration of the war. There he puttered about administratively, she busied herself with such war relief work as the ubiquitous U-boats made necessary, and they both paid frequent R & R visits to the States for shopping and entertainment. Fully luggaged, of course, and providing the British embassy in Washington with severe and continual headaches.

Doubtless to the embassy's relief, they returned to Paris in the spring of 1945. For the following six years the duke pestered the Labor government for a responsible post, to no avail. After 1951, when even Churchill, newly returned to power, ignored his pleas, he gave up. Boredom now reigned more supremely than he ever had. Once, when a friend asked him what he had done that day, he actually replied that he had gone out with the duchess and "watched her buy a hat." They fought their oppressive ennui with continual traveling and partying, with the duke desultorily coauthoring an autobiography, or apologia, and the duchess desultorily having a fling with a stunningly rich and delightful young chap who was, she informed David, quite harmless and nonthreatening because he was a notorious homosexual. That footnote was of no great comfort, but at least the duchess neglected to mention the hermaphroditic episode in her memoirs.

In May 1972, in his seventy-eighth year and the thirty-fifth year of their marriage, David, an inveterate smoker, died of throat cancer. He left Wallis rich but desolate. His life, especially the greater part of it toward the end, brings to mind words that Shakespeare put in the mouth of a royal predecessor, Richard II: "I have wasted time, and now doth time waste me." As for Wallis's life, perhaps she herself put it most ironically when she exclaimed to a friend, "You have no idea how hard it is to live out a great romance!"

Golda Meir

and

Morris Meyerson

﹏﹏

Golda Mabovitch was seventeen and living in Milwaukee when, in 1915, she joined the Labor Zionist party and started saving her money to go to Palestine and settle there. After reading of the casually cruel treatment of Jews in eastern Europe during World War I, she knew that this was something she *had* to do. The Jewish people might not continue to survive so dispersed and despised; they *must* have a homeland. Her determination to help in establishing one in Palestine was shared by many zealous young men in the local Zionist party, and, according to a friend, four out of five of them who met Golda fell in love with her.

Why, then, two years later, did she marry quiet, diffident, introversive, apolitical Morris Meyerson, who found Zionism tiresome, futile, even "ridiculous"? She did so for the same reason that he agreed to go to Palestine with her despite all his deeply anxious misgivings. They loved each other. She loved him for his honesty, his kindness

and gentleness, his knowledge of and absorption in art, music, literature. He loved her for her strength and energy, her directness, her
compassion, her integrity, all seasoned with a sense of humor. They
loved each other too much not to try the impossible.

Since they were both employed irregularly and not very gainfully,
the first two years of their marriage were a time of stern frugality and
assiduous thrift. But finally, by the spring of 1921, they had accumulated enough money to join a group of Zionist Jews, including
Golda's sister Shana, for the trip to the Promised Land. The voyage
was the first of many tests of Morris's love. Instead of a normal sailing
time of about three weeks, it took two months. At sea mutineers
flooded the engine room (causing the ship to list dangerously),
destroyed most of the larder, laced the drinking water with salt, and
finally were seized by loyal seamen and thrown in the brig. The
captain's brother broke under the pressure and screamed intermittently throughout the rest of the trip. A passenger broke a leg and
had to wait until the ship reached port to have it set. Another
passenger was thrown overboard, and a third died of presumably
natural causes. In the end the captain, faced with charges of incompetence, killed himself. Not even the ebullient Golda was prepared to
call this a pleasure trip.

It was a very glum group that arrived in the new Zionist town of
Tel Aviv in July, with Morris probably the glummest of all. The sight
of Tel Aviv did little to brighten them up. Despite the oasis promise
of its name ("Spring Hill"), it seemed to be simply a sparsely inhab-
ited patch of sand surrounded by uninhabited, boundless wastes of
more sand. The group surveyed the bleak prospect in disheartened
silence until someone said, "Well, I'm going back home." Although
the words were those of the group's self-appointed jester, they expressed Morris's sentiments exactly.

But not Golda's. Although she was the first of the new arrivals to
be offered a job, as a teacher in Tel Aviv's only high school, she
turned it down. She had come to Israel to *work*, she protested. After
some bureaucratic delay, she and Morris were accepted as probation-
ary members of a kibbutz, an agricultural community where she was
set to picking almonds and Morris to clearing a stone-laden hillside.
For Golda the gregarious visionary, this working for a common
purpose, the washing and eating together, the frequent communal
meetings and social get-togethers, the reliance on committees for

every sort of decision, all were stimulating and even inspiring elements of their new life. For Morris the leisure-loving introvert, it was
all a nightmare. Only his love for Golda held him there. When he and
Golda were accepted as permanent members of the kibbutz, he was
appalled.

But he stuck it out until Golda remembered her wish to have
children born and raised in Palestine. They would be his children,
too, he pointed out with more asperity than he usually could summon
up, and he would *not* have them raised in a kibbutz "Children's
House" presided over by communal "mothers" on rotating assignment. A serious bout with malaria, which was chronic if not epidemic
in the kibbutz, weakened his constitution but strengthened his case.
He loved Golda too much to leave her, yet bringing up children in a
kibbutz he would not even try, not even for her.

And so they moved to Jerusalem. Golda's love of her husband and
of children proved too much for her. Morris would have been only
too happy to return to the States, but they compromised on Jerusalem, the City of Peace. Compared to Tel Aviv and the kibbutz,
Jerusalem was a tropical garden. The beauty of its setting lifted
Morris's spirits, and on their evening walks together Golda, too,
could relax enough to enjoy it. Yet their life was hard. Morris had a
bookkeeping job that barely kept them alive in a two-room apartment
which they had to share with boarders in order to pay the rent.
Nevertheless, in November 1924 their son Menachem was born.
Morris was ecstatic.

But Golda's ecstasy was shorter-lived. Within six months she had
grown so restless in her housewife role that she returned to the
kibbutz, taking the baby with her. Morris's reaction was mild but
adamant: He would stay in Jerusalem. Perhaps he counted on their
love to conquer all. If he did, in this instance he counted well, for
within another six months Golda and Menachem were back with
him. Golda now seemed determined to be the kind of wife he
wanted. After their daughter was born in May 1926 and they had to
give up the extra income from boarders, Golda took in washing to
earn a little supplementary wherewithal. This meant heating an endless succession of pots on their primitive stove (Jerusalem had no
electricity or gas) and endless hours scrubbing clothes on a wash-
board in the bathtub. To this was added the chore of stalling off
creditors—the milkman, the grocer, the butcher, the landlord.

When she was offered a job, therefore, she was quite ready to take it, especially since it meant working for the cause. As secretary of the Women's Labor Council, she would be part of the action again. Morris tried to understand and cooperated, although by 1929, after the authorities had discovered that Golda was eloquent on the podium and fluent in English, he saw less and less of her at home. Indeed, her proselytizing trips to England grew ever more frequent until a family crisis arose in 1932, when she received a cable from Morris announcing that their daughter Sarah, now six years old, was "desperately ill." She rushed home.

Sarah had a congenital kidney disease that had now grown worse. The doctors gave her little time to live. Golda and Morris talked it over. Why not take her to the United States for treatment? Morris, who had been offered a job in Haifa, his most lucrative ever, would have to stay in Palestine while Golda took the two children to New York. It would mean still further separation for them and a risky trip for Sarah, but it also could bring her recovery. Golda made her first personal request of the Women's Council: Was there work for her to do in the States? There was: to alert American Jewish women to the needs of Israel. She and the children soon therefore arrived in New York, where Sarah entered Beth Israel Hospital. Two years later Golda was a well-known and successful promoter of the cause of Israel, Menachem was homesick, especially for his father, and Sarah was well. It was time to go home. Their arrival in Israel was a time of joyful tears and fond embraces.

But the old problem remained. There is a kind of wife, Golda once wrote, who cannot stay home under ordinary circumstances, who cannot separate herself from a broader social and political life. "And for such a woman there is no rest." Morris still had his job in Haifa, and Golda now was offered an excellent opportunity in Tel Aviv with the powerful and very active Histadrut, the General Federation of Jewish Labor, as a member of its executive committee. The couple agreed that, in their equation at least, great mutual love did not equal compatibility. A trial separation was in order. Golda would work and live in Tel Aviv, with the children, and Morris would continue to work and live in Haifa, some sixty miles to the north, but would commute by bus each Sabbath for a family get-together.

Such an arrangement, of course, is not likely to nourish love and marriage. As the years passed, the couple slowly drifted further apart, seeing each other now and then until Morris died—"in my house in 1951 (when symbolically enough, I was away)," Golda wrote in her autobiography. With his death, she added, "I realized once again what a heavy price I had paid—and made Morris pay—for whatever I had experienced and achieved in the years of our separation."

Not long afterward she changed her name at the insistence of Israel's strongman Ben-Gurion, who insisted that government officials must have Hebrew names. She changed hers to Meir, which means something like "illumining" and which she chose because it came closest to her married, not her maiden, name. Her wistful love of Morris's memory, she remarked many years later to Oriana Fallaci, was mixed with a sense of guilt. They could not live without each other, but, because of her zeal for Israel, they finally did just that. She did not regret that zeal, of course, but she found it hard to talk about her marriage. "It was a tragedy," she told Fallaci. "A great tragedy."

Zelda Sayre
and
F. Scott Fitzgerald

Zelda Sayre was ahead of her time, a feminist in thought, word, and deed in a time when feminism generally was socially unacceptable in thought, much less in word or in deed. But her feminism suffered from two serious flaws. One was that she idealized, and idolized, the flapper of the gaudy twenties, a figure whose aimlessness and shallow self-indulgence alienated most homebodies of her day, just as such qualities would surely turn off most of the purposefully liberated women of our own era sixty years later. The other flaw was that she took her feminism personally, inviting it into her life with her erratically talented husband, matching her fantasy of independence against the reality of her helpless love. It was a contest designed for tragedy.

As a child and young woman she was a wild 'un. Her father was a judge, a justice (after 1909, when Zelda was nine) on Alabama's supreme court, a man of awesome respectability, and a stern though ineffectual disciplinarian. But her mother, an amateur nonconformist in Montgomery's staid middle-class society, indulged her lively daughter's eccentricities. Whether turning in false fire alarms as a child or gyrating about in racy versions of popular dances as a teenager out of control, Zelda could be counted on, as she put it herself later in her autobiographical novel *Save Me the Waltz*, to "give a damned good show." Not long after he met her at a country-club dance in July 1918, Scott Fitzgerald described himself as "in love with a whirlwind."

He thought her beautiful. Although, curiously, she was not photogenic, all the men who met her seemed to find her beautiful, including John Dos Passos and Ernest Hemingway. Most women did also, the notable exceptions being Dorothy Parker, who considered her expression too "sulky," and Rebecca West, who described her as plain and even craggily homely. Her beauty indeed may have been almost as mercurial as her temperament. When she was gay, she was lovely; but depression could darken her countenance, and her face could take on a stark look of unspoken fear and pain. Her black moods, however, would come later in her life. In her late teens and twenties she was consistently bright, vivacious, articulate, unpredictable. Scott had resolved never to marry, lest the responsibilities of marriage interfere with his career as a writer. While awaiting his army discharge in New York in 1918, he had plenty of time to think about this resolution and about Zelda. He could not get her out of his mind, or heart. In a letter to a friend he wrote of his determination never to marry. "Still," he added, "she *is* remarkable."

This conflict, this tension between career and marriage, would pervade their enduring love-hate relationship, as would his conventional assumption that a wife's prerequisite role was that of helpmeet to her husband. Zelda's failure to share the assumption and to meet his job specifications remained unnoticeable under the romantic passion of their courtship days. Her self-assertiveness made her all the more attractive to Scott, whose ideal woman would surely have disdained his ideal wife. On his return to Montgomery they indulged their mutual attraction, going everywhere together, to picnics and plays and movies and parties. Especially parties, with plenty of drinking.

Meanwhile he had been doing some writing. After his discharge in February 1919 he returned to New York, got a job with an ad agency, and in his spare time began collecting rejection slips on his short stories. Zelda's letters, although frequent and affectionate, also were full of news concerning her extravagant exploits on her frequent dates—dressing in men's clothes and going to a movie with a gang of boys, running a trolley off its tracks, even getting herself "pinned," briefly, during a spree with a young golfer at a weekend tournament. She and her companions were, of course, thoroughly lubricated on such occasions. Her frankness in her reports to Scott was refreshing but not very reassuring. In an effort to stabilize their relationship somewhat, Scott sent her an engagement ring, which she accepted with loving gratitude but without letting it change her behavior. A few months later, in July, Scott could stand the strain no longer. He caught a train to Montgomery and desperately asked Zelda to marry him at once.

She refused. In the stormy scene that followed, she even returned his ring. We do not know her reasons, not even the ones she gave Scott. But she undoubtedly needed someone with "good prospects"—if not a king, then at least a crown prince—to fulfill her dreams, and Scott's prospects at the time were clearly miserable. Utterly dejected, he went back to New York, quit his job, and embarked on a three-week spell of concentrated drinking that ended only because Prohibition closed all the bars. With this failure to drink himself to death (as he later described it to Edmund Wilson), he decided to go home to St. Paul, where he had been born almost twenty-three years earlier, and there to rewrite a novel that he had been working on for some time. By September he had sent the manuscript to Scribner's and soon thereafter received a publication contract. Excitedly he wrote Zelda, telling her in effect that his prospects had brightened considerably and asking if he could visit her in Montgomery. She replied, also excitedly, that she was eager to see him again. And she asked, incidentally, that he bring along a quart of gin.

His visit was brief but highly successful. Zelda was impressed with his new self-assurance. They renewed their engagement, agreeing to marry soon after his novel was published. Back in New York, he began rewriting his short stories with gusto. With the publication of his novel, *This Side of Paradise*, his dreams began to come true. The book sold well enough to pave his way to many editors, who began buying his short stories at a very satisfying rate and for very satisfying rates. Soon he could afford that newest of status symbols, his own bootlegger. One story even brought him a bonus in the form of a contract from Metro-Goldwyn-Mayer for the movie rights. He used the proceeds to buy Zelda an enormously expensive platinum wristwatch sparkling with diamonds. He savored the role of spendthrift and would never lose his taste for it. Suggestions that he might save something he rejected with puzzled contempt.

They were married in New York, early in April 1920, took a suite at the Biltmore, and embarked on a career of high living. These two hicks from the sticks, from the Deep South and from the antipodal Midwest, became pacesetters for the zesty sophisticates of New York society. There were lionized at parties, and on their way to and from parties, not simply because of Scott's growing literary reputation but also because they were becoming known as models for the heady hedonism that was part of the reaction to a long, cruel, and bloody war. Even after they left their New York hotel for a house in Westport, Connecticut, the partying, and the lionizing, and of course the drinking, continued unabated.

Scott was working on a second novel, but he and Zelda were drunk almost every night. A friend described Scott's going on the wagon for about a week and talking "as if it were a century." They were chronically in debt ("My God, debt is an awful thing!" Scott was to write pathetically fifteen reckless years later). With all the distractions, Scott took two years to finish *The Beautiful and Damned*; it was published in March 1922. To his other distractions were added those of traveling. In May 1921 he and Zelda, now two months pregnant, took off on a tour of Europe. The tour was uneventful, as was Zelda's pregnancy, although she went through a long and difficult labor. Frances Scott Fitzgerald, nicknamed Scottie, was born in October, in St. Paul. Six months later Zelda quietly cut short her second, and last, pregnancy with an abortion.

She had begun to act strangely, especially in her relationship with Scott. Shortly before their departure for Europe she had egged him into a confrontation with a bouncer in a New York speakeasy, from which he emerged quite badly damaged. Soon after the publication of *The Beautiful and Damned*, in a *New York Tribune* review bylined "Zelda Sayre," she revealed some resentment over Scott's borrowing from her richly descriptive diary and letters. "Mr. Fitzgerald," she wrote, "—I believe that is how he spells his name—seems to believe that plagiarism begins at home." She was too talented to enjoy being relegated to the rumble seat on Scott's ride to glory, and her precariously stable personality began showing some tiny but ominous cracks. It was about this time that John Dos Passos, on meeting her, found her attractive and bright—but "there was also this little strange streak." One evening at a carnival, during a ride on a Ferris wheel, Zelda turned to him and made a remark that stunned him. In later days he tried to recall it but could not; he could remember only that it was "so completely off track" that he had an impression of "peering into a dark abyss. . . . I thought to myself, suddenly, this woman is mad."

Her worsening condition might have been more noticeable in a demure, quiet type, but in Zelda it must have seemed merely more of the same as she and Scott strenuously maintained their image and position in the vanguard of the antic society. During a visit to southern France in 1924, however, after an abortive affair with a French naval aviator, she attempted suicide with her now ever-present sleeping pills. Many years later the aviator, asked about the affair, insisted that Zelda had never been unfaithful and that the Fitzgeralds had later dramatized the situation out of their "unhealthy imagination." (They did report, for example, that he had committed suicide, although he actually lived to enjoy a long and successful career with the French navy.) Zelda's slowly suffocating ego may have been calling out to Scott for recognition. Scott's ego survived, but he felt that their relationship could never be repaired. Zelda's condition, at least, was not repaired. The next year, during dinner with friends at a fancy restaurant on the Riviera, when Scott was elsewhere in the room lavishing attention on Isadora Duncan, Zelda suddenly stood on her chair, leaped over their table, and disappeared into the dark stairwell behind it. Having attracted Scott's attention, she retired to a washroom to wipe off her bloody knees and clothing.

Not that her behavior contrasted sharply with Scott's at this stage. They were the Fitzgeralds, dynamos of social eccentricity fueled inexhaustibly by alcohol. Hadley Hemingway described them as "inconvenient friends" who, for instance, would not hesitate to drop in unannounced at four in the morning to round out a playful evening. On one occasion, at a party given by two of their best friends, a drunken Scott began throwing the hosts' precious Venetian wineglasses over a parapet until his friend stopped him and asked him not to come back again for a while. Ernest Hemingway considered him a great nuisance, but also the possessor of a great talent which he, Hemingway, went out of his way at times to preserve and foster—but which, Hemingway maintained, would never flower so long as Scott stuck with that crazy Zelda.

Scott had his irrational moments—in short, especially in his cups. But he did not have Zelda's harrowing insecurity, her deep feeling of inadequacy. When they returned to America and crossed the continent to California in December 1926 (he had contracted to write a screenplay) and after he had a fling with a young actress in Hollywood, on their way back east she threw her fabulous platinum-and-diamond wristwatch, which he had given her before their marriage, out of the train window to climax a particularly violent quarrel. On their return they embarked on ceaseless rounds of drinking, quarreling, and making up until Zelda quite abruptly decided to give up her amateur writing and painting for a professional dancing career. Determined to be a second Pavlova, she practiced relentlessly at a New York studio and, when they went to Europe again, in Paris. But she was twenty-seven years old.

Her frenzied persistence drove her into a state of physical exhaustion and nervous prostration. She began having hallucinations, hearing voices, and throwing fits controllable only with morphine injections. In May 1930 Scott took her to a clinic and then, after a diagnosis of schizophrenia, to a sanitarium in Switzerland for long-term psychiatric treatment. She was pathetically aware of her condition, saddened by it, embarrassed by it, terrified by it. Putting her in an institution was like caging a swallow. Yet that was to be her lot, almost as often as not, for the rest of her life.

She was totally dependent on Scott now, emotionally as well as financially, yet separated from him emotionally as well as physically. Her letters tremble with the ceaseless aching of her soul, her frantic yearning for recovery and her return to freedom, and to him. On one occasion, after one of his telephone calls, she wrote him, "I walked on those telephone wires for two hours after, holding your love like a parasol to balance me." Scott supported her and Scottie financially and emotionally as well as he could, but the strain of precarious income and burgeoning debt so unnerved him that the bottle became an habitual escape hatch. In 1937–38 he wrote scripts for M-G-M in Hollywood, where he started his final novel, *The Last Tycoon*. There also he met the columnist Sheilah Graham. Their love affair, which she affectionately described in *Beloved Infidel*, lasted the rest of his life. He died of a heart attack in December 1940.

That Zelda knew of this liaison, at least specifically, seems unlikely. But she clearly sensed the estrangement in the letters which he faithfully wrote to her every week. Perhaps this softened the shock of his death: She took the news more calmly than expected. Nor was she bitter in the remaining years of her own life. Despite his problems—with writer's block, with debt, with alcoholism, with his gnawing ambition and emotional instability—Scott had managed to provide for her and Scottie throughout his life. She never stopped loving him, and he did not forsake her. He was, she wrote on Christmas Day, a few days after his death, "the best friend a person could have been to me."

One night in March 1948 a fire broke out in the sanitarium where Zelda was staying. Nine women were trapped in the flames and died. Among them was Zelda.

Helen Hayes
and
Charles MacArthur

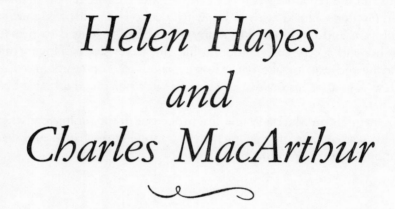

They were obviously two people who could never be happy
together. Everybody said so. His father, a fundamentalist preacher,
condemned any association with a woman who, as a professional
actress, was destined for hellfire. Her mother condemned any association with a newspaperman who would probably spend his life
drinking more money than he could earn. Their friends warned them
of their incompatibility: he the wild roué, she the shy young thing.
When they were married, in August 1928, they were destined to
spend the next twenty-eight years proving everybody wrong.

"Everybody" was right enough about their differences. Helen
Hayes, although in her mid-twenties and already an established
Broadway actress with more than a dozen years of stage experience,
was demure, retiring, and so properly brought up that, a friend once
commented, the mere mention of a farmer's daughter would send her
scurrying from the room in high color. Charles MacArthur, in sharp

contrast, was a congenital rapscallion whose chronic resort to liquor thoroughly loosened his already unraveled inhibitions. His irrepressible sense of humor was laced with a ribald wit; as a Chicago reporter, for instance, he once covered a story about a dentist convicted of raping a patient and proposed his own headline, "Tooth Doctor Fills Wrong Cavity." In his role of indomitable madcap he fascinated many women, including Dorothy Parker and Bea Lillie. And he totally captivated Helen.

From their first encounter at a cocktail party, when he poured some peanuts into her hand and told her he wished they were emeralds, she was irrevocably smitten. Over the next several months she saw him only rarely and casually, to her dismay. But one Saturday night he unexpectedly appeared in her dressing room at the Guild Theater after her performance in Shaw's *Caesar and Cleopatra*. Had he enjoyed the show? Well, no, actually he happened to be passing by the theater, and when he saw her picture on the poster he decided to stop in and say hello. Impulsively she asked him to come out for the weekend at the house on Long Island that she and her mother had rented for the summer. Just as impulsively, he suggested driving there with her that night. That weekend became one of many that summer, as Charlie became even more hopelessly ensnared.

Marriage naturally came up as a subject of their conversation. Helen was eager for it day before yesterday, but Charlie wanted first to write a hit play, a real stunner, for Broadway. He also had to divorce an almost forgotten wife. His success as a husband had been no greater than hers as a wife, and his success as a playwright had been much less solid than Helen's as an actress. Doubtless he preferred a marriage of equals. Early in 1928 *The Front Page*, by MacArthur and Ben Hecht, thoroughly stunned Broadway, and a new equality paved the way for the August wedding.

The ceremony was an unceremonious, two-minute affair squeezed in between performances of Helen's play of the moment, *Coquette*. They had to wait several weeks for their honeymoon, but by that time Charlie's royalty checks had grown fat enough to buy them a week in Bermuda. Their time there would have been idyllic except that, soon after their arrival, a shipboard friend died in their hotel under briefly suspicious circumstances. As a result, they spent most of their week giving testimony to the police and the coroner and were rather glad to get back to the peace and quiet of New York.

Helen soon had to go on tour with *Coquette*, in the first of many road-show roamings. Their frequent separations were grist for the mills of the marital Cassandras, who were sure that the marriage could not possibly stand the strain: Charlie would quickly resort to wine, women, and song. He did, indeed, resort to wine and perhaps some song, but not to women, and even the wine was kept under some control. When Howard Hughes bought the movie rights to *The Front Page* for a princely sum, Charlie was able to buy a cooperative apartment in New York's Upper East Side, symbol of his new, settled respectability—relatively speaking, of course.

This aura of respectability grew thicker after July 1929, when Helen informed him that she was pregnant. He immediately slipped into the role of oversolicitous father-to-be, scolding her for diving for pennies tossed into the pool by Maurice Chevalier at the Fairbanks-Pickford estate in Hollywood. (Once reassured, he scolded her for diving for anything less than quarters.) He had reason for his concern. Her pregnancy eventually became precarious enough for her doctor to order her to bed—for two months, as it turned out. Jed Harris, producer of *Coquette*, closed the show rather than hire another actress. This brought the pregnancy, which Helen had kept even from her mother as long as she could, a good deal of unwelcome publicity. Harris refused to pay the company any severance pay on the grounds that the contract called for none if the play were closed by, among other things, an act of God. The players filed a grievance, and the Actors Equity Association ruled in their favor—much to Charlie's satisfaction, since he had protested that he should be given credit where credit was due. Even more satisfying for him was Helen's formal presentation of their daughter, Mary, in February 1930—a result, she later confided, of their getting that apartment some nine months before.

Charlie spent a few of those months in Hollywood, writing the script for Ethel, Lionel, and John Barrymore in *Rasputin and the Empress*. When the script was finished, his fellow artists threw a farewell party for him. They then took him to the depot for his return to New York but, in their state of inebriated confusion, put him on the wrong train. In *his* state of inebriated befuddlement, he stayed on the train, was transferred to a ship, and woke up to his whereabouts during a stop at Havana. He finally made it to New York, where Helen, fortunately, was still only about eight months pregnant.

They were indulgent parents. They did not shower Mary with gifts, they engulfed her—dolls, books, building blocks, a regulation-size pool table, and a separate apartment so that, Charlie explained, she could live her own life whenever she felt ready for it. Neither the billiard table nor the apartment ever proved very useful.

Indeed, within a year they had leased out the apartments and bought an estate in California, near the MGM studio. Charlie had decided that what Helen needed was a movie career, over her protest that Hollywood was for glamor queens, and she was just a plain little thing. Her mentors in Hollywood agreed with her and tried to compensate with gaudy cosmetics and gaudier publicity (she was, briefly, the love child of a famous Broadway producer and actress), but they gave up when she obdurately refused to cooperate. When her first move, *The Sin of Madelon Claudet*, thoroughly rewritten by Charlie, was booed by the audience and panned by the critics, she was deeply disappointed and Charlie was devastated. Each felt some guilt over failing the other, but Charlie's was compounded by the knowledge that he had persuaded her to forsake a substantial and very promising career on Broadway. All this was soon forgotten, however, when a slightly revised version of the film was released in 1931, at Irving Thalberg's insistence, and became an instant hit with both audiences and reviewers. It even brought Helen an Oscar.

The plain little thing was on her way, starring with Ronald Colman in *Arrowsmith*, with Gary Cooper in *A Farewell to Arms*, and with Clark Gable in *The White Sister*, all in the space of a couple of years. Meanwhile Charlie, between bouts of well-oiled ennui, continued writing, usually in collaboration with good friend Ben Hecht. After much delay they produced a splendid script for Laurence Olivier and Merle Oberon in *Wuthering Heights*, and they provided Broadway, as a follow-up on their newspaper drama, *The Front Page*, with a hit play on show business, *Twentieth Century*, which in 1934 was translated into a classic movie.

Although Hollywood brought them a measure of artistic satisfaction, as well as some fame and wealth, the MacArthurs were never really comfortable in the rhinestone arena. According to Charlie, it was six-year-old Mary who persuaded them to move back to their New York apartment. It was not that she especially wanted to go, but rather that she wanted to keep up, in conspicuous transportation, with her best friend, a young lady who was chauffeured about in a

Dusenberg limousine with some twenty-seven cylinders and a bulging refrigerator. They started packing, said Charlie, within seconds after she broached the subject.

In New York the MacArthur-Hecht team went into the movie production business, renting a studio on Long Island and bringing out three movies in about as many years. *The Scoundrel*, with Noël Coward, earned them critical acclaim and an Oscar, and *Crime Without Passion*, with Claude Rains, was favorably reviewed. But a comedy called *Once in a Blue Moon* was mercilessly panned, labeled by a Boston critic as the worst movie ever made, and *Soak the Rich* was similarly received, labeled by the same critic as the second-worst movie ever made. None of the films made any noticeable money.

Meanwhile, Helen was doing much better on Broadway, starring in *The Good Fairy* and *Mary of Scotland* and in 969 performances of *Victoria Regina*, in each of which she aged, cosmetically, more than fifty years. This play's success was as historic as its subject. On the road it was welcomed with AOK reviews and SRO audiences, grossing over two million dollars. Quite incidentally, Helen demonstrated her perennial innocence in New Orleans, where the cast was put up at the lavishly appointed Roosevelt Hotel. No, she said, she would rather stay in the French Quarter, at a picturesque old inn with white columns supporting a classically ornate second-story balcony. It was only after her more sophisticated husband arrived to join her that she learned she was staying at a very classy, heavily atmospheric bordello.

On their return to New York they began to have doubts about their Upper East Side apartment as a place to raise a child. Mary needed some outdoor living beyond Central Park, Helen felt, and a home with an attic. And they became frightened when a child in their building became the victim of a brief but nonetheless real kidnapping. In Nyack, a small town on the Hudson River some thirty miles north of Manhattan, they bought a fine old Victorian house with an attic and twenty rooms besides. It was a rather large house for so small a family, but they had not been able to increase and multiply as they had hoped, and their future in this respect seemed bleak. As so it was that Mary, shortly before her ninth birthday, was presented with an adopted baby brother, James Gordon MacArthur.

They doted a lot, Charlie especially. The children's need for entertainment was just what *he* needed, giving him plenty of opportunity for antic embroidering. Like many fathers, for example, he made a snowman for his children; unlike many fathers, he dyed it purple and gave it a beard and an Indian headdress. When he demonstrated to Mary the use of a spoon as a catapult for mashed potatoes, he could not resist using the forehead of her rather straitlaced governess as a target of opportunity. Except for a couple of trips to Europe, he and Helen stayed home with the children as much as their busy careers would permit. He and/or Helen, that is, since their different careers often pulled them apart, sometimes with the whole continent between them. On one of Charlie's trips to Hollywood, he and Ben Hecht wrote the script for *Gunga Din*; perhaps because he found it hard to write anything tolerant of British imperialism, this was also the visit during which, in one evening, Charlie and John Barrymore drank everything, but everything, in the latter's capacious cellar.

World War II brought a long separation, with Charlie flitting about Europe and Asia as a major in the Chemical Warfare Service and general cutup in any service he might be attached to, and with Helen at home with the children, her role as Harriet Beecher Stowe on Broadway, and her benefit appearances. His letters softened her pangs of loneliness for him, as did his occasional unexpected appearances, as when he returned from India with a small package of emeralds and told her he wished they were peanuts.

Before the war, and during it, Helen and Mary had appeared on stage together, and the summer of 1949 found them in Westport, Connecticut, in a tryout performance of a comedy, *Good Housekeeping*. Several days after Mary began feeling vaguely ill, she died of bulbar poliomyelitis. Helen might have died of grief but for Charlie's efforts to rescue her. First he arranged with Josh Logan for a play and tried to persuade her to appear in it. She would not, could not. Then he took her to an isolated spot in New Mexico for uninterrupted rest. When that failed to revive her, he tried travel, to California and Hawaii. When that failed too, he brought her back to Nyack and tried again to interest her in the Logan play, *The Wisteria Trees*. This time she agreed, wanly, and two months later was again the darling of critics and audiences. But what really brought her back to an interest in life was her work with other parents of polio victims and with the March of Dimes Foundation.

As Helen gradually recovered, however, Charlie gradually succumbed. His flashes of merriment grew less frequent, more subdued. His drinking crept into the morning hours. As the years passed, a reminder of Mary still would bring tears to his eyes. Helen, although she cut down on her theater work to be with him, could do little more than watch helplessly at his side in the hospital, holding his hand. Her last words to him were "I love you." And his last words to her, delivered with a wink, were "You should." But of course "should" never entered into it.

Once again she had to struggle up from the depths. This time Charlie was not there to help. But she had her devoted actor son Jim and her grandchildren and her friends and her work—and a comforting return to her Roman Catholic religion. The combination brought her to the surface once again. She missed Charlie terribly but found great solace in lovely memories. When they were contemplating marriage, Charlie had promised her that at least she would never be bored. And she never was.

Katharine Hepburn
and
Spencer Tracy

It did not start off very well. Although Katharine Hepburn had long admired Spencer Tracy's work, especially in *Captains Courageous* and *Dr. Jekyll and Mr. Hyde*, she had never met him. Now, in 1942, at her suggestion, they were to work together in *Woman of the Year*. She could not resist wearing her male-intimidating platform shoes to their first meeting and saying, when the producer Joseph Mankiewicz introduced him, "I'm afraid I'm a little tall for you, Mr. Tracy." Tracy, an inch or two short of six feet, glowered as only Tracy could, but silently. He would, Mankiewicz assured the as yet untamed Kate, cut her down to size.

He did. Or perhaps it would be more accurate to say that she cut herself down to size, to fit his standards. She was notorious for imposing her standards on others through sheer force of overpowering personality, but not on Tracy. She could be an iron-willed terror with studio heads, producers, directors, other star performers, and lesser lights, but with him she was uncharacteristically subdued, receptive, even submissive. She was actively stubborn, he passively. She was vibrantly energetic, while he could make shuffling seem a triumph of willpower, yet it was she who succumbed, the irresistible force sitting at the feet of the immovable object.

It was love that did it, the love that grew between them during the making of *Woman of the Year*. It was Kate's idea that they should work together; she was sure that he was just right for the role of the hard-bitten sportswriter against hers of the dynamic political columnist. At first it seemed that he would not be available, since he was in Florida for *The Yearling*, but when production of that picture was suspended (to be resumed four years later, with Gregory Peck), he was only too glad to leave the hot and sticky swamplands for the comparative comfort of Hollywood. Kate was greatly relieved. She seemed to have her heart in the project, one way or another.

By the time the movie was finished, this unlikely pair had become a loving couple and a celebrated professional team. As a team they were welcomed by the critics, who enjoyed the balancing act between the two very different personalities that they brought to their roles. Clearly they had a bright future together. But as a couple they faced an obstacle, since Spencer and his wife, Louise, were churchgoing Catholics. The romance was long gone from their marriage, yet divorce was simply out of the question. They were united, furthermore, in their concern for their son, John, who was deaf from birth and was the inspiration for Louise's generous efforts on behalf of deaf children in the community, efforts that earned her Spencer's enduring admiration and support.

It was, indeed, her generosity that melted the obstacle down to manageable size. Neither jealous nor possessive, she could see no reason to make Spencer's life miserable, nor Kate's for that matter. She softened their predicament into an arrangement, an unspoken agreement, with Kate as the other woman, the most important woman, in Spencer's life. For Kate, as the daughter of a militant feminist for whom marriage rated quite low on the distaff totem pole, and as an actress bent on an uncluttered career, the arrangement was just fine. And since she could live with it, so could Spencer.

What he could not live with was liquor, because he could not live without it. When he and Kate met, he was in his early forties (she in her early thirties), and his drinking had already made him a chronically sick man. Kate nursed him tenderly, compassionately. She helped cure him of the addiction, although she could not restore his health. When he was in the hospital, she and Louise spelled each other at his bedside. (It was indeed an extraordinary triangle, alive with several kinds of love.) Spencer, for all his star status, was hardly the matinee-idol type, like Clark Gable or Robert Taylor. It was not as an Adonis that he attracted Kate, yet neither was he a man to bring out a woman's mothering instinct, of which Kate had precious little anyway. He did have his own brand of quizzical, incredulous masculinity, often expressed in films with lowered head, raised eyebrows, intent stare, and compressed lips. It was expressed also, on screen and off, in a refreshing but sometimes staggering directness of speech. Kate accepted from him more abusive teasing than she would have taken from a score of other people. Any tendency she might have toward self-inflation was regularly corrected by Spencer's ever ready needle. Nevertheless he was plainly devoted to her, dependent on her, delighted with her company, grateful for her love. At times, for instance, he would rib her mercilessly about her thinness, calling her "a bag of bones," but he clearly was happy with every bone in the bag. Maudlin he was not.

Their next movie, *Keeper of the Flame*, was released later in 1942. It flopped. A movie with a message against closet fascists, it was notably deficient in humor, presented Kate in a role in which (according to George Cukor, the director) she seemed merely highfalutin, which for the new team was (according to the reviewer for *Time*) "a high point of significant failure." Spencer's performance received better notices than Kate's; he may not have taken the picture as seriously as his partner, who was, for instance, an ardent supporter of Henry Wallace, currently the darling of the Democratic left wing. For Kate, the failure was compounded when she returned to the New York stage in *Without Love*, a critically roasted turkey that kept her away from the theater for the next eight years.

Yet the play, somewhat revamped, was destined to become a hit movie. After appearing separately in war-related movies—Spencer in *A Guy Named Joe* and *Thirty Seconds Over Tokyo* and Kate in *Dragon Seed*, the rather labored version of the Pearl Buck novel—the team came together again early in 1945, transforming *Without Love* into an entertaining and successful comedy. But the roller coaster dipped down once more, for both of them.

For Spencer the summer of 1945 was torture. The agony came in the form of his first stage play in fifteen years, Robert Sherwood's *The Rugged Path*. For the first tryout performance in Providence, Rhode Island, he came down with an almost paralyzing case of nerves. Despite a high fever and a nest of stabbing butterflies in his stomach, he got through the play, with Kate standing anxiously in the wings, ready to comfort him between the acts, even to do whatever cleaning up was necessary after he upchucked. She stuck with him through the entire ten weeks, in Providence, in Boston, in New York, giving him courage when he wanted to give up, keeping his dressing room livable, and keeping a comfortable house for him and his brother Carroll. On their return she got trapped in a sentimental mishmash of a movie called *Song of Love*, and it was not until 1948 that the roller coaster started up again.

State of the Union, a Broadway hit by Lindsay and Crouse, had attracted the notice of Frank Capra, the Hollywood director. The play's protagonist, a neophyte presidential candidate resembling the 1944 campaign's Wendell Willkie, seemed an ideal role for Spencer Tracy. For the role of his wife, a woman devoted to keeping him on the straight and narrow, Capra pictured Claudette Colbert. He bought the movie rights to the play, signed Spencer and Colbert, and set up a production schedule. On the day before shooting was to start, Colbert, who had broken an ankle, informed Capra that her quitting time every day would have to be five o'clock, at the insistence of her doctor-husband and her agent-brother. Capra, by now too fully committed, told her to pick up her marbles and go home.

He reported the situation on the phone, uneasily, to Louis B. Mayer, who suggested that he call Tracy, at least to let him know that the film was missing a leading lady before he read about it in a gossip column. Capra did so, adding a desperate plea that the actor come up with some names for replacement purposes. Well, there's Kate, replied Spencer—she's been working with me on my lines here at home, taking Colbert's part, and she'd be readier than anybody. Capra could not believe that a prima donna would fill in for someone else, as second choice, without using the emergency as an opportunity for a little extortion. When Spencer said that he would put Kate on the phone, Capra braced himself for lots of talk about money, perquisites, billing, what have you. What he got, instead, was Kate saying, "Sure, what the hell—when do we start?" And they started right on time. And, despite some friction with Adolphe Menjou, a right-winger who played a machine-type pol in the movie and who had fingered colleagues for the House Un-American Activities Committee, *State of the Union*, played by professionals, was a solid hit.

When their work on the picture was over, Kate joined Spencer in a visit to England, where he made a forgettable movie called *Edward, My Son*, with Deborah Kerr. (He stayed with the Laurence Oliviers while Kate discreetly slept at Claridge's.) Meanwhile, Louis B. Mayer was pressing for another Tracy-versus-Hepburn comedy along the lines of *Woman of the Year*. (Spencer usually got first billing; once, when Garson Kanin asked him if he had never heard of "ladies first," he replied that they were talking about movies, not lifeboats.) In response, Kate and Spencer on their return revived a script, written by their talented friends Garson Kanin and his wife, Ruth Gordon, that told a story of two lawyers, husband and wife, finding themselves on opposing sides of a murder case. They were in their element again. *Adam's Rib* was a smashing success and has become a classic.

That was in 1949. In 1950 and 1951 Spencer was busy with *The Father of the Bride* and its sequel, *Father's Little Dividend*, with Joan Bennett and Elizabeth Taylor, while Kate played Rosalind in *As You Like It* for a year's run at the Cort Theater in New York. (His visits east were conspiratorially discreet.) As the play's run ended, Kate was visited by John Huston and Spencer's old friend Humphrey Bogart with a proposal that she play the spinster missionary in *The African Queen*, to be shot that year in Africa. She accepted with delight and spent most of 1951 putting up with the Belgian Congo and with Bogart, who shared Tracy's intolerance for any affectation. She and Lauren Bacall, who was along merely for the dubious ride, served heroically as Florence Nightingales ministering to the tropically ailing weaker sex (for a while Kate herself was down with dysentery). The nightmare produced a splendid picture, of course, and this pleased Kate enormously. But she was also pleased to learn, on her return to New York late in 1951, that the team of Kanin and Gordon had dreamt up a new movie for the team of Tracy and Hepburn, to be shot entirely within the comfortable confines of southern California's Riviera Country Club.

The movie gave Spencer an opportunity for a little more ribbing of his beloved "bag of bones." At one point the script called for him, playing a sportswriter, to refer to Kate, playing a professional golfer, as "well stacked." He objected to the line as unrealistic. Under pressure to offer some alternative, he came up with one, more realistic and much more memorable: "There ain't much meat on her, but what there is is cherce." It helped to make *Pat and Mike* a popular film, with both critics and audiences. And the film let Kate look a lot chercer than she had looked in *The African Queen*.

Then came a period of separation. During 1953 and 1954 Kate was at first in London, doing Shaw's *The Millionairess* on the stage, and then in Venice for David Lean's movie *Summertime*, with only brief visits from Spencer. She spent much of 1955 in Australia doing Shakespeare with the Old Vic Company, and during that time they saw each other not at all. Spencer had a rather bad time of it, making two pictures consecutively that required him to work in mountainous country, and the high altitudes made him ill. He began drinking heavily again and was even dropped from one of the movies. Kate could not be of much help to him even after her return from Australia, since she had to leave almost immediately for England to make what turned out to be a disastrous film, *The Iron Petticoat*.

But in the spring of 1956 she was able to go with Spencer to Cuba, where he was slated for the starring role in the movie version of Hemingway's *The Old Man and the Sea*. It might have been a pleasant time for them, but the weather was generally disagreeable and the people involved in the production even more so. It was an unhappy experience for all concerned, except that Kate found some comfort in painting a number of sunny seascapes. For Spencer the misery continued on their return to Hollywood, where much of the movie had to be shot again in an immense studio tank, leaving him worn-out at the end of each day. Since Kate also was working in Hollywood, rather ill cast in *The Rainmaker* opposite Burt Lancaster, she and Spencer could be together after work, and that was when he needed her most.

What they both needed was the fun and relaxation of doing another comedy together. It came in 1957 in the form of *Desk Set*, with Spencer playing an efficiency expert bent on automating Kate's television research department. It was a delight for all concerned— the critics, audiences, distributors, cast, and especially the stars. Kate was filled with joy to see Spencer relaxing, enjoying his work once more.

Yet their careers separated them again when Kate went to Stratford, Connecticut, on a rescue mission for the American Shakespeare Festival company, playing Portia in *The Merchant of Venice* and Beatrice in *Much Ado About Nothing*, and to England for a movie version of Tennessee Williams's *Suddenly Last Summer*. The moviemaking proved an ordeal, largely because Montgomery Clift, not yet recovered from his terrible auto accident, distracted Kate the actress with unspoken but irresistible appeals to Kate the nurse.

Kate the nurse was anxious also, of course, about Spencer, and on her return from England—and after stopping off at Stratford to play Viola in *Twelfth Night* and Cleopatra in *Antony and Cleopatra*—she relegated Kate the actress to temporary retirement while she focused her efforts on her beloved's health and welfare. It meant more traveling. After making *Inherit the Wind*, he went to Hawaii for *The Devil at Four O'Clock* and then to Germany for *Judgment at Nuremberg*. Since he disliked traveling and hated flying, he needed her support, which she gave unstintingly. She accompanied him on both trips—as usual, discreetly.

Discretion has its limits, and so does journalistic restraint. Early in 1962 *Look* published an article on Tracy alluding to their hitherto unpublicized affair. It hurt them personally but not professionally. Spencer was asked to do the narration for the epic *How the West Was Won*, and Kate was asked to play Mary Tyrone in the movie of Eugene O'Neill's *Long Day's Journey Into Night*, a role that brought her a ninth nomination for an Academy Award.

In the summer of 1963, as the couple were on their way to have a picnic at Malibu Beach, Spencer went limp, complaining of sharp pains in his chest. In the ambulance on the way to a hospital, he registered another complaint. "Kate," he asked, "isn't this a hell of a way to go to a picnic?" He recovered, but the two of them disappeared into virtual seclusion for the next three years. They emerged from it only in response to a compelling offer from Stanley Kramer, who asked them late in 1966 to appear together in *Guess Who's Coming to Dinner*. Although Kate was up to it, Spencer was not; yet they could hardly turn it down.

It was hard on Spencer, whose energy level had fallen so low that he could work only in the morning. The picture could not be insured with him in it, so Kramer assumed the risk himself. But Spencer stuck with it until finally one day he was able to point out to Kramer that the script did not call for anything more from him—"if I died tonight at home it wouldn't make any difference—you could still release the picture." He did live long enough to know of the film's great success, though not long enough to know that it would bring Kate an Oscar.

Very early one morning in June 1967, Kate, sleeping in a small room not far from Spencer's bedroom, heard him go to the kitchen and open the refrigerator door. But another, strange sound alarmed her, and she hurried out to the kitchen, where she found him sitting at a table with a glass of milk in front of him. He was dead. Discreetly, she did not attend his funeral. And thus ended, wrote Charles Champlin of the *Los Angeles Times*, "an association as beautiful and dignified as any this town has ever known."

It was by no means the end of Kate's career—within a year she had thrown herself into *The Lion in Winter* and won another Oscar—but it was the end of her love life. She had had a quarter of a century "of perfect companionship with a man among men," she once told a reporter, and she had "never regretted it." In addition, she said, there was a "tiny thing about Spencer—he made the best cup of coffee in the world."

Eva Duarte
and
Juan Perón

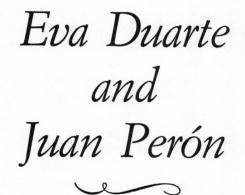

One day in the fall of 1934 Maria Eva Duarte, sweet fifteen and eminently kissable, arrived in Buenos Aires to seek fame and fortune. She had come from the little city of Junin, some 150 miles to the west, where her widowed mother and three sisters and brother lived in modest, respectable circumstances. She had high hopes and colorful dreams, sprung largely from her addiction to Argentine movie magazines, but she had only a sixth-grade education, a reedy and unreliable voice, a very small command of the piano, a rustic accent, and no training or experience in any kind of public entertainment. For the next six years she would live in the same cramped boardinghouse room in the great metropolis. But she was pretty, smart, and relentlessly ambitious. Six years after she left that boardinghouse, she became First Lady of Argentina.

Her first two years in Buenos Aires were a time of scrabbling poverty and continual rejection at theaters and booking offices, a

213

time of misery relieved sporadically only by the restrained generosity of *señores amigos*. In 1936 she landed a small part in a Spanish version of Lillian Hellman's *The Children's Hour* and during the next three years appeared in a number of stage and musical-comedy roles ranging from insignificant to inconsequential. But in 1939 she broke into radio, whose mass audiences were not so particular about unsophisticated accents and lack of talent. By 1943 she had risen to the status of soap opera star. By that time, too, she had begun to appear in movies, in minor roles at first although her radio reputation increasingly furthered her movie prospects, and vice versa. Later that year she became hostess of a radio talk show on which current topics were discussed, including political topics. Among the latter the most popular and recurrent subject was the inexorable rise of Colonel Juan Perón in the latest junta. He was coming to be known as Argentina's strongman, a man with a very promising future. He was a widower, conspicuously vigorous in his forty-ninth year and known to be fond of sweet young things. Eva Duarte set her cap.

She was already acquainted and perhaps quite familiar with several members of the junta, having met them through the officer charged with control of the airwaves. Perón's position in the predominantly fascist government—"neutral" Argentina was the only Latin American country to maintain diplomatic relations with the Axis powers almost to the end of World War II—was that of minister of labor. He had lost no time in solidifying his control of the politically powerful trade unions, in the Mussolini style. Meanwhile, Eva was furthering her movie career through her friendliness with the junta, which controlled the country's supply of raw film as well as almost everything else. In the summer of 1943, having left the boardinghouse three years earlier for posher shelter, she took an apartment in an excruciatingly fashionable district bordering downtown. Although she had yet to meet Juan Perón, she was already promoting his interests at every opportunity.

They finally met that October, at a party given for the junta members by her radio station. Although they became friends and doubtless occasional bedfellows, it was not until early the following year that he grew interested enough to desert his current teenager and take up residence in Eva's apartment building. She made full use of this arrangement not only to distract him from government business but also to participate in it, playing a crucial role in his transformation from first among equals to first amid subordinates.

After Juan became vice president in 1944 during a round of musical chairs, she began going with him to union meetings, where her lower-class accent and feverish hostility toward the country's entrenched, parasitical plutocracy soon made her a very persuasive speaker in his behalf. Her political devotion to him was manifest, and their personal relationship was generally known or suspected. One evening on the radio, just as she took up her position in the studio, an announcer's voice was heard saying into an inadvertently open mike, "The tart is on." (The government immediately canceled all the station's commercials for forty-eight hours.) When Juan was told that some conservative officers were worried over the effect of the scandal on governmental and military authority, he came out with a public statement. "My adversaries charge that I associate with women," he complained, "and I do, of course. Do they expect me to go out with men?"

The interweaving of the political and personal in the bond between them was highlighted in October 1945. Uprisings against his despotic rule had become so uncontrollable that he was forced to resign and was imprisoned on the 6th. Eva spent the following ten days visiting friendly labor leaders, urging them to action. On the 17th a general strike forced the government to release him and restore all his offices and perquisites. And on the 22nd, gratefully, he married Eva. (A lack of public announcement suggested that they had been married all along.)

Argentina had not had a national election since 1928, and the iron was hot for striking. After a campaign reminiscent of elections in Nazi Germany, Juan (who had become a civilian, briefly, for the occasion) led his party in a spectacular victory. Although he himself received only about 55 percent of the popular vote for president, his party took all fifteen provincial governorships, all the seats in the upper house of the national legislature, and 70 percent of the seats in the lower house. Eva, who had fully shared in the burdens of campaigning with him, fully shared in his triumph.

And she more than shared in his government. Her office in the Labor Secretariat became the administrative hub of that government. While the president wrestled with the big problems, she handled appointments, favors, executive orders (for his compliant approval), bribes (her jewelry and furs were more than she could wear), deposits for their Swiss bank accounts, and personal vengeance. While busily skimming, the exultant couple did not forget who had put them in power. He doubled and in many cases tripled military officers' pay within his first three years. In their first five years, under her auspices, the workers' share of the country's national income increased almost 100 percent, bringing them to a level of food, shelter, clothing, and recreation that they had never known. Since prices were controlled, the money for all this came chiefly from those who had it, the notoriously rich owners of manufacturing and agricultural industries. Small wonder that, in the palatial houses and apartments of Argentina's plutocrats, Eva was referred to as "she" or "her." Or perhaps occasionally as "it."

The Peróns were, conspicuously and doubtless genuinely, a loving couple. Certainly they were mutually protective. Just as she had come to his rescue during his imprisonment, so he now used his status as autocrat to protect her from any physical danger, to silence her critics, to punish any signs of disrespect. During her tour of Europe in 1947, an Argentine plutocratic family living in Paris failed to throw a party for her and soon thereafter lost all their property, valued at a quarter of a billion dollars, to government seizure. When she learned that the British royal family would be vacationing in Scotland during her scheduled stay in London, she angrily canceled her visit to England, and a few months later, after prices of Argentine beef and wheat to the United Kingdom had been increased by 20 percent over those charged on the Continent, British railroads and other properties in Argentina were abruptly nationalized.

Yet just as she was riding highest, she was struck down. In June 1951 she began feeling ill. Although she continued to drive herself in such activities as her highly publicized charity work and her supervision of the government's indispensable mass-media propaganda machine, her energy was on the wane. In August she had to deny reports that she would run for vice president with her husband in the November election; her illness, although it was not mentioned, was a major reason, the other being that Juan had been warned by the military panjandrums that her appointment to the ticket might spark a rebellion in the officer corps. Her public appearances grew fewer. On October 17 she helped celebrate the anniversary of her man's return to power by showing herself beside him on a Casa Rosada balcony to the adoring thousands below while he gave her the country's most prestigious decoration and proclaimed the date as a national St. Evita's Day. Just before going to the hospital in November she recorded a lachrymose speech urging his reelection.

The results of the election were more satisfying than those of the surgery, but she did rally briefly afterward. Yet she was doomed. Although official medical reports of her condition were sparse and uninformative, the consensus of historians appears to be that she was suffering from a neglected breast cancer which had slowly spread through her body. Her condition seemed to alienate Juan, whose adherence to his recreational schedule as well as his official calendar demonstrated something less than overwhelming grief and concern. On one occasion shortly before her death in July, as her weeping family hovered around her bed, she emerged long enough from her drugged state to notice him standing to the side, dry-eyed and abstracted. "Everyone weeps for me," she said to him, "except you."

The nation after her death was more demonstrative. Mourning was quite literally the order of the season, not merely of the day. A youth who made the mistake of laughing in a crowded streetcar drew three years in prison. The vast collection of toadies accumulated by the Peróns over the previous nine years acted out paroxysms of fawning grief at hundreds of official mourning ceremonies. Eva's body was embalmed especially for enduring public veneration, like Lenin's. Two weeks elapsed before the final obsequies.

Even then the body was not buried but was stashed in a large, heavily guarded room where a Spanish anatomist-taxidermist worked day after day to complete the embalming process for what he called "absolute corporeal permanence." Meanwhile, Juan sought to bury his grief in a return to teenage distractions. The body, it was announced, would be housed in a stupendously monumental tomb. Like many, or most, of the regime's grandiose projects, this one never got beyond its cornerstone, which Juan laid two years and many teenagers after Eva's death. During those two years the corrupt tyranny caved in before the pressure of its enemies and its own follies (inflation, for instance, had lately burst out of control). Juan and Eva's family fled the country, quite separately, leaving Eva's body behind. Finding no one eager to claim it, the new government shipped it to Europe, and eventually it was buried, secretly and unceremoniously, in Milan. In Argentina the cornerstone of Eva's gargantuan sepulcher was destroyed.

When Juan returned to Argentina in November 1972, at the age of seventy-seven, he had another wife, Isabel, aged forty-one. The incompetence and venality of the plutocracy paved their way. A year later the couple were overwhelmingly elected president and vice president by a disillusioned, deluded, desperate electorate. When Juan died the following July, Isabel succeeded him as president. She lasted as figurehead until early in 1976, when an inflation rate of over 200 percent and a military coup persuaded her to take early retirement—but not before she had Eva's body found and brought back to Argentina in the hope of providing her own brief incumbency with an aura of sainthood by association. After the coup, the body was finally buried in the Duarte family plot.

Lauren Bacall
and
Humphrey Bogart

⌒

Everybody was against the marriage. But everybody. In 1943
Humphrey Bogart was forty-four; Betty Bacall was only nineteen
("Lauren" was never more than a melodious moniker for Hollywood
and Broadway). He had been married three times, she was romantically and sexually about as experienced as Little Bo Peep. His
fondness for alcohol was as chronic as her indifference to it. He and
his current wife, an authentic alcoholic, had earned a resounding
reputation for spectacular brawling in a town noted for boisterous
domestic relations. Betty's mother vociferously opposed her daughter's interest in such a man (she had been hoping for a clean-cut
Jewish boy like that nice Kirk Douglas). Her brothers, Betty's uncles,
warned against expecting happiness or permanence in the marriage.
Howard Hawks, her mentor and the director of *To Have and Have
Not*, in which she and Bogart were starred, was furious over his
protégé's infatuation, seeing it as a serious threat to her career and to

the success of his considerable efforts on her behalf. Even her long-absent father interrupted years of relentless neglect long enough to write her a letter objecting to the marriage.

As for Howard Hawks, he had only himself to blame. It was he who took his wife's suggestion that he bring that pretty young *Harper's Bazaar* fashion model out to Hollywood. And it was he who decided to cast her opposite Bogart in *To Have and Have Not*. That, of course, was as far as his responsibility went. Betty and Bogie took it from there. One day soon after she had taken the screen test that got her the part, as she was approaching Hawks's office, Bogie emerged from it and announced that he had just seen the test and that he expected that they "would have a lot of fun together." This must have been, at least, the understatement of the week.

He meant it professionally, of course. He enjoyed his work and was looking forward to doing this movie. Romance was not so much as a glint in his eye, nor in hers. He was much too busy with his tumultuous marriage to get serious with a starlet. As for her, she had greatly preferred Hawks's earlier, very tentative decision to cast her in a movie with Cary Grant. She saw it then as a choice between yum and yuck, but when Hawks assigned her to yuck, she accepted his judgment with good grace. Bogart was, after all, a twenty-four-carat superstar.

The change may have come as early as their first scene together, the memorable matchbook scene with the line ". . .just whistle. . . You do know how to whistle, don't you?" Bacall was shaking with stage fright, so badly that she could not light her cigarette at first. To keep her head from trembling conspicuously, she lowered her chin somewhat (and thus gave birth to "The Look," the forties' contribution to smoldering seductiveness). Bogart tried to calm her nerves, to ease her tension, with laughter. He joked with her, kidded with her in a gentle, friendly way, until she had relaxed enough to get through the scene. He was very good at this sort of thing, had a natural talent for it that caused her to write, years later, that throughout their life together, "the most fun was where he was."

She had not expected such kindness from the silver screen's foremost tough guy, nor had he expected such sparkling responsiveness in the give-and-take of their working together. Three weeks into the shooting schedule he asked for her phone number. They began seeing a good deal of each other, and by the end of the schedule the affair had become quite serious. Not only serious but grim, since Bogart's wife could easily fly out of control under the influence of jealousy laced with alcohol. In their anxiety to keep the affair inconspicuous, the actors resorted to such timeworn devices as furtive phone calls and secret rendezvous. In addition, Bogart became quite demanding when drunkenly depressed, phoning at odd hours of the night or early morning, usually from bars, to request companionship and transportation. This treatment infuriated Betty's mother, but Betty was too much in love to do anything but eagerly comply.

The lovers' anxiety was complicated by other considerations. Bogart was tormented by the difference in their ages. This young girl's infatuation, he feared, could not last very long. He was only moderately comforted by his friend Peter Lorre's suggestion that he might be able to hold on to her for "maybe five years—isn't five years better than none?" He worried, too, about her being in show business. His various and sundry marriages had foundered chiefly on his actress-wives' ambitions—why should he expect anything different this time? Betty shared this latter concern, from another angle. She was obsessively in love with Bogie and felt that he was similarly in love with her. She wanted to marry him and considered the marriage far more important than anything in her possible career. Yet, given Bogie's highly adhesive wife, she had no way of knowing when, or even if, such a marriage might take place. She was by no means indifferent to her career, and she was terrified that Howard Hawks might carry out his threat to have her exiled to Monogram Pictures, the B-movie graveyard for unruly actors.

A final complication was Bogart's solicitude for his wife, who would occasionally emerge from her alcoholic trances long enough to promise to reform and to beg for another chance. He felt obliged to give her several other chances, thereby delaying the inevitable divorce but also earning Betty's reluctant admiration for his resilient compassion. Eventually the wife, admitting that she had had her last chance, went to Reno, and in May 1945, two years after that fateful meeting at the door of Howard Hawks's office, Betty Bacall became Mrs. Bogart.

She really was Mrs. Bogart, loving spouse and housewife. Although she had starred with Bogart in the highly successful *To Have and Have Not* and *The Big Sleep* and with Charles Boyer in the not so successful *Confidential Agent*, and although her public image as a *femme fatale* had spread throughout the country, she became quite a homebody, doing very little acting over the next few years. The outstanding exception was her work with Bogart in *Dark Passage*. They were utterly, serenely happy in each other's company. For the first eight years of their marriage, they were never apart. When he left Hollywood to shoot a film on location, she went along. Even John Huston's notorious passion for inaccessible sites—notably the mountain fastnesses of Mexico for *The Treasure of the Sierra Madre* and the jungle recesses of the Dark Continent for *The African Queen*—did not dismay her. Nor did the corridors of darkest Washington, where they went (also with Huston, and others) to protest against the ravages of the House Un-American Activities Committee in 1947.

In addition, the loving spouse and housewife also became a loving mother. Their son, Steve, was born in January 1949; their daughter, Leslie—named after Leslie Howard, who in 1935 had given Bogart his start in movies by refusing to play in *The Petrified Forest* without him—in August 1952. She also became an enthusiastic hostess, giving talk-of-the-town parties which often started as soirees for a few close friends (the David Nivens, Frank Sinatra, Spencer Tracy and Katharine Hepburn) and burgeoned into y'all-come social jam sessions. "Y'all" generally consisted of assorted denizens of the film colony together with visiting literary and show biz celebrities from the East Coast. And she learned to share his passion for sailing.

The first separation occurred in early 1953, when Bogart had to go to Italy to make *Beat the Devil*, again for John Huston. Betty had been offered a splendid part in *How to Marry a Millionaire*, to be shot in Hollywood. They agreed that their marriage had proved more than strong enough to survive the separation, but they also agreed that she would join him in Italy just as soon as *Millionaire* was in the can. She did so, the marriage survived quite intact, and the good life continued. In 1956 they were delighted when Warner Brothers offered to cast them together in a movie based on John P. Marquand's *Melvin Goodwin, U.S.A.* They had lived together in loving contentment for more than ten years, but they had not worked in a movie together in eight years, and they were looking forward to it.

But it was not to be. One day in the fall of 1956 Greer Garson happened to meet Bogart at lunch and was terribly disturbed when he went into a fit of coughing, so disturbed that she insisted on his seeing her doctor at the Beverly Hills Clinic. He had had the cough almost all his life—an unusually sensitive throat, he had told Betty—but now it was diagnosed as a symptom of cancer of the esophagus. This diagnosis inaugurated a year of drastic surgery, hospitals, doctors, and nurses for a man who had hardly known a sick day in his life, a year of personal suffering for him and vicarious suffering for Betty. She stayed at his side throughout his ordeal, at the hospital and at home, providing what therapy she could, nursing him, feeding him, tending to his wants, arranging for visits from his friends. She had made a happy home for him, and she meant to keep it as happy as possible till the very end. He may have had a sense of this on his return from the hospital, when, as he was being carried up the stairs, he saw her waiting on the landing with Steve and Leslie. "This," he said, "is what it's all about. This is why marriage is worth it."

He died in January 1957. The marriage that could not possibly work had worked just splendidly. There were some tears in it, but mostly laughter. Lots of laughter, lots of love. Making love, Bogie once said, is "the most fun you can have without laughing." Over the ensuing years, Betty could treasure, along with her memories of that delightful time, the words of Moss Hart in his letter of deep sympathy and encouragement: "You and you alone were the one person in all of his life that Bogie loved the most tenderly and the most deeply—that he took the most pride in and that he relished and enjoyed above all other human beings."

Ingrid Bergman
and
Roberto Rossellini

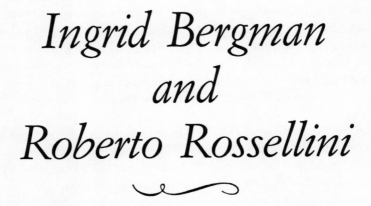

From the start, even before they met, Roberto Rossellini felt that his relationship with Ingrid Bergman would not be purely professional. Perhaps he had, Italian style, overinterpreted her remark, in her first letter to him, that the only Italian she knew was *ti amo*. Even without the letter, Anna Magnani, his ladylove at the time, suspected enough to be jealous. When he received a wire from England while they were having dinner at a restaurant, her temperature began to rise, since she knew that Ingrid was in England. His elaborate pretense of pocketing it indifferently further infuriated her until, after mixing the spaghetti thoroughly in a bowl with the usual colorful condiments, she dumped the contents over him, Italian style, and left in triumphant dignity. "I suppose," Ingrid wrote years later in her autobiography, "you could call that moment the start of our actual relationship."

That moment was in the fall of 1948. One evening the previous spring she and her husband Petter Lindstrom had seen the Rossellini film *Open City*, and shortly thereafter she had seen *Paisan*. She was deeply moved by both movies and enormously impressed by the quality of the directing. This man's talent, she thought, deserves a wider audience. To get that audience, he needs an international film star. And where could he find such a star? Well, a survey recently had placed her at the top in current popularity, ahead of even Garbo and Tracy. And so she wrote him a brief letter, that fateful letter. She showed it to Petter, who felt it sounded all right, and sent it off. In it, after mentioning her appreciation of the two movies, she wrote that if he could use a Swedish actress able to speak fluent English, passable German, understandable French, and only those two words in Italian, she was prepared to come to Italy and make a movie with him.

Her reputation had not reached Roberto, who rarely went to the movies. Only the strenuous efforts of a determined secretary persuaded him to recollect the blond girl he had seen opposite Leslie Howard in *Intermezzo*. That actress, he was informed, had starred in about a dozen European films and more than a dozen American, including *Dr. Jekyll and Mr. Hyde, Anna Christie, Casablanca, For Whom the Bell Tolls, Gaslight, Spellbound, Notorious, The Bells of St. Mary's,* and *Joan of Arc*. He thereupon cabled Ingrid an enthusiastic response.

A letter followed, describing a proposed movie for her. The description was fervid but rather incoherent, at least by the elaborate Hollywood planning standards to which Ingrid had become accustomed (with the famous exception of the ad hoc production of *Casablanca*). Rossellini's moviemaking was downright casual in comparison; it relied heavily on improvising, on the seizing of opportunities (and often actors) along the way. Ingrid decided that they would have to meet somewhere and discuss the project if it was ever to get anywhere. She suggested Paris, since she expected to be in London for the filming of Alfred Hitchcock's *Under Capricorn*, and she and Petter could conveniently fly over for the meeting. Roberto agreed. Although no contract was signed at the meeting, Ingrid felt committed to make the picture.

The commitment may already have been personal as well as professional. Her relationship with Petter had been strained for several years. His practical, concerned protectiveness had been invaluable to her, but it had soured somewhat into bossiness and even nagging. Or so it seemed to her, and as a result she was especially vulnerable to Roberto's undisciplined, easygoing charm, his open emotionalism, his colorful imagination, his magnetic eloquence even in unfamiliar languages. The man intrigued her, fascinated her. As she returned to London and finished the Hitchcock film, as she returned to California and resumed her Hollywood and Beverly Hills routine, she realized with some alarm that she could not get him out of her mind.

Absence had no chance to make her heart grow fonder, or otherwise. Within a few weeks Roberto was in New York to receive the New York Film Critics Award for *Open City*, voted the best foreign film of 1948. Soon thereafter he was in Hollywood, where Ingrid had persuaded Sam Goldwyn to consider backing the projected movie. Goldwyn, although dazzled by Roberto, eventually pulled out because he could not fathom the inchoate scenario. Yet he was soon replaced. When Howard Hughes, one of Ingrid's most ardent fans, bought RKO, there was no longer any problem of financial support. Meanwhile, within a month of his arrival on the coast, Roberto had fallen passionately in love with Ingrid, enough to propose a kind of elopement to the Mediterranean island of Stromboli, where the movie would be shot. The most she could bring herself to do was to promise that she would come to him soon in Rome. When she arrived there in March 1949, she was greeted by the press and the people of that amorous land not only as a movie superstar but also as the new woman in Roberto's life. She was deeply touched, almost overwhelmed, by the joyously affectionate welcome. She had never been so happy.

Yet there were those nagging pricks of her Lutheran-trained conscience. What of Petter and their daughter, Pia? Her romance with Roberto was the talk of the tinseltown, she knew. Surely it would be best to tell Petter directly that she was hopelessly ensnared, that she would not be coming home. She did so, and when he read her letter, despite the forewarnings in the newspaper columns, despite a picture in *Life* magazine of the lovers holding hands in a romantic setting on the Italian coast—and although she had asked for a divorce three years before—he could not believe his eyes. Would she really give up all *this* for *that*? Hurriedly he arranged to have Pia stay with a friend, closed up the house, and took off for Italy. But when he arrived, he found that he could not get to Stromboli because of heavy weather.

They met in Messina, Sicily. Roberto went with her to the hotel.

During the meeting he drove in circles around the hotel, dramatically prepared to foil any attempt to spirit her away. When she finally emerged, he zoomed away with her and promptly ran out of gas because of all the circling. But at least the meeting had produced a compromise: Petter would let Ingrid finish the picture without interference and then Ingrid would return to the States to discuss the situation as calmly as it would allow. Meanwhile the scarlet-letter, scarlet-woman press coverage of the affair burgeoned uncontrollably, making much of the fact that the nun of *The Bells of St. Mary's* and the young-girl saint of *Joan of Arc* had taken a lover amid worldwide titillation and consternation. In the States, Senator Edwin Johnson of Colorado led a posse demanding that she be refused reentry into the country as an undesirable alien, on the grounds of moral turpitude. When she finally left Stromboli in August, shocked and appalled by the worldwide turmoil over what she had naively thought of as a private matter, she knew that her reputation, personal and professional, was in ruins. She also knew that the situation would surely get worse, for she was three months pregnant. She would not return to America after all.

A few days earlier she had issued a public statement that she had instructed her attorney to initiate divorce proceedings and that she now intended to retire from public life, to give up her career. Shortly afterward a newspaper in Rome breathlessly informed its breathless readers of her pregnancy. Suddenly Hedda Hopper materialized in Rome and interviewed Ingrid, who obliquely denied the story of the pregnancy ("Do I look pregnant, Hedda?"), to the gossip's chagrin. But the lawyer hired by Ingrid and Roberto, an American working and living in Rome, turned out to be more a publicity agent than an attorney. Arriving in America with a great deal of private information from Ingrid about her life and her marriage, he eagerly fanned the flames of publicity in an effort to put Petter in the role of heavy before going to court. This tactic tattered the tatters of Ingrid's reputation and thoroughly alienated Petter. By the time another lawyer took over and completed the litigation more quietly, even the ruins had crumbled. Of all the devastating news stories, the most devastating for Ingrid was the report, quite false, that she had said she was willing to give up her child by Petter. Knowing that Pia would probably read the story—or have it told to her by inquisitive friends—she wrote a frantic letter to reassure her. It was especially frantic because she finished it just in time to be rushed off to the hospital, where she gave birth to her son, Robertino. Reporters and photographers, who had kept her confined in her Rome apartment for five weeks, engulfed the hospital. Ironically, most of them arrived after taking hurried French leave from the premiere of Anna Magnani's latest film. After twelve days of their implacable siege and occasional sneak attacks, Roberto managed a getaway for himself and family without a single photograph being taken.

It was February now, 1950. The two lovers found a little peace and quiet in Rome with Roberto's family, despite the ceaseless intrusions of the press, despite the incessant flow of nasty letters, despite the scathing reviews of a ruinously edited *Stromboli*, and, for Ingrid, despite the thought of Pia. At least things were settled by November, in the sense that all the necessary legal relationships were more or less cleared up, including Roberto's annulment of his marriage, Ingrid's Mexican divorce from Petter, Petter's American divorce from Ingrid, and Ingrid and Roberto's Mexican marriage. The rearrangements were a bit labyrinthine, but traceable.

Within a year she was back at work, for all her resolve to retire. They needed the money (they did not live frugally). Roberto directed, she starred with Alexander Knox, the movie was variously entitled *Europa '51* and *The Greatest Love*, and it did nothing for her career. The production had been rather hurried, since she was ballooning with the twins expected in June 1952. For that event she had hoped that Pia would pay her and her new half sisters a visit in Italy and had petitioned a California court to that effect. But Pia did not want to come. Although she liked her mother, she testified, she did not love her. She loved her father.

It had to be hard for Pia to watch her proper but very human father struggling against, bowing under, the weight of the scandal. He had become a highly competent brain surgeon, eventually achieving an international reputation, but the scandal had cost him hard-earned promotions and brought him acute embarrassments. To her mother's pleading invitations she responded with a recommendation that Ingrid concentrate on caring for her three other children, stop seeing lawyers, and leave her and her father alone. Ingrid, deeply hurt, wrote back that she would not bother her again. (She did not, but later they were reconciled.)

She had other worries. She and Roberto and the three children spent about eighteen months, from late 1953 through early 1954, traveling about Europe with a Rossellini production of Paul Claudel's oratorio, *Joan of Arc at the Stake*. Toward the end the tour took them to Sweden, to her great delight, but the delight was cut short by brutal treatment from the press. They also made two movies, neither successful. It was becoming increasingly clear that their careers were incompatible, that his directing talent and her acting talent were an impossible—or at best a nonlucrative—combination. Their debts were growing alarmingly—alarmingly at least for Ingrid, who was more sensitive about such things. Their professional incompatibility began to enter their personal relationship. It was becoming noticeable to others, such as the German actor who played her husband in one of the movies. She was heading for a nervous breakdown, he warned her, unless she left Roberto. The suggestion shocked her deeply.

The break came over her appearance on the Paris stage in Robert Anderson's *Tea and Sympathy*. Roberto forbade her, Italian style, to be associated with a play concerning homosexuality. She ignored his demand. The play and her performance were enthusiastically received. And during the run the movie *Anastasia* was released. Since it had been shot in Europe, she had been able to appear in it (also over Roberto's objections) without going to America. It was an instant hit, bringing her an Oscar and the New York Film Critics Award as best actress of 1956. Roberto took off to do a film in India. He would be gone nine months.

In India he became involved with a married woman, and Ingrid knew that he was when he called to indignantly deny the rumors. A new man had entered her life as well, a successful theatrical impresario. On Roberto's return they agreed that the marriage was finished. But not their lives. He had a great deal of work ahead, she a spectacularly successful resumption of her career. And they would always be friends.

Nancy Davis
and
Ronald Reagan

F ittingly or ironically, it was Communism that brought Nancy
Davis and Ronald Reagan together.

In 1951, a year in which Red was a perilous color to be in show
business, the twenty-nine-year-old movie actress found her name in a
list of "Communist sympathizers," although her interest in political
and social questions was virtually nonexistent. Knowing that such
attention could be a professional kiss of death, she sought advice and
help from one of her directors, Mervyn LeRoy. LeRoy knew her well
enough to suspect that there must be some mistake. The president of
the Screen Actors Guild, he reassured her, could probably straighten
the thing out for her. He had been in the thick of the battle with
Communists over control of the Guild and knew about such things.
Perhaps all it would take would be a phone call.

That was, indeed, all that it took. In his return call Ronald Reagan
informed LeRoy that the confusion was caused by the existence of

three other Nancy Davises in show business. Assure Miss Davis, he added, that she can count on the Guild to defend her if the allegations ever crop up again. (They never did.) Next morning, after LeRoy had given her the happy news, Nancy realized that her relief was tinged with regret. She had expected a direct, personal response. She had seen Ronald Reagan in several movies, she had found him very attractive, and she knew that he had been divorced from Jane Wyman a couple of years before. She decided to take the initiative— but discreetly, for she was a very properly brought-up young lady from Smith College.

She was still rather worried, she told LeRoy, and would like to have some personal reassurance. He got her drift without further prompting. Early that evening, after what seemed a long wait, her phone rang; it was Ronald, asking her to have dinner with him. She protested the short notice in maidenly style, briefly and faintly enough not to jeopardize the invitation. During dinner, at a Sunset Strip restaurant, after a quick disposition of the multiple Nancy Davis problem, she discovered that this man's interest ranged far beyond his own career, beyond Hollywood, beyond acting. And she found her reaction to him ranging well beyond a casual attraction.

He responded in kind. Although he was on crutches, having broken his leg in a charity baseball game, their expected brief evening together lengthened well into the morning, at Ciro's, where they saw Sophie Tucker's show two—or was it three?—times, and then into successive evenings at other restaurants and clubs, and later at the homes of close friends such as William Holden and his wife, Brenda Marshall. Gradually the pace slackened a bit, if only in the interest of healthful tranquillity, but the togetherness remained. Marriage, though never a formal topic of discussion, became a widespread assumption among their friends and soon between them as well. Ronald finally formalized the situation by asking her father for her hand in marriage, an old-fashioned gesture that utterly charmed his old-fashioned girl.

After twice trying to squeeze a formal wedding into his rather hectic shooting schedule (he made some fifty movies between 1937 and 1964), they finally settled for a quick, quiet ceremony at the Little Brown Church in the Valley, in March 1952, with the Holdens as matron of honor and best man. They honeymooned briefly in Phoenix, Arizona, where her parents were vacationing. Although her folks were amiable in-laws, Nancy wrote later of its being "a tribute to Ronnie that he took this in his stride." But then he had his innings on the way home through the deserts of Arizona and southern California. During a vicious sandstorm the top of his convertible began to rip apart, and Nancy had to kneel up on the seat and hold the top together with half-frozen hands. They drove out of the storm, fortunately, before she could become permanently fixed in that position.

The next twenty years or so were particularly a period of domestic bliss. Indeed, the Reagans were and are not only a loving couple but also essentially happy, buoyant people, and domestic bliss has been a hallmark of their relationship. Soon after their marriage they went house hunting in the hilly Pacific Palisades area just north of Santa Monica. Their first house proved too small, but their second, which they built in the same area in 1956, is the one in which they raised their children—daughter Patti, born in 1954, and son Ron, born in 1958 (Michael and Maureen being his children from the previous marriage)—and in which they lived for more than a quarter of a century, as much as professional schedules would allow. With only three bedrooms, it was an unpretentious house, especially by Beverly Hills standards, but it was a comfortable one for a family not inspired by conspicuous consumption. Later they bought a modest ranch at Lake Malibu, where Ronald could indulge his love of horses and Lincolnesque rail splitting.

Gradually they abandoned their movie careers, she for home and family, he for television's *General Electric Theater* and *Death Valley Days*. But before they quit Hollywood completely (she in 1958, he in 1964), they did have a chance to make a movie together, *Hellcats of the Navy*, a war picture in which she played his fiancée and found the love scenes deliciously easy to do. When it was released in 1956, Ronald had already for two years been host of, and occasional actor in, the *GE Theater*, a role he was to fill until 1962, when he moved to *Death Valley Days* for a two-year stint. As GE host he was contracted also to spend ten weeks per year visiting GE plants and speaking to employee groups around the country. This experience, which entailed a good deal of speaking at other business and civic functions, gave him plenty of practice in projecting his amiable personality and uttering sweet nothings over public address systems, although at the time he had no thought of a political career. But his continual dealings with business executives transformed the Roosevelt Democrat in him into a Landon Republican, while those same business executives, and others, came to recognize what a political opportunity he represented.

In the early 1960s he was offered Republican support if he would run for political office, twice for the U.S. Senate, once for the California governorship. No, he replied, get yourselves another candidate—but I'll campaign for him. He did campaign, vigorously, getting himself known throughout the state and whetting many a Republican appetite. After his celebrated speech for Barry Goldwater in 1964, the pressure grew more intense. Throughout 1965 his sleeves and lapels grew ragged with insistent plucking, very flattering plucking, by people desperate for a candidate to defeat Democratic incumbent Pat Brown in the 1966 race for governor. He said no just as insistently until the summer, when he asked the party to arrange speaking tours for him over the next five months so that he could get some feel for his chances as a candidate. He would let them know his findings, and his decision, before year's end. It was a deal.

On December 31, at a press conference, he announced his decision to run. The announcement was not greeted with unanimous enthusiasm within the state's Grand Old Party, chiefly because of resentment against a newcomer, especially a theatrical ham who could hardly be expected to cut the political mustard. But this was a campaign that saw the birth of the eleventh commandment, "Thou shalt not speak ill of another Republican." As the campaign progressed, he managed to charm most of the skeptics into at least guarded support, and in this he was greatly helped by Nancy, another charmer who, like her husband, revealed a gift for expressing opinions that seem to come simultaneously from the bottom of the heart and off the top of the head. Although hardly eager to trudge the campaign trail and refusing adamantly to make a political speech, she was persuaded to hold question-and-answer meetings throughout the state, at which she greatly enhanced his image as well as hers. By election day both images were well burnished, and Ronald was elected governor by a 58 percent majority.

Their life together changed, of course. For financial and political reasons they had to sell their treasured Lake Malibu ranch (later replaced by their Santa Barbara retreat). As public figures, they found that even private decisions would have to bear public scrutiny. When Nancy discovered that the eighty-seven-year-old governor's mansion was coming apart at the seams and had been officially declared a fire hazard, she insisted on renting another, less perilous house in Sacramento, at their own expense, and Ronald readily agreed. Their decision, although made in the interest of family safety, provoked a good deal of criticism from denizens of the political woodwork, but they moved nonetheless. A new governor's mansion was eventually built, but not soon enough for them to occupy it before the end of his second term.

The governor's office at the state capital, though safe, was about as dilapidated as the old mansion. It hurt Nancy to think of Ronald's trying to work in such depressing surroundings. (Always an unabashed sentimentalist, she had been accused by her husband of crying when she sent out the laundry.) The interior decorator in her got to work. The carpet was replaced; the sofa was repaired; the walls were stained a softer brown; English prints of horses were hung. Perhaps her most effective piece of work was the simplest. The office had windows overlooking a remarkably beautiful landscape, but the blinds were always kept drawn, for what reason nobody knew. She had them opened, and kept open, to the governor's vast delight. When the work was completed early in February 1967, she wished him a happy birthday.

Their eight years in Sacramento were busy years. He gained some invigorating experience as a political chief executive and she used her influence on behalf of worthy causes such as her favorite, the Foster Grandparent program. But those years were prelude, and the rest is recent history. After a close defeat in the 1976 Republican National Convention, in 1980 she saw her husband nominated and then elected President of the United States. For years his political preoccupation, his obsession, had been the U.S. government's habit of spending more money each year than it received. Through the 1970s, in his speeches and radio talks, especially during the presidential campaign, he had harped continually about those outrageous federal budget deficits. Now he would be president and could *do* something about them.

His reliability in this respect is a matter of public record, but so is the Reagans' success in bringing a measure of grace and elegance to the White House that had not been seen there since the Kennedys. More important for our consideration here, their personal relationship remained undamaged by the discomforts and hazards of the goldfish bowl. Despite criticism, she continued gazing at him during his speeches as though he were creating heaven and earth by fiat. Despite criticism, they continued to hold hands during public functions, discreetly but not surreptitiously. As son Michael put it, "You'd think they just got married yesterday."

Jacqueline Bouvier
and
John F. Kennedy

∽℮∾

Thtere is an element of Greek tragedy in the story of Jacqueline Bouvier and John F. Kennedy, an ironic twist of self-determined destiny. She was determined to become Mrs. Kennedy, and he was determined to become President of the United States. And there was a Lee Harvey Oswald in their future.

Her determination did not spring suddenly out of nowhere, nor was it any sort of single-minded, ruthless ambition. It grew slowly, and it never went much beyond an ardent, single-hearted hope. She first met Congressman Jack Kennedy, very briefly and casually, in 1948. In 1952 she met him again, at a party given by mutual friends who had invited them both in the fond expectation that they would "hit it off." If they did, they gave no indication. But Jackie's job as inquiring reporter for the *Washington Times-Herald* involved frequent visits to Capitol Hill, where they became, quite literally, passing acquaintances in the congressional corridors. After Jack's election to the Senate in 1952, in a rare Democratic victory amid the Eisenhower landslide, she interviewed him for her column in the *Times-Herald*. This time her obvious attractions—her demure beauty, her soft voice, her quick and well-stocked mind, her agile wit, her grace and poise—really caught his attention, and he began squiring her about with growing frequency. Among other things, she was quite conspicuously his "date" at the Eisenhower inaugural ball. Since he was the Senate's most eligible bachelor, their companionship soon drew the notice of the gossip columnists, giving Jackie her first experience with the kind of relentless harassment that would plague her throughout her life.

She was nonetheless delighted with the senator's obvious interest in her. Although at thirty-five he was twelve years older than she, he looked and acted much younger than his age and was an addictively attractive man. Before long she was inextricably hooked. Marriage began to fill her thoughts (these were staider times than now). Jack gave no indication that she could seriously compete with his political preoccupations, but in May 1953, when she went to London to cover Elizabeth's coronation for her column, her absence suddenly made his heart grow acutely fonder. He began telephoning her, assuring her how much he missed her, urging her to hurry back, and finally proposing marriage on her return. With her assignment completed, she canceled her return-trip boat reservation and flew back, eagerly. Jack was waiting at the airport, eagerly. They were formally engaged the following day, although the public announcement was delayed until June 25 to allow the *Saturday Evening Post* time to publish a long-scheduled article on "Jack Kennedy: The Senate's Gay Young Bachelor." (In staider times, "gay" was staider too.)

The wedding took place in September, a modest little affair with Boston's Archbishop Richard Cushing officiating amid twelve hundred guests whose importance ranged generally from impressive to staggering. As Jackie walked down the aisle on the arm of her stepfather, Hugh Auchincloss, her happiness was marred only by her mother's ill-suppressed disdain for the Boston Irish Kennedys and her natural father's absence. Jack Bouvier, apparently depressed by the contrast between his own relative lack of affluence (stemming mostly from Wall Street, 1929) and the lavish display of Auchincloss wealth, had drowned his anticipated embarrassment in alcohol the night before and was now unconscious in his hotel room.

After their all too brief honeymoon in Acapulco, the newlyweds returned to Washington, where she entered into the routine of being a senator's wife. Dinners, teas, cocktail parties—both giving and attending them—became her weekly fare, and planning for them her daily fare, while Jack spent long days and most evenings on Senate business. Much of their social life was connected with that business, often boring for both of them but especially for Jackie, who much preferred artistic and literary types to political types of people. She also had to organize not only their household but also her thoroughly disorganized husband, whose wardrobe, for instance, she had to transform into Neatly Turned Out from Forgetfully Rumpled.

Meanwhile his back, injured during the war in the famous PT-boat episode, was growing ever more painful and troublesome, requiring him to use crutches in the summer of 1954. That October he underwent spinal surgery, incurred an infection, and nearly died. A few months later, since the operation had been unsuccessful, he went through it all over again, this time with the hoped-for results. With the help of a brace and daily therapy, he could still expect to be president.

Jackie was close by, of course, throughout this ordeal and the months of convalescence in Palm Beach that followed it. Jack, restless as always, used these months to work on his book, *Profiles in Courage*, a collection of stories of politicians who risked and destroyed their careers for the sake of a principle. The project became a highly organized operation, with aides like Ted Sorenson and banks of stenographers and with Jackie in the thick of it, reading to Jack, translating for him, combing bookstores and libraries for research material. She knew that the creative work involved provided him with a welcome distraction, good therapy in itself. In awe of his remarkable courage and patience, she stood by to offer him support in the moments when those qualities failed him. She tolerated his Irish pals and political cronies, even encouraged them to visit and keep his spirit up—particularly Dave Powers, the Boston politician and raconteur whose lifelong friendship with the Kennedys was based on the maxim, "Three things in life are real: God, human folly, and laughter. The first two are beyond our comprehension, so we must do what we can do with the third."

She had married Jack for better or worse. This was the worse, though not the worst. Part of the better was the Kennedy money, which allowed her to indulge her most publicized weakness, extravagance. During Jack's convalescence, when he was resting or having visitors, she would sometimes seek her own form of distraction in a shopping tour of the town. Although she had been born and raised in an atmosphere of aristocratic wealth, her mother, always wary of spoiling the children, held tightly to the purse strings. Jackie's newspaper job had earned her about fifty dollars a week, a tolerable salary for the times but hardly conducive to profligacy. The sudden accessibility of the Kennedy millions was more than she could readily handle, and shopping became a mild but expensive addiction. She would spend several thousand dollars a month, for months on end, on clothes and household items and gifts. Jack, whose share of the Kennedy fortune was limited by paternal control and sibling claims, protested at times, occasionally with some effect, but he had to accept that, in general, quality would always stand higher in her vocabulary than cost.

Another thing that he had to accept, he and his family, was that she was not a Kennedy and was not about to be refashioned into one. The fabled fun and games, the boisterous exuberance, the competitive high jinks at Hyannis Port, were not her style. Although she enjoyed the informality and lively camaraderie, she generally resisted being drawn into the varsity-squad pastimes, and in this she was supported by none other than the patriarch and genial tyrant, Joe Kennedy himself, who admired spirited independence wherever he found it. Her friendship with him deepened over the years, and his stroke in December 1961 and subsequent paralysis were almost as great a blow for her as the death of her own father four years earlier.

By 1956 Jack was again well and vigorous enough to make his nearly successful bid for the vice presidential nomination. Meanwhile, Jackie suffered a miscarriage and then a cesarian stillbirth, misfortunes that were downright frightening amid the celebrated Kennedy fecundity. Her anxiety that she might never bear a child successfully was only deepened when she became pregnant again, but this time a healthy daughter, Caroline, was born in November 1957, though by cesarian section. Indeed, Jackie was destined never to give birth normally; The premature birth of John Jr. ("John-John," as his father was to christen him informally) in late November 1960 was by cesarian section, as was that of their last child, Patrick, who was born prematurely in 1963 and who lived only a day and a half.

Because her pregnancies were precarious, her condition in 1960 prevented her from participating fully in the Kennedys' feverish efforts to install Jack in the White House. Unable to travel very much, she cooperated by doing campaign work at home, sending out letters to political workers across the country, writing a weekly newspaper column called "Campaign Wife," appearing on TV talk shows, attending political teas. It was all a considerable effort for her, and hardly an undiluted joy, but she was bothered by the possibility that, in a close election, a wife's apparent aloofness might make a crucial difference. The election was indeed a close one, although it was not contested because neither side was eager for any detailed scrutiny of the vote counting. Jackie joined Jack on the morning after, when the late returns brought him to victory. "So now," he told the assembled media people, "my wife and I prepare for a new adminis-tration and a new baby."

Jackie had less to do with the new administration than with the new baby, of course, but her job as first lady was no sinecure. The mail alone was more than any one person could handle. The variety of her duties is suggested by the composition of her staff, which was headed by a social secretary, a press secretary, and an executive housekeeper (in addition to a nurse for the children). She and Jack made a handsome couple, adding a touch of glamor to White House affairs that was soon hyperbolized into Camelot by public relations, press, and public. She especially enjoyed two projects that gave scope to her artistic bent, redecorating the rooms for her children and re-storing the White House for its owners, the U.S. public. The execu-tive mansion, she insisted, must not be merely redecorated but should rather be restored to give it an air of historical continuity. After studying a great deal of research material on the White House from the Library of Congress and obtaining the cooperation of Congress, which classified the White House as a national museum (eligible for tax-deductible contributions), she embarked on a pro-gram of retrieving bits of the mansion's past from its basement and forgotten storage rooms and from private collections all over the country—a James Monroe desk and table, a Dolly Madison sofa, an Andrew Jackson portrait, a Lincoln settee and chair, and so on. By the time the project was completed, furnishings worth an estimated million dollars had been contributed and another million dollars' worth purchased with cash donations. To make all this more meaningful for the visiting or otherwise interested public, Jackie conducted a "TV Tour of the White House" in February 1962, shown to more than fifty million people on all three commercial networks, and later had a guidebook prepared by the new museum's curator. The guidebook provoked even more criticism than the restoration project had (so expensive!), but again she prevailed, and after its publication in July it sold 600,000 copies over the next eighteen months. Her efforts to make the White House something of a national cultural center were similarly successful, bringing Shakespearean players, ballet dancers, opera and musical-comedy singers, and artists like Isaac Stern and Pablo Casals to delighted audiences in the East Room.

The President, who had been skeptical and rather negative at first, was pleased with the results and with Jackie's unsuspected organizing ability. He was pleased, too, with the dignified informality that she brought to state dinners and other functions held in honor of guests with names like Nehru, Selassie, de Gaulle, Macmillan, Adenauer, and Rainier. From the outset he had been obviously proud of her as First Lady, and he was especially impressed with the welcome that she received on their visit in 1961 to France, where she utterly charmed the public and the de Gaulles. He paid tribute to her there in a celebrated compliment, "I am the man who accompanied Jacqueline Kennedy to Paris, and I have enjoyed it." About a year later she visited India, this time accompanied by her sister Lee, with similar results.

Jack's admiration for Jackie was not diminished by his obvious interest in other women. The nature and extent, and the intensity, of that interest has been the target of much titillating conjecture over the years among the prurient and prudish. It may be that the Washington press corps tolerated Kennedy's improprieties much as Gerald Ford tolerated Nixon's a decade later. It is a fact that Jack and Jackie were apart a great deal and that they had separate, though adjoining, bedrooms in the White House. It is an even better documented fact that Jackie became pregnant again early in 1963.

That pregnancy ended with the tragic premature birth of Patrick in August and his death less than two days later. Jackie's sister Lee, Princess Radziwill, relayed an invitation from Aristotle Onassis, the prepossessing Greek shipping tycoon whom Jackie had met in 1958, to use his yacht for a period of recuperation. Although she and Jack had grown much closer after the baby's death, she needed to get away. And so in October she flew to Greece, where she joined Onassis, the Radziwills, and Mr. and Mrs. Franklin Roosevelt Jr. aboard the yacht for a leisurely, highly therapeutic cruise of the Aegean Sea. In a couple of weeks she returned to Washington much rested, ready to brace herself for the fast-approaching 1964 presidential campaign.

That campaign really was already under way, with presidential visits scheduled for politically critical areas over the next several months. One of these areas was Texas, where the presidential couple visited San Antonio, Houston, Fort Worth, and, on November 22, Dallas. The Secret Service people were nervous about Dallas, a hotbed of political reaction with a boisterous minority of firearms enthusiasts and hostile mental and emotional defectives. Kennedy, always a fatalist on the chances of assassination, brushed aside their concerns and opted for riding in an open car in the fateful motorcade. He and Jackie sat in the back seat, with Governor John Connally and the wife on the jump seats in front of them. Jackie was wearing a wool outfit, too hot for the unexpectedly warm day. She was uncomfortable, she remembered later, and as they approached an underpass the thought briefly crossed her mind that it looked invitingly cool.

First they had to pass by the Texas School Book Depository building, where Lee Harvey Oswald lay in wait by an open window. A moment after they passed, shots rang out, almost like irrelevant backfires. Jack lurched forward, crying out "I've been hit!" as he clutched at his throat. Blood from his head spattered the upholstery. Connally, wounded in the arm, shouted as Jackie screamed and caught hold of Jack, cradling his bloody head in her lap. After a moment, as the motorcade began to speed up, she climbed dazedly across the back of the car, stretching an arm toward her assigned Secret Service agent, who was sprinting and then climbing onto the car trunk. By the time he reached her and pushed her back into the seat, the motorcade was speeding to the nearest hospital.

Over the next several days she showed her strength and courage to the people of America and the world. As she put it, she would not cry until it was all over. And as a not overly friendly biographer put it, she was magnificent. With the help of others, especially Robert Kennedy, she bore up splendidly, participating in the funeral arrangements so that the occasion would invest the tragedy with the historical significance and the somber beauty that it deserved.

As might be imagined, the departure of a husband possessing such vitality and charisma left a great emptiness in her life. But gradually she began filling it as best she could, losing herself in the practical decisions that follow hard upon such personal tragedies. Soon she and the children, toward whom she now became more militantly protective than ever, moved to an apartment in New York City, where they could find some relief from the remorseless pressures of idle and often hostile curiosity. Here, too, she would find fewer reminders of her loss and more distractions better suited to her tastes than Washington could provide. And she could devote much more of her time to the Kennedy Memorial Library at Harvard.

After five lonely but healing years, she married Aristotle Onassis, whose anxious, thoughtful attentiveness had contributed much to that healing, especially after Robert Kennedy's death. As usual, her behavior raised eyebrows, creased foreheads, and pursed lips all over the country, but sturdy old Cardinal Cushing defended her ("Why can't she marry whomever she wants to marry?"), and the matriarchal Rose Kennedy praised Onassis as "a fine man." Jackie's motive in marrying a man so much older and richer provided a field day for psychological interpretations, but her own explanation was simply that she was lonely. Onassis, she said many years later, "rescued me at a moment when my life was engulfed in shadows. . . . He brought me into a world where one could find both happiness and love."

Coretta Scott and Martin Luther King Jr.

~~~~~

Obadiah Scott was the only black man with his own truck in the little community of Marion, Alabama. White truck owners resented the competition that he offered in the hauling and delivery business, and they threatened to kill him. Often. In 1942, during the war against the other Nazis, his house was burned to its foundation, as was a sawmill that he had laboriously saved enough money to buy and—briefly—to operate. With courage and perseverance he survived and eventually even prospered; yet, like millions of other blacks, he lived in constant fear of his life. Years afterward, his daughter Coretta would write in her autobiography that the relentless, underlying fear that she felt as a child for her father's life would prepare her well for the fear that she would feel later for her husband's.

In January 1952 Coretta Scott was a twenty-four-year-old Fellowship student at the New England Conservatory of Music in Boston.

244

Behind her were six years at Antioch College, six intellectually and artistically invigorating years which also prepared her well, though differently and much less unpleasantly, for her future life. Her first decision, to teach, had been abandoned for a singing career, since she loved music and had a lovely voice. That month, however, she met Martin Luther King Jr., a twenty-three-year-old Boston University graduate student working toward his doctorate in theology. Martin had been asking one of her friends about her, and by the time of his first telephone call, he had learned, as he put it, "some very wonderful things about you." After talking with her on the phone for a while, he became irrevocably smitten, impulsively blurting out, "You know every Napoleon has his Waterloo. I'm like Napoleon—I'm at my Waterloo, and I'm on my knees." This on the first phone call!

If this was a line, she enjoyed it. Indeed, she enjoyed *him* and could see no reason to avoid a modest commitment, like lunch the next day. When he arrived to pick her up in his green Chevrolet, she thought him rather short and not very impressive, but that was before he began to talk. During lunch he grew rapidly in her eyes. He seemed to glow with a masculine self-assurance, softened by a tongue-in-cheek sense of humor. He spoke of his pastoral ambitions with a determination untinged by fanaticism—fluently, sincerely, appealingly. She quickly realized that "he was very special," and this recognition must have been mutual. On the way back to the conservatory he remarked that he wanted four things in a wife: "character, intelligence, personality, and beauty—and you have them all." When, he asked, could he see her again?

She was having some trouble keeping her balance but managed a call-me-later response. At home she began shoring up her defenses to protect her career from this impetuous besieger. From the conversation, she had gathered that he would expect a full-time wife and mother, old style, not a career woman with only a sideline interest in home and family. After working so hard and so long, did she really want even to consider giving up her career for a *man*? Even for *this* man? Well, she would have to think about it. Meanwhile she did want to see Martin again.

She did see him again, of course, and often. She not so much saw as heard, and it was especially the hearing that made the difference. He was a genuine student, interested in ideas, familiar with a wide variety of concepts in philosophy and theology, erudite without being stuffy, compelling in conversation. He had become especially fond of Thoreau and Gandhi. Their provocative arguments for civil disobedience and nonviolent resistance might well be applied, he felt, to relieve some of the oppression of blacks in the United States. And he had long been dedicated to the message of Jesus Christ, the message of a love that included even one's enemies. People could resist mistreatment, he believed, without being guilty of it.

He dispelled her reservations about him as a Baptist minister, reservations arising from her own more liberal viewpoint. He was certainly no fire-breathing fundamentalist, as well as no stickler for the niceties of ritual. When she heard him preach at a local Baptist church, she was greatly taken with his quiet, reasoned approach to this reserved northern congregation (he would be more emotional in his sermons in the Deep South). And he increased her doubts about her commitment to a singing career. She would not be simply giving up that career but would, rather, be exchanging it for another which might well prove more important and more satisfying. Anyway, she finally decided, she was in love with Martin and he was obviously in love with her. After the obligatory family introductions—Martin's formidable father resisted a bit but was soon won over—they were married in June 1953. The bride's promise to obey was omitted from the ceremony.

They spent their wedding night at a funeral parlor, owned by family friends, because the region of the land of the free offered no suitable hotel accommodations for blacks. In September, after a summer spent mostly with the hospitable King family, they returned to Boston to complete their respective studies and share housekeeping chores in a small apartment. (He was a passable cook but in laundering showed more diligence than competence.) In addition to their burdensome studies, he preached at churches and she sang at concerts. When her mother visited them toward the end of the academic year, she was greatly impressed with his Sunday morning sermon—and equally but differently impressed by his clowning at a roller-skating rink that afternoon. His love of fun was the joy of Coretta's life.

At the end of that summer of 1954, the couple, their formal studies completed, went back south to Montgomery, Alabama, where Martin had accepted the pastorship of the Dexter Avenue Baptist Church. Coretta was disappointed to be returning so soon to that region of overt racism, but whither he went, thither she. The next fifteen months were busy but would prove to be the most tranquil of their married life. While he spent three hours before breakfast and another three hours after dinner on his doctoral dissertation, and the rest of each day on his pastoral duties, she took up on-the-job training as cook and house-keeper, parish secretary, choir singer, ministerial assistant, and, in the spring of 1955 (soon after he received his Ph.D.) as mother-to-be. The first of their four children was born that November.

Three weeks later their fifteen months of tranquillity ended when Rosa Parks, a Montgomery seamstress and part-time secretary for the National Association for the Advancement of Colored People, was arrested for wearily violating a Montgomery segregation ordinance requiring her to give up her seat to a white man and get to The Back of the Bus Where She Belonged. For most of Montgomery's fifty thousand blacks, this was the last straw in their burden of relentless humiliation. Rosa Parks's lawyer, after getting her released on bail, enlisted the help of Martin and Ralph Abernathy, Martin's lifelong friend, and others in a campaign for a black boycott of the city's bus system.

Martin's eloquence at a succession of meetings soon put him in the forefront of the movement. ("We have been amazingly patient . . . but we come here tonight to be saved from that patience which makes us patient with anything less than freedom and justice.") Soon, too, especially after he was elected to the formal leadership of the boycott effort, all tranquillity disappeared from the King household. The phone rang without letup, bringing messages of cooperation and encouragement as well as vicious threats not only against him but also against his wife and family. To minimize the chances of their daugh-ter's being hurt in a bombing of their home, Coretta kept the child in a bedroom in the rear. Fortunately, no one was hurt when the front of the house was demolished by a bomb on the night of January 30, 1956, some eight weeks after Rosa Parks's arrest.

It had been a frustrating eight winter weeks for the black commu-nity, weeks of pooling cars and vans and taxis, riding in buggies and on horses and mules, often trudging miles on foot to work, to the store, to church, to the doctor. A crowd of incensed people gathered in front of the Kings' damaged home that January evening, many of them armed and most of them ready to tear up much more than the nearest pea patch. But Martin calmed them with a characteristic "love your enemies" speech that persuaded them to go home quietly. Yet not he nor his father nor her father could persuade Coretta to return to her family in Marion for safety's sake. This was her man, the man she loved, and she was not about to abandon him when he most needed her. He did need her, as he told her later after the immediate danger had subsided, not only then but thereafter.

The boycott continued for nine months more while the white establishment tried various ploys to end it—and while the case against the constitutionality of Montgomery's and Alabama's bus segregation laws was being carried through the federal courts. In November the city went to a local court for an injunction against "car pools or transportation systems growing out of the boycott." Martin felt that this probably was the end, that the long-suffering blacks could not be asked to avoid using the buses when nothing else was available, not after all those grueling months. But the injunction, although issued readily enough, made little difference. On the same day, the U.S. Supreme Court declared the bus laws unconstitutional.

A benefit concert to support the boycott had long been planned for early December in Manhattan. It was held, with Coretta as featured performer and Harry Belafonte as one of the stars. This was her first meeting with the celebrated singer but not her last; he was to prove one of the Kings' most faithful and cherished friends. The concert was a success, giving her the satisfaction of making a distinct, practical contribution of her own.

In Montgomery, Martin appealed to blacks to "respond to the [Supreme Court] decision with an understanding of those who have oppressed us and an appreciation of the new adjustment the court order imposes on them." Nevertheless, the desegregation of the buses was followed by a few weeks of sporadic beatings, shootings, and bombings. Gradually the pleas of newspaper editors and white ministers for obedience to the law began to take effect, gradually redneck violence began to lose community support and tolerance. By the spring of 1957 the desegregated buses were operating without serious incident. To Martin's and Coretta's immeasurable relief, not a single life had been lost in the battle.

As his fame grew, and as more and more demands were made on his time and talents, the movement continually separated the young couple (still only in their twenties) physically but united them spiritually. Had she been less dedicated to the cause, his frequent absences might have strained their marriage beyond recall. In a twelve-month period in 1957–58, for instance, he traveled some 780,000 miles, gave more than two hundred speeches, and at home was usually closeted with the manuscript of his first book, *Stride Toward Freedom*. To her fell the task of raising their children, of trying to explain to them why they could not go to a particular school, a store, a theater, an amusement park, and why their daddy was so often arrested and hauled off to jail. (The reason for the jailing, she told them, was so that some day they *could* go to the store, etc.; and when the amusement park was desegregated, Martin took her and the children there and had the time of his life.)

Although she was able to join him, through the kindness of relatives and friends, on his visits to Africa and India, she could not be with him on his organizing and fund-raising trips in the States without neglecting the children. She shared a great deal in his activities, whenever she could, during the formation of the Southern Christian Leadership Conference (with Martin elected president), the student sit-ins to desegregate eating places, the Freedom Rides, the campaign in that citadel of racism, Bull Connors's Birmingham. She visited him in courtrooms, in jails, and in the hospital after he was stabbed in Harlem by a demented black woman. He could always count on her loving concern, wherever he was, and she could always count on his need for it.

Events moved swiftly—the famous march on Washington in August 1963 and the November assassination of the president who had been so kind and had meant so much to the Kings; the Civil Rights Act of 1964, Martin's Nobel Peace Prize, and the first of Coretta's Freedom Concerts; the bloody confrontations in Selma, Alabama (with the sheriff screeching, "Get those goddam niggers!"), and the Voting Rights Act in 1965; the Mississippi march and the Chicago campaign in 1966; Martin's controversial condemnation of the U.S. role in Vietnam in 1967; and the Poor People's Campaign early in 1968. Through all the turmoil—the marches, speeches, riots, threats, physical attacks, criticism, and the stories of his distant infidelities—their love remained impregnable, resting as it did in love of God and neighbor.

In his visit to Memphis in early April 1968, in support of a strike by the city's sanitation workers, he told a black gathering, "I may not get there with you, but I want you to know tonight that we as a people

will get to the Promised Land." He may have had a premonition—
the week before, he had sent Coretta a bouquet, as he often did, but
this time, for the first time in their life together, the flowers were
artificial and would last. He had planned to lead a march in Memphis
on Easter Monday but was murdered on Holy Thursday. That Monday Coretta marched in his place.

*Joanne Woodward
and
Paul Newman*

～◦～

They can hardly be blamed for being withdrawn and reticent about
their private lives. Nasty little experiences have made them so. One
day, for example, during the shooting of the movie *From the Terrace,*
in which they appeared together, Joanne Woodward and Paul Newman used a coffee break to find a secluded spot on the set for a
moment of private communion. The seclusion was illusory, however.
During an ardent, nonprofessional embrace their picture was
snapped by a drooling photographer for the Peeping Tom set.

Whatever the justification as the price of celebrity, this sort of
experience hardly nourished abiding trust. At the suggestion of
publicity, the Newmans do tend to hunker down. When the writer
Lionel Godfrey informed Paul of his intention to do his biography
and asked for his help, the actor guardedly declined. Although he
disliked being uncooperative, he explained, he wanted no part of any

251

such attention-getting project. The book was written, surprisingly well, from a respectful distance.

When they met in 1952, both had left television for Broadway. He was a twenty-seven-year-old contentedly married man with three children; she was twenty-two, unmarried, and devastatingly attractive. Her attractions might not have been so kismetic if their meeting had been brief and casual. Instead, it extended into daily association over more than fourteen months in the Theater Guild's production of William Inge's *Picnic,* which ran for 477 performances. He was playing a subordinate role (Alan Seymour, played by Cliff Robertson in the movie version); she was understudying a couple of the female parts. Neither of them felt comfortable with their growing emotional involvement. When the play closed and Paul went to Hollywood in the spring of 1954, having signed a five-year contract with Warner Brothers, their separation promised to solve their problem, but soon afterward Joanne followed, having signed with Twentieth Century-Fox. This only intensified their problem, of course, and the hazards of proximity eventually proved too much for them. Joanne would later describe the six years before their marriage as a time of running away from each other—figuratively and futilely—and Paul would comment in an unguarded moment that the breakup of his first marriage left him with a feeling of guilt that he would carry with him to the grave.

When they were married in January 1958, they had both achieved star status, he for his performance in the movie version of *Somebody Up There Likes Me,* the Rocky Graziano story, and she for her Oscar-winning portrayal of the multiple personalities in *The Three Faces of Eve.* They also were acting together in *The Long Hot Summer,* the Faulkner-inspired film story of burning barns and searing emotions, the first and probably the best of the eight pictures in which they were to appear together. After a honeymoon in England, the first of several affectionate visits to the sceptered isle, the newlyweds returned to Hollywood to wrestle with the problems of two careers, three stepchildren, and the Tinseltown atmosphere of nervous, multi-layered narcissism. They partly solved the problem of atmospheric pollution, chemical as well as psychological, soon after their return, when they bought a 180-year-old house in Westport, Connecticut, complete with apple trees and brook trout, for use as a retreat at every opportunity. The problem of the stepchildren, like most such problems, abated with time, especially after the arrivals of their own three daughters. (Paul's son Scott, however, died tragically in 1978.)

The problem of the two careers could never really be solved, but they learned how to live with it. Each enormously admired the other's professional talent, as well as respecting the other's professional opinion, so that there was never any meaningful discussion of bringing either career to an end. Joanne's, however, was dogged by absences due to her childbearing and a lack of suitable scripts. Paul's experienced its ups and downs at a generally more exalted level, largely because of his sex-symbol status, which at first made her jealous and made him chronically uncomfortable. They found that they could work well together, especially in movies which he directed and in which she starred—*Rachel, Rachel* in 1968 and *The Effects of Gamma Rays on Man-in-the-Moon Marigolds* in 1972. They found that they could work well apart, too, although her film successes never quite reached the blockbuster levels that some of his attained, notably *The Hustler, Hud,* and *Butch Cassidy and the Sundance Kid.* And they found that they could live apart without liking it when the separation, sometimes a continent wide, was unavoidable and reassuringly temporary. In a sense their profession, having led them into their marriage, was not likely to lead them out of it.

They also found that they could tolerate and even participate in each other's interests, short of Paul's beer-drinking habit. They found no incompatibility in their attitudes on political and social questions; both were, and are, ardently active liberals in such matters as minority rights, environmental quality, nuclear disarmament. Joanne has been a nervous spectator, but a spectator nonetheless, at car-racing events in which Paul has indulged his passion for suicidal velocities, and he has accompanied her to ballet performances as an alternative to watching the fights on TV.

Their own fights, not on TV, could be spectacular without doing irreparable damage, since both had learned the art of timely self-restraint. They could sense the times when tension precluded closeness: While he was directing her in *Marigolds,* for instance, she despised the character she was playing so deeply that their flare-ups on the set followed them home—where "Paul and I avoided each other as much as possible." In that particular case, too, they doubtless wanted to be especially careful, since someone else very dear to them was involved. Their thirteen-year-old daughter Elinor, stage-named Nell Potts, was playing Joanne's daughter, a major role, in the movie.

Their acting together in films has proved less successful than the director-actress relationship, at least in the sense that the movies in which they appeared together received less critical acclaim and public attendance. *Winning* was fairly well accepted, but its subject, race-car driving, surely attracts less widespread devotion than Paul doubtless thinks it deserves. *WUSA* was too preachy to be popular. And *The Drowning Pool* apparently was considered merely a weak sequel to *Harper*. They had better luck on Broadway, where they played for four months in 1964 in *Baby Want a Kiss*, although this was hardly enough to give them a Lunt-Fontanne reputation.

Their disappointments in this respect discouraged further joint ventures. Indeed, their careers have diverged. Joanne, after appearing in the Burt Reynolds movie *The End*, turned to television drama with gratifying success in such meaty roles as the psychiatrist in *Sybil* and the courageous teacher in *Crisis at Central High*. She also played Broadway, in Shaw's *Candida*. Paul, meanwhile, stayed with the cinema, enjoying similar gratification in the role of the booze-soaked lawyer in *The Verdict*.

Their separations have regularly stimulated a conditioned reflex of ravenous curiosity in the peep-show press. Is this a trial separation? Are they breaking up? Is there someone else in his life? In hers? During the filming of *Cat on a Hot Tin Roof*, the gossip columns vibrated persistently with rumors of a torrid romance between Paul and Elizabeth Taylor, rumors that eventually ended not with a bang but a whimper. The recurrent gossip was aggravated by their living on the East Coast, which some professional Hollywooders interpreted as an intolerable rejection of their celebrated community, and this often added bite to the scandalmongering.

Both partners have made sacrifices for their marriage. Joanne interrupted her career often for home and family, on one occasion in 1960 taking the infant Elinor to Israel so that they could be with Paul during the filming of *Exodus*. In 1977 Paul took a year off and stayed home to allow "one of the greatest actresses in the world" to do her thing. They have been united by their children, but even more by a deeply felt, very mutual romantic love. They have managed to use their differences, their incompatibilities, to nourish that love. Paul believes in arguments that "clear the air." And as Joanne once commented to an inquisitive reporter during the making of *From the Terrace,* "We get all our hostilities worked out on the set. Then when we get home—wow!"

Maybe that's why their 1991 joint effort, *Mr. and Mrs. North,* was such a splendid piece of work.